THE
ELEPHANT
IN THE
ROOM

THE ELEPHANT IN THE ROOM

EVANGELICALS, LIBERTARIANS, AND THE
BATTLE TO CONTROL THE REPUBLICAN PARTY

Ryan Sager

John Wiley & Sons, Inc.

Published by John Wiley & Sons, Inc., Hoboken, New Jersey
Published simultaneously in Canada

Design and composition by Navta Associates, Inc.

For general information about our other products and services, please contact our
Customer Care Department within the United States at (800) 762-2974, outside the
United States at (317) 572-3993 or fax (317) 572-4002.

Wiley also publishes its books in a variety of electronic formats. Some content that
appears in print may not be available in electronic books. For more information about
Wiley products, visit our web site at www.wiley.com.

Library of Congress Cataloging-in-Publication Data:
Sager, Ryan, date.
   The elephant in the room : evangelicals, libertarians, and the battle to control the
Republican Party / Ryan Sager.
        p. cm.
   Includes index.
   ISBN-13 978-0-471-79332-8 (cloth)
   ISBN-10 0-471-79332-9 (cloth)
   1. Republican Party (U.S. : 1854–) 2. Libertarianism—United States. 3. Conservatism—
United States. 4. Conservatism—Religious aspects—Christianity. 5. Christianity and pol-
itics—United States. 6. United States—Politics and government—2001– I. Title.
   JK2356.S27 2006
   324.2734—dc22
                                                                        2006013298

Printed in the United States of America

10 9 8 7 6 5 4 3 2 1

In loving memory of
Zachary Mackenzie Sager
and
Goldie and Abe Fish

CONTENTS

1

Live from the Reagan Building

In February of 2005, less than a month after George W. Bush was inaugurated for his second term as president of the United States, more than four thousand conservative activists from all over the country gathered in Washington, D.C., for the thirty-second annual Conservative Political Action Conference—or CPAC, for short. While most Americans have never heard of CPAC (it's pronounced like C-SPAN and features a similar number of congressmen), its organizers have called it "the conservative movement's yearly family reunion." That's a pretty accurate description. And with the Republican Party having just held on to the presidency by a convincing margin and increased its majorities in the House and the Senate, this was one big, influential, happy family.

In fact, maybe it was a little too happy.

As the devotees of the party of small government and anti-Washington fervor pitched their tent for three days inside the palatial Ronald Reagan Building and International Trade Center—a billion-dollar federal boondoggle in downtown D.C. that the Republican Congress named after the Gipper in 1995, in an act of unintentional irony—a question hung in the air: what on earth are we doing here?

Not just in the giant government building, of course—though these were the swankest digs the conference had ever had. But what was the party of Ronald Reagan ("Government is not the solution to our problem, government *is* the problem") and Barry Goldwater ("I fear Washington and centralized government more than I do Moscow") doing dominating Washington in the first place? What does a movement do when it has spent decades arguing that the government should have less power, and then it takes control of the government? Does it stick to its principles and methodically find ways to tax less, spend less, and interfere less in the lives of Americans? Or does it slowly but surely—day by day, issue by issue, bill by bill—succumb to the temptations of power and start to wield it toward new ends?

These were unfamiliar and uncomfortable questions for conservatives—questions, quite frankly, that they had been doing their best to avoid.

For months after the 2004 election, the main pastime of the conservative movement was simply basking in the afterglow of a stupendously successful campaign season. And conservatives had every right to gloat. The Republican Party had certainly held its share of power over the past few decades, but it had never seen anything like this. Bush might not exactly have won in a landslide by any conventional standard, but 51 percent of the popular vote over John Kerry's 48 percent certainly felt like a landslide after four years spent living under the cloud of the 2000 Florida recount. And the Republicans now had 55 seats in the Senate (a gain of 4 seats) and 232 seats in the House (a gain of 5 seats).

President Reagan had to deal with a Democratic Congress in the 1980s; George H. W. Bush faced similar problems. The Republican Congress could only rein in President Clinton, not set an agenda of its own, in the 1990s, and even George W. Bush's first term was a wash for the GOP when liberal Republican senator James Jeffords of Vermont defected and became an independent, briefly giving Democrats back control of the Senate.

But now this was the Republicans' hour, and they weren't going to let anyone forget it.

Days after the election, presidential adviser Karl Rove took to the airwaves, trumpeting the president's "strong, convincing" vote on NBC's *Meet the Press* with Tim Russert. "This country was a narrowly divided country in 2000," he said. But no longer. "The country has slid to a 51–48 Republican majority."[1]

Comparing Bush to Franklin Delano Roosevelt—the last president to win reelection while adding to his party's numbers in the House and Senate—Rove said that while there are no literal "permanent majorities" in American politics, there are some that last for a couple of decades. Or, as in the case of the Roosevelt coalition (which brought together small farmers in the Midwest, urban political bosses, intellectuals, organized labor, Catholics, Jews, and African Americans in support of the New Deal), they can sometimes last fifty or sixty years.

"Would I like to see the Republican Party be the dominant party for whatever time history gives it the chance to be? You bet," Rove told Russert. In an interview with the *Washington Post* that appeared the same day as his *Meet the Press* appearance, Rove said that America was likely witnessing a "rolling realignment" toward total Republican Party dominance of national politics.[2]

Cue scary music.

By smoothing off its rough, small-government edges, Rove's theory goes, the GOP can pick off ever-bigger chunks of the Democrats' base: working-class voters can be won over by dropping traditional Republican objections to generous spending on entitlement programs; black, Hispanic, and Catholic voters can be won over with ever-harsher attacks on abortion and homosexuality; big business can be kept on board through ever-larger corporate subsidies and tax breaks, and so on and so forth. By being as many things to as many people as possible, according to the theory, the Republican Party may be able to eclipse the Democratic Party for decades to come. Bush is the test case.

If anyone was listening more closely to Rove than the president whom he'd twice helped elect, it was the Democrats, terrified that these rumblings about "realignment" and a "permanent" Republican majority—which had been going on for years, and which had only been amplified by the tragedy of 9/11 and the American public's lack of confidence in liberals on national security—were more than just rumblings.

In fact, it would probably be fair to say that liberals entered full panic mode. After the 2000 election, there had been a lot of talk about Red America vs. Blue America—Red being Republican, religious, and rural, and Blue being Democratic, secular, and urban. But after the 2004 election, people started drawing up new flags and currencies. One map circulated on the Internet annexed the West Coast and the Northeast to the "United States of Canada"—located just north of "Jesusland."

On a slightly more serious note, the *Stranger*—a liberal alternative weekly newspaper in Seattle—wrote about what it called the Urban Archipelago. "Liberals, progressives, and Democrats do not live in a country that stretches from the Atlantic to the Pacific, from Canada to Mexico. We live on a chain of islands," the editors wrote. "We are citizens of the Urban Archipelago, the United Cities of America. We live on islands of sanity, liberalism, and compassion."[3]

More mainstream moping by Democrats could be seen all over the American media landscape: from *New York Times* columnist Maureen Dowd ranting about a "jihad in America" that "controls all power in the country," to New York's senator Chuck Schumer appearing on Comedy Central's *The Daily Show with Jon Stewart* the day after the election and complaining that Democrats keep getting "paddled" and "outfoxed," to the liberal online magazine *Slate* running a series of articles on the topic of "Why Americans Hate Democrats."

Despair was the order of the day for Democrats, jubilation the order of the day for Republicans. But did either side even begin to comprehend the fix that the Republican Party was now in? If only they could have seen the scene at CPAC.

.   .   .

If the conservative movement is a family, it's a far-flung, rowdy, dysfunctional one. But CPAC brings it all together.

If only for three days.

But for those three days, all the brothers and sisters, crazy aunts and sleazy uncles, barely tolerated in-laws and disgruntled step-children, black sheep and golden boys, and grandmas and grand-pas of "the movement" (as those in the family are known to call it) are under one roof. It's a bit like the holidays—inasmuch as there's a reason the suicide rate spikes around the holidays.

Various bizarre scenes unfold all around. An iMac plays footage of Ronald Reagan on a loop. Republican committeemen from the Midwest can be overheard debunking the theory of evolution while waiting in line for dinner ("What do you call an animal with a half-fin–half-wing? Kibble."). Al Franken and G. Gordon Liddy face off over at Radio Row. And books full of Antonin Scalia's dissenting opinions are given out as party favors.

Meanwhile, a walk around CPAC's convention floor takes one on something of a whirlwind tour of the Right. There, the ninety-plus organizations and corporations that sponsor the conference set up booths to push their pet causes: Americans for Tax Reform ("reforming" taxes to within an inch of their lives), Americans for Immigration Control (keeping Mexicans in Mexico), the Family Research Council (keeping gays out of marriage), the Log Cabin Republicans (wedding gays to the GOP), the Clare Boothe Luce Policy Institute (grooming the next generation of Ann Coulters), the National Rifle Association (defending the right to shoot), the Drug Policy Alliance (defending the right to shoot up), the Objectivist Center (deifying Ayn Rand), and the National Right to Work Foundation (demonizing the unions). Just to name a few.

As in most large families, however, there is one marriage that undergirds the entire enterprise: for the conservative family, that is the marriage between social conservatism and small-government conservatism. There is no one group at CPAC—or anywhere else, for that matter—that fully represents either of these philosophies. Rather, these are the two main currents of thought that push the conservative movement along. Social conservatives (a.k.a.

traditionalists, the Christian Right, the Religious Right) place the highest value on tradition and morality—or "Western values," as they often put it. Small-government conservatives (a.k.a. libertarians) value human freedom and choice above all else.

These two kinds of conservatives, whose fundamental views of the world are at odds as often as not, were brought together in the 1950s and 1960s by a concept known as "fusionism," the brainchild of conservative thinker Frank Meyer, an editor at *National Review* from its earliest days and a tireless movement activist until his death in 1972. In Meyer's formulation, social conservatives and libertarians should be natural political allies. Not only are their goals compatible, he argued, but also their philosophies are complementary, if not codependent. Either philosophy, if not reined in by the other, risks veering wildly off the tracks.

At CPAC, watching anti-immigration activists frothing at the mouth and calling illegal immigrants "burglars" and "wage thieves" and watching libertarians selling T-shirts urging "Capitalists of the world unite," it's not hard to see how that might happen.

Meyer began expounding his theory in a series of essays in *National Review* in 1956. It boiled down to a simple formulation: no act is truly moral unless it is freely chosen. While Meyer agreed with social conservatives about the importance of moral order, he feared that they were so wrapped up in preserving Western tradition that they were willing to resort to authoritarianism to achieve their goals. At the same time, while Meyer was in sympathy with libertarians and their emphasis on the need for a limited state, he feared that their philosophy was prone to degenerate into the pursuit of freedom for its own sake, free of any moral boundaries.

As Meyer wrote: "Truth withers when freedom dies, however righteous the authority that kills it. . . . Free individualism uninformed by moral value rots at its core and soon surrenders to tyranny."

What's more, Meyer argued, social conservatives had a vested interest in the small government pursued by libertarians. It was the government, particularly the federal government, that was to blame for what many perceived at the time to be America's moral decay. As conservative writer David Frum summed up Meyer's thinking: it was federal judges who were banning prayer in schools; it was city planners destroying inner cities with their highways and public-housing projects; it was New Deal welfare programs fostering illegitimacy. The way to achieve social conservatives' goals, Meyer argued, was to beat back big government. In other words, in a conservative society, libertarian means would achieve traditionalist ends.[4]

It was a clever argument, especially in light of the threat from "Godless" international communism, which was despised equally by libertarians and social conservatives. And to the extent that the conservative movement has congealed and succeeded in the decades since Meyer began pushing it, that success—first within the Republican Party and then on the national stage—has been due to the libertarian and social-conservative factions sticking together.

These partners got the Republican Party to nominate Barry Goldwater, a libertarian-conservative and militantly anti-Communist U.S. senator from Arizona, for president in 1964. While Goldwater lost that race in a spectacular fashion, getting less than 40 percent of the popular vote, his candidacy committed the Republican Party to the cause of conservatism.

Out of Goldwater's failed campaign rose many of the pillars of the modern conservative movement. An out-of-work actor and former Democrat named Ronald Reagan launched his political career during the 1964 campaign with a rousing, nationally televised speech, "A Time for Choosing," in support of Goldwater. The antifeminist icon Phyllis Schlafly, best known today for her fight against the Equal Rights Amendment, first became known for writing a pro-Goldwater book, *A Choice, Not an Echo*, attacking the liberal Republican establishment that had elected Dwight Eisenhower and nominated Richard Nixon for turning the party into a weak imitation of the Democrats. And last but not least, the idea for the American Conservative Union—which founded and runs CPAC and serves as something of an umbrella organization for the conservative movement—was born in a meeting just five days after

Goldwater's defeat, with the idea of carrying on the fight begun in the 1964 campaign.

From these humble beginnings, the conservative movement went on to elect Reagan as president in 1980 and 1984. It turned over control of both houses of Congress to the Republican Party in 1994. It elected Bush in 2000. And it reelected him, with increased margins in Congress, in 2004.

So why was all not well in the Republican Party in the months after Bush's reelection? Why, as Democrats wept over the election returns, did a significant segment of the conservative movement weep with them? Why, as activists and students and journalists gathered for CPAC, was there a distinct sense that something was amiss?

Because the marriage at the heart of the conservative movement was falling apart.

To be sure, the relationship has had its rocky patches before. It has always been more *Married with Children* than *Ozzie and Harriet*. Whatever alliances have been formed, libertarians have always tended to see social conservatives as rubes ready to thump nonbelievers on the head with the Bible first chance they get, and social conservatives have always tended to see libertarians as dope-smoking devil worshippers.

The exaggeration is only slight. In 1957, the Communist-turned-social-conservative Whittaker Chambers famously wrote of libertarian favorite Ayn Rand that "from almost any page of *Atlas Shrugged*, a voice can be heard, from painful necessity, commanding: 'To a gas chamber—go!'" In 1961, Ronald Hamowy, reviewing the first years of *National Review*'s existence for the libertarian *New Individualist Review*, blasted editor William F. Buckley Jr. and his colleagues for plotting to reintroduce the burning of heretics. In 1969, a libertarian delegate to the conservative youth group Young Americans for Freedom (YAF), which was holding a convention in St. Louis, burned his draft card on the floor of the convention hall—sparking a physical confrontation and the tossing out of three hundred libertarian YAF members.

The split under way between libertarians and social conserva-tives today is less dramatic than those of the past—there are no punches being thrown (yet), and Nazi analogies in contemporary politics are usually confined to the MoveOn.org crowd—but it is far more profound.

This time, the split is not a spat. It is a slow but sure breaking apart.

The sides here are not arguing over one unpopular war, as they were during Vietnam. They are not arguing about any of the vari-ous vagaries and fine points of conservative thought that have fueled so many heated internal debates over the decades. They are not fighting over one administration's failure to rein in the size of government, as some conservatives did during the Reagan years.

Today, no longer bound together by the Cold War or opposition to Bill Clinton and having tasted power at the small price of bend-ing their beliefs, the two sides are fighting over nothing less than whether the Republican Party will complete its abandonment of the very principle upon which their fusionist marriage has been based these many years: a commitment to limited government.

Will social conservatives continue to accept federally funded "character education" in lieu of education reforms that would let parents choose their children's schools? Will they continue to accept billions of dollars of government money channeled to reli-gious charities in lieu of reducing the tax burden on Americans so that they could give more money to charity themselves? Will they continue to accept the idea of government as nanny, protecting children from sex and violence in TV shows, movies, video games, and every other conceivable medium, in lieu of demanding a soci-ety in which parents are expected to be responsible for their own children? Will they continue to embrace the machinery of federal power they once feared, simply because the "good guys" are the ones pulling the levers for the time being?

In other words, can social conservatives and libertarians return to the common ground they once shared, or will their differences grow irreconcilable?

The early signs are less than encouraging.

The Bush administration, steered by the thinking of Karl Rove, has adopted a philosophy of big-government conservatism, which joins unrestrained government spending to an aggressive appeal to religious conservatives. It is a philosophy that has led Bush and the Republican Congress to create a $1.2 trillion Medicare prescription-drug benefit, making Bush the first president in a generation to create a new federal entitlement program. It is a philosophy that has led the president to support a constitutional amendment banning gay marriage, which would override the decisions of several state governments on a matter that has traditionally been left to the states. It is a philosophy that has led the president and Congress to undertake a highly politicized intervention into a painful family medical decision, in the case of Terri Schiavo in Florida. And ultimately it is a philosophy that has the Republican Party running hard and fast away from the ideas that have been the underpinning of the conservative movement since before Goldwater.

Rove arrived on the first day of CPAC, following morning talks on "How the Good Guys Won" and "How the Bad Guys Tried to Stop Us," to remind conservatives of how far they'd come and to present a plan for where he promised to take them next.

Rove—the man the president had dubbed "the Architect" in his 2004 victory speech, delivered in the very same building just over three months before—reminded the crowd of how Lyndon Johnson won the presidency in a landslide forty years ago. After that election, the Democrats held 68 Senate seats, 295 House seats, and 33 governorships. Liberalism was far and away the nation's dominant political philosophy, and the Democrats were unquestionably the country's governing party.

Now all that had changed. The numbers bore repeating: Republicans now had 55 Senate seats, 232 House seats, and 28 governorships. They had won seven of the last ten presidential elections. The Republicans of 2004 weren't quite the Democrats of 1964—but they were on their way.

How had they gotten there? Where were they going?

Rove's talk was as notable for what it didn't say as for what it did. Not once did Rove proclaim the importance of reducing the size and scope of government. Not once did he echo Reagan's warning that government *is* the problem and not the solution. Nowhere to be found was Goldwater's wisdom that "a government big enough to give you everything you want is also big enough to take away everything you have."

Quite the contrary.

Far from reaffirming the Republican Party's past, Rove rebuked it. In the past, he said, the Republican Party had been "reactionary" and infected with "pessimism." He lamented that "for decades, Democrats were setting the agenda and liberals were setting the pace of change and had the visionary goals.

"But times change, and often for the better," Rove said. Now "this president and today's conservative movement are shaping history." Whereas the conservative movement was once a "small, principled opposition," it was now "broad and inclusive" and "confident and optimistic and forward-leaning" and—the word choice here might have been more revealing than Rove intended, so why not italicize it—"*most important of all, dominant.*"

There is, of course, always a trade-off in politics between "small and principled" and "broad and inclusive." The trick, for people who care about the principle part of the equation, is to balance the two so that one's party has the support to win elections and the integrity for those wins to mean something. The question, then, is whether the Republican Party and the conservative movement have come to believe that simple dominance really is "most important of all."

There's significant reason to believe that they have. Having lost confidence that they can sell the American people on the need for smaller government, both the party and the movement have shifted their strategy from fighting big government to trying to co-opt it.

If Rove was doing anything up there on that stage at CPAC, he was forcefully rejecting the image and agenda of the Republican Party as it existed during the Gingrich years. In those heady days back in 1994, the GOP took control of both houses of

Congress—after forty years of unbroken Democratic rule in the lower chamber—on the strength of the Contract with America, which promised "the end of government that is too big, too intrusive, and too easy with the public's money." The Republicans seemed ascendant back then. Not only had the American people elevated the GOP, but they had also slapped down Clinton for his overreaching national-health-care plan. But the revolution went off course, and in doing so, it provided a cautionary example that convinced many conservatives to see small government as a losing political proposition.

As conservative commentator David Brooks wrote in the *New York Times Magazine* in a piece ahead of the 2004 elections, if one wanted to put a "death date" on the tombstone of the Republican Party's commitment to small government, it would be November 14, 1995.[5] That was when the newly minted Republican majority shut down the federal government as part of a dispute with the president over the budget. The Republicans, proposing a number of cuts, were spoiling for a fight over the size of government. Clinton let them have it—in more ways than one.

While each side tried to blame the other for the impasse, the Republicans just couldn't get the better of Bill Clinton. They expected the public to be on their side. "People who know the facts overwhelmingly support our view that it is time to end big government," Republican House majority leader Dick Armey said a few days into the shutdown.[6] Republican senator Phil Gramm of Texas, never one to back down from a fight, said at one point that the government could stay shut down as far as he was concerned, joking, "Have you really noticed a difference?"[7] The public wasn't amused. The Republican Party got slammed in the polls, and the Gingrich Revolution was set back irreparably—traumatizing an entire generation of GOP legislators.

(Fittingly enough, it was also during the government shutdown that Clinton began his affair with Monica Lewinsky, setting in motion another chain of events that would end badly for the Republicans—cementing their image as, to use Rove's words, pessimistic and reactionary.)

After the government-shutdown debacle, the Republicans began searching for a new approach. The American people might hate big government in theory, the new thinking went, but at the same time they don't have much appetite for seeing government programs that they've become attached to get slashed.

Thus Texas governor George W. Bush came onto the scene in 1999, groomed by a woman named Karen Hughes and backed by a shadowy figure named Rove, with something called "compassionate conservatism." The phrase made conservative stalwarts bristle (was conservatism in and of itself somehow less than compassionate? they asked), and it made liberal partisans titter (did Republicans really think they could disguise their coldhearted agenda behind a linguistic trick, they asked?)—but there was far more substance behind the phrase than any of the skeptics realized at the time.

This wasn't the old Republican agenda of cutting taxes and the government programs they fund gussied up with a little rouge and lipstick. This was a different animal entirely. "Too often, my party has confused the need for limited government with a disdain for government itself," Bush said during the 2000 campaign. He derided the idea that "if government would only get out of our way, all our problems would be solved." He called this a "destructive mind-set" with "no higher goal, no nobler purpose, than 'Leave us alone.'" Instead, Bush said, America needed less "sprawling, arrogant, aimless government" and more "focused and effective and energetic government."[8]

To skeptics, that sounded an awful lot like saying America needed less *bad* big government and more *good* big government—with "bad" meaning Democrat-controlled and "good" meaning Republican-controlled.

The skeptics are still waiting to be proved wrong.

Judging by CPAC 2005, which dedicated virtually its entire middle day to the issue of out-of-control spending (panels included "Cutting Spending Is Tough Work, but Somebody Has to Do It" and "They Take and Spend What We Earn but Won't Let Us Save It"), it sure didn't sound like Republican big government had turned out to be any more "focused and effective and energetic" than Democratic big government.

In fact, quite the opposite. If anything, one-party big government run by Republicans has turned out to be a massively bloated endeavor. According to the conservative Heritage Foundation, federal spending grew twice as fast in Bush's first term as it did under Clinton—and the bulk of the growth was in nondefense spending. What's more, the spending hasn't been turned toward any particularly conservative ends. The president's signature education law, No Child Left Behind, boosted federal spending on education 137 percent from 2001 to 2006, while all but abandoning free-market education reforms such as vouchers and charter schools. There was nothing conservative about the massive giveaway of subsidies to farmers in 2002. And there was precious little conservative about the Medicare prescription-drug benefit in 2003.

Some conservatives may believe they are co-opting big government. In reality, it is co-opting them.

What's striking, however, is just how dependent big-government conservatism is on the War on Terror. Bush's compassionate conservatism lost the popular vote in 2000. And to the extent that Republicans succeeded electorally in 2002 and 2004, it was based on the president's decision to take a hard line in the War on Terror far more than on any domestic policy innovations.

Just what would have happened to a George W. Bush administration in more placid times? He entered office badly damaged by the election controversy in Florida. A liberal Republican senator defected, giving the Democrats control of the Senate. If not for the boost in support Bush gained after 9/11, his party might well have lost seats in the 2002 midterm elections. Come 2004, the "soccer moms" turned "terror moms" would still have been soccer moms, inclined to vote Democratic. Conservatives would have been unimpressed with Bush's conservatism; liberals would have been unimpressed with his compassion.

Of course, that's not how it happened. And to say that the Republican Party is winning elections because it's right on the War on Terror is hardly an indictment. What's worrying, however, is that conservatives who have long pined for activist government have found in the War on Terror the key to crafting an overarching theme.

In his speech at CPAC, Rove explained that the primary factor behind the realignment he sees occurring in American politics is that the Republicans are "seizing the mantle of idealism." Idealism used to be the preserve of liberals, he said, but Reagan changed all that when he vowed to end communism, not just to contain it. Now Bush was building on that legacy. "President Bush's eventual goal is the triumph of freedom and the end of tyranny," Rove said. "This vision . . . is consistent with the deep idealism of the American people."

What's more, having seized the banner of idealism abroad, it was now possible to connect Bush's domestic agenda to a more sweeping vision: spreading freedom abroad and at home.

"Our goal as conservatives must be to put government on the side of progress and reform, modernization and greater freedom, more personal choice and greater prosperity," Rove told the CPAC crowd, echoing any number of speeches Bush gave on the campaign trail in 2004. "The great goal of modern conservatism is to make our society more free, more prosperous, and more just."

These lines received light applause from the crowd. Republicans were going to need more energy than that to fulfill Rove's ambitious agenda. The Republican Party, he said, needed to "reform" the tax code, health care, pension plans, the legal system, public education, and worker training; it needed to "build" an Ownership Society of homes and businesses, and it needed to "prepare" Americans for meeting "the challenges of a free society." But that's not all. It also needed to "build" a culture of life, "support" religious charities, and "foster" a culture of "service and citizenship."

If this wasn't activist government, it's hard to say what would be. But Rove wasn't quite done. "Republicans cannot grow tired or timid," he said. "We have been given the opportunity to govern, and now we have to show that we deserve the respect and trust of our fellow citizens."

This was all a long way from thirty years ago, when California's governor Ronald Reagan told the libertarian magazine *Reason* that "the very heart and soul of conservatism is libertarianism," the desire for "less government interference," "less centralized authority," and "more individual freedom."

Conservatives had backed a wartime president in a tough reelection campaign, but were they really comfortable with resuming the era of big government, as long as it was all under conservative auspices? Was this really the new heart and soul of conservatism?

Over the course of three days at CPAC, it became clear that while conservatives were ecstatic over their recent victories, they were deeply divided as to whether to move into the new edifice the Architect was busy building.

Some were quite eager.

Take, for instance, Ohio's secretary of state (and Republican candidate for governor in 2006), Kenneth Blackwell, who spoke on "Marriage as a Winning Issue in 2004 and Beyond." Blackwell, who is African American, credited opposition to gay marriage—along with the Republican Party's general social conservatism—for boosting Bush's vote among Catholic and black voters far above his 2000 showing. Bush's share of the black vote in Ohio, he noted, went to 16 percent in 2004, up from 9 percent in 2000. "I want to be sure that there are no revisionists here among us," Blackwell said. "The reality is that the values voters won Ohio and won the presidency for George Bush."

This was a recurring theme over the three days, that "values voters," social conservatives, religious conservatives—whatever one wanted to call them—were now the real linchpin of the Republican coalition. These voters had often been ignored and treated shabbily by the Republican Party, the argument went, but now they'd proven that when the GOP caters to them on issues such as gay marriage, stem-cell research, abortion, obscenity on TV, and judicial nominations, they can deliver the vote.

There were some problems with this theory. Exit polls showed that 22 percent of voters named "moral values" as their "most important issue," a fact of which much was made in the days after the election, on the Left as well as on the Right. But the very same polls on which the moral-values story line was based showed that those who said either "terrorism" or "Iraq," taken together, added up to 34 percent of the electorate. Moral values certainly weren't *un*important, but the 2004 elections were clearly about the War on Terror. It was evident not just from the polls, but also from the campaigns both parties ran, which overwhelmingly focused on who was better suited to protect the homeland and fight terrorism overseas.

Still, social conservatives weren't all that far off. Whether or not so-called values voters had been the deciding factor in 2004, they were certainly of primary importance to Rove's electoral strategy moving forward. One of his central insights was that the Republican Party had to start making inroads with minority voters, and while blacks and Hispanics have long voted Democratic based on economic issues and historical loyalty, they might be persuaded to vote Republican by an aggressive appeal to them on social and cultural issues. There were other components to the Republican Party's minority-outreach strategy, of course, such as not harping on illegal immigration—lest the GOP look hard-hearted or racist—but God and family were the keys.

What's more, one simply can't overestimate the religious fervor of the Republican Party's existing base. There was a sentiment among many at CPAC that George W. Bush had been picked by God to lead America. In fact, this claim was made so many times during the conference, both from the stage and from the audience, that the incidents were almost beyond counting. In one particularly partisan prayer before one of CPAC's formal dinners, God was thanked specifically for the Republican majority in Congress.

When God and government are on the same side, who needs restraint?

Of course, not everyone at CPAC was ready to go along with Rove's emerging God-and-government coalition. While many social conservatives are ready to make common cause with a party that has lost all concern with limiting the size of government—that spends without restraint, that sees no area of American life as too intimate for Washington's gaze, and that actively looks to expand the state to shore up its political base—other conservatives are not.

Peppered throughout the conference were signs of discontent.

Floyd Brown, executive director of Young America's Foundation and one of the organizers of CPAC, told the *Milwaukee Journal Sentinel* that while conservatives were euphoric about the elections, they were still troubled by the growth of government. "Bush is not the leader of the conservative movement," he said. "The conservative movement is going to stick to its roots."[9]

Senator Tom Coburn (R-Okla.), in a talk titled "Simply Talking about Runaway Spending Won't Cut It," blasted the president for his "failed leadership" in not having vetoed a single spending bill in his time in office. He also blasted some of his colleagues as "careerist" lawmakers, more concerned with getting reelected than pushing a bold conservative agenda. Coburn was introduced by former congressman and current MSNBC talk-show host Joe Scarborough, who had just written an election-year book blasting the Republican Party for having gone native in Washington and having abandoned the legacy of Ronald Reagan.

Pat Buchanan, never one for understatement, came out guns blazing. "We do not consider 'Big Government Conservatism' a philosophy," he told the crowd. "We consider it a heresy."[10]

The biggest gap, however, was generational. If the kids at CPAC are the future of the conservative movement, then big changes are on their way—at least when it comes to cultural issues.

Take, for example, two students from the College of New Jersey, Thomas Sales and Eric Pasternack, at CPAC representing their College Republicans group. Sales described himself as "a big fan of God" who finds homosexuality "reprehensible" because of his Christian beliefs. Asked his opinion on gay marriage, however, his response was simple: "From a liberty perspective, I can't find any reason you'd ban it." Pasternack, chiming in, added that most people their age are more in favor of civil unions than opposed to gay marriage. "It won't be an issue in twenty years," Sales added.

And these two were hardly a deviation from the mean. When

Senator Rick Santorum (R-Pa.) spoke on the first day of CPAC, he knew some of the younger people would be skeptical, so he addressed himself to those "economic conservatives who may not be cultural conservatives." He presented an argument that gay marriage would lead to social decay, which would in turn lead to a need for more government. But at least some of the students were unimpressed. Asked about the talk the next day by the *St. Petersburg Times*, twenty-two-year-old Deb McCown identified Santorum as "one of the speakers everybody hated." McCown, editor of the *Carolina Review*, a conservative magazine at the University of North Carolina, continued, saying "he got up there and started talking about marriage as if it was the biggest issue, but it's not. It's taxing and spending." She added that Republicans are not living up to their ideals of "cutting spending and smaller government and personal responsibility."[11]

Perhaps most confounding to CPAC's organizers were the results of the straw poll held at the end of the conference, in which six hundred respondents (two-thirds of them college students) picked the candidates they thought would win the Republican and Democratic presidential nominations in 2008. Hillary Clinton got the Democratic nod, of course. But the Republican nod went not to a traditional conservative, such as Florida's governor Jeb Bush or Senate majority leader Bill Frist, but instead to the fiscally conservative, socially liberal, tough-on-terror Rudy Giuliani.

What those voting probably didn't know was that American Conservative Union chairman David Keene had pointedly rebuffed an offer by Giuliani to address the conservative faithful, sans his usual speaking fee. "I would assume he wanted to come here to boost his conservative credentials, but we didn't think that would be useful," Keene told columnist Deroy Murdock after CPAC.[12]

So just what is it about a Rudy Giuliani that so upsets the old guard of the conservative movement? Is it the potential for a new kind of fusionism—really, a rejuvenation of the old kind—that is committed to small government in economic and personal affairs and that, at the same time, is unflinching in the face of the terrorist threat?

Can the Republican Party and the conservative movement really conceive of no way forward other than to concede the bulk of their long-held convictions to the opposition? Do they have so little faith in the principles of the movement of Goldwater and Reagan?

The history of modern conservatism is the history of a marriage, with all of the attendant ups and downs, spats and make-ups, flirtations and frustrations, and distance traveled together by souls sharing a common purpose.

Or at least something vaguely resembling a common purpose. If you squint really hard.

For as long as there has been a self-aware conservative movement—that is, since roughly 1955, when William F. Buckley Jr. founded *National Review*—a debate has raged as to whether its two main factions, traditionalists and libertarians, truly share the same goals or whether they share only common enemies. Surely, in the decades after World War II, people from both camps, as they wandered in the political wilderness, cursed the name of Franklin Delano Roosevelt. They also despised the specter of totalitarian communism. And they would instinctively band together to oppose any massive expansion of the federal government, such as Lyndon Baines Johnson's Great Society. But beyond that, it has remained a perennially open question just why these two groups would ever choose to be in a political movement together.

The traditionalists—typified by political philosophers such as Russell Kirk and Richard M. Weaver—placed the highest value (as their label might suggest) on tradition and social order. Repulsed by the rise of mass society and horrified by the depravity of the "total" war waged by and against Nazism and fascism, they radically rejected their own age. Seeking solace in the past, they exalted concepts such as a rigid class structure, elitism, and obedience to authority—especially the authority of God. As Kirk put it, this brand of conservative believed, first and foremost, that a divine intent rules society and that "political problems, at bottom, are religious and moral problems."[13]

The libertarians, on the other hand—typified by economists such as Milton Friedman and Murray Rothbard—placed the highest value on human freedom. These men, too, were aghast at the age in which they lived, though for very different reasons than those of the traditionalists. They believed that, if anything, society had grown too authoritarian. In the march toward greater and greater state control of the economy, first during the Great Depression and then during World War II, the libertarians made out what the Austrian economist F. A. Hayek called, in a slim volume published in 1944, "The Road to Serfdom." Control over the economy, Hayek argued, meant control over every aspect of man's being—which could only lead to totalitarianism. The government, libertarians believed, must be kept as small as possible, and individuals must be restricted in their actions as little as possible.

Libertarians considered traditionalists little dictators, aching to subject their fellow man to one particular view of God's will. Traditionalists considered libertarians imitation anarchists, isolating man from society and reducing him to nothing more than the sum of his material desires. Yet somehow by 1964 these two warring factions would ally to take over the Republican Party. By 2004, forty years later, they would dominate the entire country.

On the road to dominance lay a cantankerous Arizona senator, a genial out-of-work actor, and a swaggering pretend cowboy. Yet few conservatives—and even fewer liberals—remember the role played by a chain-smoking, home-schooling, nocturnal ex-Communist named Frank Meyer, who, from his house tucked away in the Catskill Mountains near Woodstock, New York, showed the movement how it could fuse together into something far greater than the sum of its parts.

The world was a lonely place for conservatives only a little more than fifty years ago. But Meyer showed them it didn't have to be. Tradition and liberty were complementary. Freedom and virtue were inextricably linked. And "Godless" communism was a moral affront and a mortal threat to traditionalists and libertarians alike. A limited federal government pursuing a strong national defense would be the ideal scenario for all.

Meyer's fusionism is a tradition and a formula that contemporary conservatives have largely forgotten or set aside, especially since the end of the Cold War. But as the Republican Party gains in power, and the old alliances shift and crack and twist and fray under the tumult of wielding that power, it's worth remembering just how the alliance at the heart of the party came to be in the first place.

There are many in the Republican Party who believe that now is the time to enjoy the spoils of victory. In truth, however, this is just the beginning of a new war—a war for the heart and soul of conservatism.

On one side are those conservatives who think that the cause of small government is lost. And if they can't beat big government, they might as well run it. They believe that the battles of the past have been a foolish diversion and that now is the time to adapt to the world as it is and to cease imagining the world as it could be. Some of these people have begun to simply seek power for its own sake. Others have sold their souls in the hope of buying them back one day. Still others have glimpsed a golden opportunity to impose their idea of morality on their fellow citizens. The road to victory has been long and arduous, all of these people recall, and so in their minds there can be no turning back to the discarded ideas of the past.

Yet there are other conservatives. They are just now waking up to what their party has become: an echo, not a choice. They are realizing that big-government conservatism is no longer an ill-conceived theory, it is the creed of the Republican Party. And they are realizing that far from being "confident and optimistic and forward-leaning," as Karl Rove would have it, this brand of conservatism is weak-kneed, defeatist, and retrogressive to a time before giants fused together the coalition that in four decades defeated communism abroad, halted the march toward socialism at home, lowered taxes, and reformed welfare—just to name a few of its accomplishments.

This is the story of a movement—an extended family, really—that rose from humble beginnings to heights it could never have imagined. It's the story of idealists tempted and eventually corrupted by power. And it is the story of old friends torn apart by the pressures and possibilities and pitfalls of success. Most of all, however, it is the story of how these old friends might renew the bonds that have tied them together these many years and recall the ideals and the ideas and the passions that once united them.

The Republican Party stands at a pivotal moment in its history, as was becoming clear to those on the convention floor at CPAC. It can learn to live with big government, determining that it's not so bad, just as long as it's Republicans intruding into the lives of Americans instead of Democrats. Or it can remember its roots and realize that a majority set against its own bedrock principles of limited government and individual liberty is not one worth having—and thus not one that can long be sustained.

The marriage between libertarians and social conservatives would certainly not be the first torn apart by power and fortune and success. But the consequences of such a divorce would be uniquely far-reaching. They would be of concern well beyond the expanses of the conservative family—most acutely, perhaps, to those moderates and liberals already profoundly uncomfortable living under Republican governance, who can only dread what this new, expansionist conservatism might become.

Most aggrieved, however, would be those conservatives who have remained faithful to their small-government vows—those who know the nobility of what conservatism can be when it holds to its ideal of a limited government that leaves Americans to work and prosper and love and pray, free from the daily diktats of the meddlesome minds in the nation's capital.

The differences between libertarians and social conservatives are not yet irreconcilable. There is a way open toward reconciliation—a way that revives the old fusion of liberty and tradition, freedom and responsibility, small government and strong government.

But to find it, conservatives of all stripes will have to begin by acknowledging the elephant in the room.

2

United against Communism

In the era of Fox News, *National Review*, the *Weekly Standard*, Ann Coulter, Rush Limbaugh, Sean Hannity, Bill O'Reilly, the Heritage Foundation, the Cato Institute, *Reason* magazine, and literally hundreds of other right-wing magazines, editorial pages, personalities, think tanks, and pressure groups, it's hard to imagine an America without the modern conservative movement.

Pleasant for liberals, no doubt, but a real stretch of the imagination.

Nonetheless, such was the landscape of American political thought as World War II came to a close. The very word "conservative" was hardly a part of the American political vocabulary, except perhaps as an epithet to be hurled at Republicans by New Deal liberals—and for Republicans to run away from at a clip. The few prophets of what would one day come to be known as conservatism, iconoclastic writers such as Albert Jay Nock and H. L. Mencken, preferred other terms: "classical liberal," "radical," even "anarchist."[1]

The reasons the Right was so decimated were hardly obscure: The combination of the Great Depression and World War II served as a one-two punch to the old Right's twin creeds of laissez-faire at home and isolationism abroad.[2] People didn't want to hear about the virtues of the free market after losing all their money in the stock market, being robbed of their life savings in bank failures, or watching their jobs disappear with the rest of the economy; and no one wanted to hear about the wisdom of noninterventionism after having saved half the world from tyranny at great cost in blood and treasure.

The spirit of national unity during the war, in fact, was so strong that liberalism essentially became the only "respectable" point of view among intellectuals. Liberals simply stopped taking dissenting views seriously. In 1950, the liberal critic Lionel Trilling famously proclaimed that in the United States at the time, liberalism was "not only the dominant but even the sole intellectual tradition." He confessed that a conservative "reactionary impulse" did exist still in America, but dismissed it as something that expressed itself only in "irritable mental gestures which seek to resemble ideas."[3]

Trilling wasn't being terribly unfair. Following the war, conservative publications in America could be counted on one hand. The only explicitly conservative journal was *Human Events*, an eight-page weekly newsletter founded in 1944, the first office of which was one of its founding editors' apartments. By 1947, its circulation was only about five thousand.[4]

There were grumblers of various stripes, upset with Democratic mishandling of the Cold War, the loss of American sovereignty to the United Nations, the growing power of the labor unions, and what they saw as creeping socialism and immorality at home. But these grumblers hardly knew one another existed; polite, liberal society did its level best to ignore them, condescending to recognize their existence only to denounce the scourge of McCarthyism. Conservative direct-mail pioneer Richard Viguerie and fellow conservative movement founder David Franke have called this period in the history of the Right the "conservative non-movement," a state of utter "grass-roots anarchy."[5]

There were, running through those gnarled grass roots, the three strands of what would come to be the thread of the conservative movement: anticommunism, libertarianism, and traditionalism. But they were, in the decade after World War II, largely tangled, muddied, and difficult to see with the naked eye.

The clarifying, unifying moment came in August of 1948, when a pudgy-faced, rumpled, graying senior editor at *Time*, Whittaker Chambers, told the House Un-American Activities Committee that he had been an underground agent for the Soviet Union in the 1930s and that one of his contacts during that time was a man named Alger Hiss—then a young State Department official, now president of the Carnegie Endowment for International Peace and a fixture of Washington society.

Hiss sued for libel. The Left closed ranks. Truman called the case a "red herring." Eleanor Roosevelt said Hiss was the victim of a smear campaign. But Chambers was able to back up his charges with documentary evidence, and by January of 1950 Hiss was convicted of perjury (and, by implication, spying) and sentenced to five years in prison.

The Hiss affair, in a profound way, alienated many conservatives even further from the liberal establishment. They were, in a word, shocked. It was "the 'best people' who were for Alger Hiss," Chambers wrote in his memoir *Witness*, published in 1952. "It was the enlightened and the powerful . . . who snapped their minds shut in a pro-Hiss psychosis."[6] The Left in America had never hated communism in the visceral way conservatives thought necessary and proper, but now they were apologizing for out-and-out treason. Just after Hiss was convicted, Truman's secretary of state, Dean Acheson, declared his solidarity, saying: "I do not intend to turn my back on Alger Hiss."[7] In turn, few conservatives would turn their backs on Senator Joseph McCarthy when, barely two weeks after the Hiss conviction, he showed up in Wheeling, West Virginia, to inform a group of Republican women that he held in his hand a list of known Communist spies in the State Department.[8]

Anticommunism, however, was not enough on its own to draw together a coherent conservative movement. The ex-Communists

who would come to make up a good deal of the conservative movement's anti-Communist wing—men such as Chambers and Frank
Meyer—were still migrating to the Right in the late 1940s and
early 1950s.

Meyer, who had broken with the Communist Party in 1945, was
converted into a full-fledged member of the Right in large part by
reading the works of the patron saint of the libertarians, F. A.
Hayek.[9] That American libertarians of this period had to look to
an Austrian professor living in London for inspiration and leadership is a pretty good indicator of the trouble they faced at home.

When a group of nearly forty European and American scholars
got together in 1947 to found an organization devoted to the
preservation of "private property and the competitive market," the
ten-day conference happened not in New York City or Washington, D.C., but nestled away high in the Swiss Alps. Thus was born
the Mont Pelerin Society. "It showed us that we were not alone,"
Milton Friedman told *Fortune* magazine three decades later.[10]

Slightly less isolated than the poor libertarians were those souls,
deeply troubled by modernity and longing for a distant past, who
formed the strand of conservatism that would come to be known
as traditionalism. Mostly ensconced in the universities—and thus
not quite reduced to pecking out newsletters to each other while
eating cat food, like some of their conservative brethren—these
thinkers decried materialism, mass society, and the worship of the
common man. Thinkers such as University of Chicago English professor Richard Weaver idealized the Old South, which he dubbed
"the last non-materialist civilization in the Western world." In his
most famous work, *Ideas Have Consequences*, he traced the
decline of Western civilization to the late fourteenth century and
William of Occam's theory of nominalism.[11] Russell Kirk, who
gave the modern conservative movement a name and its first sense
of self-awareness, so despaired for the future of concepts such as
tradition and hierarchy and class that he nearly named *The Conservative Mind*, published in 1953, "The Conservatives' Rout."[12]

But while Kirk may have decided to go in a slightly more optimistic direction with his title, the fact remained that—for the time

being, at least—the conservatives had indeed been routed. While hope was on the horizon, there would still be some significant indignities left to suffer.

One Low after Another

The year 1952 was a jubilant one for Republicans, but it marked the beginning of a long period of depression for conservatives— what conservative-movement historian Lee Edwards called in an interview, "one low after another." Eisenhower, of course, captured the White House, and with it the Republicans gained narrow majorities in both houses of Congress. It was the first time since 1930 that Republicans had controlled both the White House and Capitol Hill. Eisenhower, if only by virtue of his smile, had finally gotten the GOP out of the national dog house.

The convention that nominated Eisenhower over the more conservative Robert A. Taft had been a contentious one, with disputed delegates and supporters of the Ohio senator certain their man had been robbed. But Taft, ever the loyal Republican, had closed ranks with Eisenhower, while doing what he could to pull the genial general to the right. In what came to be known as the Morningside Declaration (after Eisenhower's headquarters in Morningside Heights in New York City, where the two men met), Eisenhower made a series of assurances to Taft over a two-hour breakfast. In turn, Taft went across the street to a hotel and made a ringing endorsement of his rival, declaring that both he and Ike agreed the fundamental issue of the campaign was turning back "the creeping socialism in every domestic field." Liberal Republicans were dismayed, calling the meeting the "Surrender at Morningside Heights." For Taft, it was a triumph.[13]

When Eisenhower won, and Taft became the Senate's majority leader, it looked as if the party's liberal and conservative wings might form a powerful alliance to govern the country, one that could last for an administration or even a generation. But it was not to be. Eisenhower and Taft worked closely together in the first months of 1953. Some suggested Taft was acting almost as a prime minister to the president. But one day while playing golf with the president, Taft felt a severe pain in his hip. He had cancer. He quickly stepped down as majority leader, and not long after that died on July 31, 1953.[14]

Without Taft, there was no effective counterweight to the liberal Republicans in the Eisenhower administration, and there was also no one to keep extremists on the other side, particularly McCarthy, in check. When McCarthy went on the attack against the Eisenhower administration shortly after Taft's death, he brought the wrath of a popular president down on himself. Hearings to investigate and then censure McCarthy were initiated in Congress, with Ike's blessing. Televised live, the hearings beamed McCarthy's "menacing monotone" and "perpetual 5-o'clock shadow," as McCarthy's chief aide, Roy Cohn, put it, into some 20 million homes daily. McCarthy made the "perfect stock villain."[15]

With Taft dead, and McCarthy as good as dead at the end of 1954, the conservative movement was without a leader—or even a good, drunken rabble-rouser.

Conservatives were at such loose ends with all of this that some came completely undone. In 1958, a fanatic named Robert Welch founded the John Birch Society, named after a Protestant missionary who had been killed by Chinese Communists at the end of World War II. Welch, a retired Massachusetts candy maker (he was named Candy Industry Man of the Year in 1947 and, like Willy Wonka, apparently had something of a dark side), believed that everyone everywhere was a dupe of a Communist conspiracy aimed at world domination. In one of his main works, he claimed that Eisenhower had been "consciously serving the Communist conspiracy for all of his adult life." (To this, Russell Kirk retorted, "Ike's not a Communist—he's a golfer!"[16]) Despite such nuttiness, the society won a membership in the tens of thousands in the late '50s and early '60s, with chapters all over the country. Members would get together in each other's living room to watch films of lectures by "The Founder," as members invariably referred to Welch, and to carry out letter-writing campaigns aimed wherever Communist infiltration reared its ugly head—for instance, say, in the ranks of the Boy Scouts.[17]

Clearly, in the intellectual free-for-all of the 1950s, the conservative movement needed some form, some focus, some center of gravity to keep its constituent parts from flying off into space. It needed a person or an institution that could bring together the strands of the protoconservative movement and tie them into something more coherent. That person would be William F. Buckley Jr., and that institution would be the magazine he founded, *National Review*. Buckley, who in 1951 (at age twenty-five) had written *God and Man at Yale*, decrying his alma mater's hostility to Christianity and capitalism, was uniquely well suited to the task of uniting the diverse factions on the Right. Believing in tradition, economic liberty, and the righteousness of America's struggle against communism, he was, in and of himself, a living, breathing, rapier-witted synthesis of the ideas that would come to unify the Right.

When *National Review* debuted in 1955, it did so with a pugnacious publisher's statement: the magazine was to stand "athwart history, yelling Stop, at a time when no one is inclined to do so, or to have much patience with those who so urge it." It also struck a note of comradery, declaring that the diverse group of editors Buckley had brought together were "non-licensed nonconformists . . . dangerous business in a Liberal world, as every editor of this magazine can readily show by pointing to his scars."[18] The magazine's masthead included traditionalists such as Russell Kirk and Richard Weaver, libertarians such as John Chamberlain and Frank Chodorov, and anti-Communists such as James Burnham and Frank Meyer. They came from different ideological backgrounds, but now, Buckley urged, they must come together against a common enemy.

Individual conservatives were now part of something larger than themselves—they were part of a self-conscious *movement*. They now had a meeting place, a debating chamber, a way to figure out who belonged and who didn't and, most important of all, a means of learning *what to do*. The founding of *National Review*, after all, was more than the launch of a magazine. As longtime publisher William Rusher put it, *National Review* combined for conservatives the roles of church, university, and political party.[19]

Circulation started small: fewer than twenty thousand in its first three years, only thirty thousand by 1960.[20] And the magazine has always had financial difficulties, having to turn to readers for contributions above and beyond the price of a subscription. It dropped from being a weekly to a biweekly in 1958. But circulation jumped to ninety thousand by 1964, the year of the Goldwater candidacy, and since then *National Review* has remained at the center of the conservative movement.[21]

Other signs of life and organization on the Right followed. In response to the challenge from *National Review*, *Human Events* began focusing more on political activism, started holding political action conferences in Washington, D.C., and converted from a newsletter to a weekly tabloid newspaper.[22] At the tenth annual convention of the Young Republicans in Washington, D.C., in 1957, conservatives took over and adopted a platform opposing federal interference in education, opposing membership in the United Nations for Communist China, and opposing compulsory union membership as a condition of employment.[23] The Intercollegiate Society of Individualists, founded in 1953, over the course of eight years expanded its mailing list from six hundred to more than thirteen thousand and distributed conservative literature to about forty thousand students.[24]

But it would be *National Review* to which the intellectual and political development of modern conservatism would most closely track in coming decades. While it's only human to see the current state of the world as preordained, the conservative world was still very much being formed at this point. Buckley's project involved quite a bit of cat herding and saw more than a little fur fly. One man above all others, Frank Meyer, would be there to tend the flock through the tumultuous and crucial 1960s.

Winning by Losing (and Fusing)

The moment Barry Goldwater heard that President Kennedy had been shot, he knew he would never be president of the United

States. The American people weren't going to endorse an assassination. Goldwater hadn't killed Kennedy (just ask Oliver Stone), but that didn't stop the public from blaming him—or at least blaming the extreme Right—even if it was a lunatic with ties to Soviet Russia, not the John Birch Society, who had pulled the trigger.

When news moved across the wires at 1:32 P.M. Washington time on Friday, November 22, 1963, that shots had been fired at Kennedy's motorcade in Texas, a whole nation asked: What's the matter with Dallas? Writer Rick Perlstein describes the scene in vivid detail in his book on the Goldwater years, *Before the Storm*: the Voice of America bulletin announcing the shooting described Dallas as "the center of the extreme right wing." Clips of Adlai Stevenson being jabbed with anti–United Nations picket signs and spat on by "conservatives" a month earlier in Dallas were shown again and again on TV. Under the headline "Dallas, Long a Radical's Haven," the *New York Herald Tribune* pointed out that "Texas is one of the few states that has a senator ranking with Arizona's Barry Goldwater in conservatism." That senator was John Tower, who had to put up his family in a hotel because of the threats against them. In Washington, D.C., the National Draft Goldwater Committee off Farragut Square was inundated with angry phone calls ("You sons of bitches, you killed him!") and surrounded by an angry mob. The Goldwaterites shut down the office, locked the doors, and retreated to the back room to watch the news.[25]

And it wasn't by any means just liberals who saw a conservative hand in the killing. According to historian Lee Edwards (who had started his first day of work as the Draft Goldwater Committee's publicist that very morning), the first reaction of many conservatives was, "Oh, my God, it must have been one of ours." When, later in the afternoon, Lee Harvey Oswald was identified as the assassin, conservative organizations all over America began checking their membership rolls and donor lists for his name.[26]

They wouldn't find it. But it didn't matter. Conservatives would receive the brunt of the outrage anyway. "When right wing racist fanatics are told over and over again that the President is a traitor, a Red, a 'nigger-lover' . . . that he has traduced the Constitution and is handing America over to a mongrelized world-state, there are bound to be some fanatics dull-witted enough to follow the logic of the indictment all the way and rid American of the man who is betraying it," columnist Max Lerner wrote. Chief Justice Earl Warren, a frequent target of right-wing attacks, said in a service at the Capitol Rotunda that we may never know why Oswald shot Kennedy, "but we do know that such acts are commonly stimulated by forces of hatred and malevolence, such as today are eating their way into the bloodstream of American life."[27]

Goldwater had been skeptical about running for president before Kennedy's assassination. Polls showed him behind; he once told a reporter he didn't have the "really first-class brain" necessary to be president.[28] But at least with Kennedy, he believed he would face a gentlemanly campaign against a man he considered honorable and a friend. He and the president joked about sharing a plane in 1964 and debating at every campaign stop, like Lincoln and Douglas. Johnson, on the other hand, Goldwater detested as a low-life snake and a ruthless political opportunist.[29]

Now, he wanted out. But there was the small matter of the "Draft Goldwater" movement. Since his election to the Senate in 1952, Goldwater had slowly become the hero of the burgeoning conservative movement on account of his fiery criticism of the Eisenhower administration; he accused Ike of offering Americans a "dime-store New Deal" at home and coddling communism abroad. Goldwater's 1960 book *The Conscience of a Conservative* solidified his status, combining libertarian, traditionalist, and anti-Communist themes in a way that made him an idol, a superstar, and a spokesman for conservatism nationwide. It sold 3.5 million copies before the 1964 election.[30] The draft campaign that started the year after his book was published was perhaps the first genuine nomination draft in the history of modern American politics.[31] Goldwater felt a tremendous sense of duty to his supporters, and ultimately he could not let them down.

Goldwater knew he would lose. But this was the right election to lose, and he was the right man to lose it. Specifically, he was the right *kind* of man: Frank Meyer's concept of fusionism made flesh in the person of a square-jawed, government-hating, peaceful-coexistence-mocking, fighter-jet-flying, Thunderbird-driving, western, maverick-Republican senator. As the story of Barry Goldwater can't be told properly apart from the rise of the conservative movement, so the story of the rise of the conservative movement can't be told apart from Frank Meyer and what would come to be called *fusion*.

Frank Meyer didn't choose the word "fusion" or "fusionism" to describe his theory of why the conservative movement should stick together—why it worked, why each faction needed the other, why things really couldn't be any other way. It was thrust upon him. Meyer insisted he wasn't trying to reinvent the wheel, but that he was simply describing the world as it already existed, articulating "the instinctive consensus of the contemporary American conservative movement."[32] But no such consensus existed—the movement was constantly threatening to break apart. Someone had to invent it.

Buckley and *National Review* brought three strands of conservatism under one roof, but that couldn't stop them from fighting. In fact, if anything, like throwing a bunch of cats in a sack, the magazine's founding ensured that claws would be drawn and blood spilled.

Most of the nastiest spats (as today) broke out between the libertarians and the traditionalists. Early on, Meyer himself (who often favored the libertarian side) crossed swords with traditionalist Russell Kirk in the pages of *National Review* over the issue of intellectual freedom. "It is consummate folly," Kirk had written, "to tolerate every variety of opinion, on every topic, out of devotion to abstract 'liberty.'" To Meyer, this was an outrage. "The use of force against those who propound error is wrong," he thundered, "not because it is inexpedient but because it is an outrage upon the freedom of man."[33]

In 1957, when libertarian icon Ayn Rand's masterwork, *Atlas Shrugged*, was published, the task of reviewing it for *National Review* fell to Whittaker Chambers, an anti-Communist clearly closer to the traditionalist wing of conservatism. Rand's novel, which has the productive capitalists on strike against the parasitic masses (for a change), Chambers called "preposterous," "primitive," and "sophomoric." Rand was no better than the Russian Communists she despised and fled as a teenager, Chambers said, as "Randian Man, like Marxian Man, is made the center of a Godless world." Indeed, he detected in her novel a "dictatorial tone": "From almost any page . . . a voice can be heard, from painful necessity, commanding 'To a gas chamber—go!'"[34] Chambers had declared war. Years later, in a famous 1964 interview with *Playboy*, Rand would fire back, labeling *National Review* "the worst and most dangerous magazine in America." Because "it ties capitalism to religion," she told interviewer Alvin Toffler, it slanders capitalism as indefensible without appeals to "supernatural mysticism."[35]

In 1961, another libertarian, Ronald Hamowy, launched a blistering attack on the first six years of *National Review* in the pages of *New Individualist Review*, a journal founded by graduate students of F. A. Hayek. Buckley's magazine, Hamowy wrote, promoted "the conservatism of Pharonic Egypt, of Medieval Europe, of the Inquisition . . . of the rack, the thumbscrew, the whip, and the firing squad." A return to the free market was "hardly a burning issue" for *National Review*, Hamowy wrote, and the "libertarian principle of peace and non-intervention has been replaced by the heroics of a barroom drunk who proudly boasts that 'he can lick anybody in the room.'" Clearly riled by the charges, Buckley wrote a lengthy response, retorting that "it is only because of the conservatives' disposition to sacrifice in order to withstand the enemy, that [libertarians] are able to enjoy their monasticism, and pursue their busy little seminars on whether or not to demunicipalize the garbage collectors."[36]

Clearly, someone would have to try to bring order out of chaos. All of the various feuds and temperamental splits and theoretical arguments couldn't be resolved—nor did they have to be. But at some point conservatives had to be able to look across the table and decide whether it was worth keeping the company they were keeping. One man, above all others, believed conservatives could and should stick it out together.

Kevin Smant's biography of Frank Meyer, *Principles and Heresies* (named after Meyer's long-running column in *National Review*), provides a portrait of the thinker's intellectual evolution. Born in 1909 in Newark, New Jersey, Meyer joined the British Communist Party in 1931, while studying at Oxford. During his time in the party, he accepted a number of positions of authority and various postings, including stints in Chicago and New York City. Doubts about the nature of the Soviet Union eventually led Meyer to break with the Communist Party in 1945 and begin an intellectual journey rightward, influenced by the *Federalist Papers*, libertarians such as F. A. Hayek, and traditionalists such as Richard Weaver. Meyer made contact with various conservative writers in the early 1950s, and when *National Review* was launched, he was on the masthead.

Before breaking with the party, Meyer and his wife, Elsie (a fellow Communist he met while in Chicago), had settled near Woodstock, New York, because it was known as something of a Communist hot spot. Later they would come to regret that choice, but there was no money to move. Meyer took to sleeping with a loaded rifle near his bed, for fear of Communist reprisal. He and Elsie began staying up later and later, until eventually their schedules were entirely upside down. They'd sleep all day, and then Frank would read and work all night. Once, the story goes, Meyer called into *National Review* managing editor Priscilla Buckley (Bill's sister) at noon—an unheard-of time for him. "Why are you up so late?" she asked. "I have insomnia," Meyer replied.[37]

Meyer was famous for his phone calls—at all hours—which were his means of keeping in touch with the various writers and thinkers and activists who were shaping the conservative movement and of keeping them from wandering too far afield. And, indeed, in the early 1960s, he took it upon himself in a book and in a series of articles to articulate what would come to be known as fusionism.

To Meyer, both the libertarians and the traditionalists went too far sometimes—though, it's worth noting, he reserved by far the bulk of his criticism for the traditionalists. Certainly the libertarians could air toward "anarchy and nihilism."[38] But it was from the traditionalists that one had to fear authoritarianism. "If the state is endowed with the power to enforce virtue," he wrote in one essay, criticizing traditionalist conservatives such as Kirk, "the men who hold that power will enforce their own concepts as virtuous."[39] What's more, he wrote in his book *In Defense of Freedom*, virtue by its nature cannot be compelled no matter what the mechanism: "No act to the degree that it is coerced can partake of virtue—or of vice."[40] Just as much as any liberal collectivist or Communist, he wrote, the traditionalists were willing to "reduce the person to a secondary being, whose dignity and rights become dependent upon the gift and grace of society or the state."[41]

To strike a truly *conservative* path between what Meyer called these two "emphases," one had to balance both traditions. Traditionalism and libertarianism were not "irreconcilable." They were two forces in constant tension within conservatism—yin and yang, alpha and omega . . . Itchy and Scratchy. Neglecting virtue, he wrote, "leads not to conservatism, but to spiritual aridity and social anarchy"; denying freedom "leads not to conservatism, but to authoritarianism and theocracy."[42] But both extremes are self-defeating: "Truth withers when freedom dies, however righteous the authority that kills it; and free individualism uninformed by moral value rots at its core and soon brings about conditions that pave the way for surrender to tyranny."[43]

Fusionism had its critics. Meyer's good friend L. Brent Bozell (who was married to Bill Buckley's sister and who gave fusionism its name) thought that Meyer erred in elevating freedom above obedience to God. Kirk, who placed a relatively low value on human freedom, would maintain a lifelong skepticism of any alliance between libertarians and conservatives, writing in the early 1980s that "to talk of forming a league or coalition between these two is like advocating a union of ice and fire."[44]

But in the end, the simple fact is that fusionism won. Hardly any-one could deny that whether through osmosis, acclaim, or attrition, it became the de facto consensus of the conservative movement. Traditionalist ends, most agreed, could be achieved through liber-tarian means. Partially, conservatives had Moscow to thank. While the fusionist bargain between libertarians and traditionalist conser-vatives had little to do with the Cold War at a theoretical level, anticommunism was without a doubt the cement that made all other accommodations between conservatives possible.

But conservatives also had better things to do than debate each other. They had a party to take over. Three times, conservatives had tried to nominate Taft. Three times they had been repelled by the eastern forces of Dewey and Eisenhower. In 1960, conservatives had gotten stuck with Richard Nixon—and not for the last time. But this, 1964, was to be their year. When at the 1960 Republican convention there had been a brief—and hopeless—push to nomi-nate Goldwater, the silver-haired senator took to the floor and urged his supporters, "Let's grow up, conservatives! We want to take this party back, and I think someday we can. Let's get to work!"[45]

Conservatives did just that. Goldwater urged conservatives to support Nixon, but National Review refused to endorse, largely at Meyer's insistence, to remain independent. In the fall of 1960, some eighty young conservatives, gathered at the Buckley estate in Sharon, Connecticut, formed a group called Young Americans for Freedom (YAF), whose members would serve as the ground troops of conservatism. The young activists issued a soaring declaration, called the Sharon Statement, which said that "liberty is indivisible . . . political freedom cannot long exist without economic freedom" and that "the forces of international communism are, at present, the greatest single threat to these liberties."[46] By October 1961, some twenty well-connected conservative Republicans, calling themselves the "hard core," met in Chicago to discuss how to make Barry Goldwater the 1964 Republican Party nominee. They traveled the country, enlisting old friends, political neophytes, and students, building an organization in every state and congressional district—a task made possible by the existence of groups like the Young Republicans, Young Americans for Freedom, and the National Federation of Republican Women.[47]

When their director, Cliff White, reported to the senator in January of 1963 on their activities and the formation of a national "Draft Goldwater" committee, Goldwater flatly responded, "Cliff, I'm not a candidate and I'm not going to be." Eventually, however, the zeal of his supporters—and the fact that literally millions of conservatives across the nation were looking to him to lead—won out, even after the assassination of JFK. "Our cause is lost," Goldwater told a group of his closest advisers. And with that, he joined the battle.[48]

Despite some early gaffes, such as saying that Social Security should be made optional and that NATO commanders in the field should have the ability to use nuclear weapons, knocking out his main rival for the nomination, New York's liberal governor Nelson Rockefeller, turned out to be relatively easy. The California primary turned into a showdown between the two men. Goldwater had an army of fifty thousand volunteers canvassing the state—the largest such force ever assembled. Goldwater also had a little help from Rockefeller himself; in 1962, the governor had divorced his wife of thirty-one years and taken up with a much younger, married woman, Margaretta "Happy" Murphy. The two were married, and she was expecting his child near the date of the primary. "I have a show opening on both sides of the continent the same weekend," Rockefeller joked. As Lee Edwards put it, this was too much for the Christian Right of the day; Goldwater won with 51.6 percent of the vote.[49] The nomination would be his.

Goldwater's convention speech set the tone for the campaign. Goldwater would truly offer Americans a choice, not an echo. "The good Lord raised this mighty Republic to be a home for the brave and to flourish as the land of the free—not to stagnate in the swampland of collectivism, not to cringe before the bullying of communism," he boomed, indicting the "wall of shame" in Berlin and the "sands of shame" at the Bay of Pigs. "Our people have followed false prophets. We must, and we shall, return to proven ways—not because they are old, but because they are true," he preached, railing against the decay of the nation's social order. "We are plodding along at a pace set by centralized planning, red tape, rules without responsibility, and regimentation without recourse."

At the end of his speech, Goldwater addressed, very directly, the new coalition that he was, from his place on the podium in San Francisco, helping forge that very night. Reaching back, as Republicans have so often, to Lincoln, he quoted the Great Emancipator on the state of the Republican Party in 1858: "It was composed of strange, discordant and even hostile elements." End of quote, Goldwater said, cracking, "I quote him because he probably could have said it during the last week or so." As Lincoln's party had united in its desire to end slavery, he said—to "place it in the course of ultimate extinction"—the Republican Party gathered together that night was taking upon itself "the task of preserving and enlarging freedom at home and of safeguarding it from the forces of tyranny abroad."

He concluded, as was his pugnacious way, by all but daring the American people to cast their votes against him. "Anyone who joins us in all sincerity, we welcome. Those who do not care for our cause, we don't expect to enter our ranks in any case." There could hardly have been any clearer statement of Goldwater's fatalism, and determination to plant the seeds of later victory in the soil of certain defeat. The conservatives would go down—but they would go down fighting like hell, and leaving no question what they believed, why they believed it, and what those who disagreed could go do to themselves. "Extremism in the defense of liberty is no vice," Goldwater shouted, to the loudest and most sustained applause of the night. "Moderation in the pursuit of justice is no virtue."[50]

One reporter blurted out: "My God, he's going to run as Barry Goldwater!"[51]

Goldwater never had a prayer. Johnson received 43 million votes to Goldwater's 27 million. In the House, Democrats won their largest majority since 1936. In the Senate, Democrats outnumbered

Republicans two to one. Republicans held only 17 of the nation's 50 governorships. In 1964, 25 percent of voters described themselves as Republicans (down from 38 percent in 1940); 53 percent were Democrats.[52]

Goldwater's campaign style certainly didn't help him. He gleefully, as in his convention speech, would list from the stump groups of voters he *didn't* want to vote for him. He suggested during the California primary that Communist supply lines into South Vietnam could be blocked by use of "defoliation of the forests with low-yield atomic weapons" (one of more than a few comments about nuclear weapons that would make the Democrats' famous "Daisy" ad, where a little girl picks a flower as a nuclear weapon goes off, ring true). His official slogan, "In Your Heart, You Know He's Right," was switched around by opponents to read, "In Your Guts, You Know He's Nuts."[53]

But also, as Bill Buckley said, Americans just weren't ready for such a radical, polarizing figure—even if a lot of his supporters couldn't accept that. In a speech before Young Americans for Freedom in September of 1964, Buckley referred to "the impending defeat of Barry Goldwater." It was too much for the crowd; a woman cried. Buckley tried to explain. To expect a Goldwater victory would be to "presuppose a sea change in American public opinion" that simply hadn't happened. The point wasn't so much to win, but to win recruits, "not only for November the third, but for future Novembers." No one applauded.[54]

Still, as often, Buckley proved prophetic. Thousands of young people entered and stayed in politics. Those young people went on to get elected to Congress, sit on the Supreme Court, manage campaigns, raise money, head think tanks, write books, edit magazines, and run television networks. The Goldwater campaign also greatly expanded the financial base of the Republican Party. In 1960, there had been some 50,000 individual contributors to the Nixon campaign. In 1964, there were estimated to be more than 650,000 to the Goldwater effort.[55] Conservative direct-mail pioneer Richard Viguerie, who's been called the "funding father" of the conservative movement, tells the story of how he copied the names of Goldwater donors by hand (at the time, the names of anyone who donated more than $50 to a candidate were kept on file with the clerk of the House of Representatives) to create one of the most important fund-raising lists in conservative history.[56] Barely a month after Goldwater's defeat, a group of conservative activists, including Frank Meyer, set up the American Conservative Union (the folks behind CPAC) as an umbrella organization for the conservative movement.[57] And there was, of course, the small matter of an actor named Ronald Reagan making his national political debut during the 1964 campaign with a thirty-minute taped speech called "A Time for Choosing," where he let conservatives know they had "a rendezvous with destiny."

There was one sea change in the 1964 election, however, that was impossible to ignore: that on the issue of race. It was in this election that the Democrats would permanently lose the "Solid South." One of the major structural problems for the conservative movement postwar was that a large chunk of its potential constituency wasn't in the Republican Party. Southerners were historically loyal to the Democratic Party: a Republican president had fought and won the war against the Confederacy, and Radical Republicans in Congress had imposed Reconstruction on the region; the Democrats, on the other hand, had defended segregation and poured federal (i.e., northern) resources into the South under FDR's New Deal. In 1950, the GOP had no senators from the South; in the House, out of a southern delegation consisting of 105 members, 2 were Republicans. But as the civil rights movement took hold, fewer and fewer northern Democrats were willing to continue looking the other way, even if it meant putting the old New Deal coalition in peril. The Civil Rights Act of 1964—originally introduced by Kennedy in 1963, but pushed through by Johnson—took dead aim at the entire system of southern segregation.[58] As legend has it, Johnson knew that in signing the act he was signing away the South to the Republicans for a generation.

Republicans voted for the bill by wider margins than the Democrats. But Barry Goldwater voted against it. Goldwater was, by all accounts, no racist. He'd supported the Civil Rights Acts of 1957 and 1960. With a Jewish last name, he had experienced his share of bigotry. One much-repeated, though likely apocryphal, story had Goldwater, when told he couldn't play on a golf course because he was Jewish, ask if he at least could play nine holes, since he was really only *half* Jewish.[59] In his book *Conscience of a Conservative*, he supported integrated schools.[60] As chief of staff for the Arizona Air National Guard, he pushed for desegregation two years before Truman desegregated the army. At the department store the Goldwater family owned, Barry and his brother Robert hired and served blacks without reservation. He gave generously to the Arizona branch of the NAACP and the Phoenix branch of the Urban League. One of the first staffers he hired when he came to the Senate was a black female lawyer.[61] Goldwater was certainly more progressive than *National Review*, which editorialized repeatedly and forcefully in favor of segregation, calling whites the "advanced race" and even labeling blacks "retarded."

But Goldwater believed firmly that the Civil Rights Act of 1964 was unconstitutional, allowing the federal government to tell businesses and individuals whom they had to hire and whom they had to serve. If the federal government could tell people *not* to discriminate, could it not also tell them *to* discriminate? He also was not above some cold political calculation when it came to looking at the Republican Party's prospects nationally. In 1962 he'd famously said that the GOP should "go hunting where the ducks are"—as in pandering to white, southern, racist voters. And, in fact, his vote against the Civil Rights Act of 1964 would end up assuring him virtually every state he ended up carrying. If it weren't for Dixie, Goldwater would have carried only his home state of Arizona . . . and even that barely.[62]

An incumbent president held on to his job in a landslide in 1964. But the tectonic plates of American politics had shifted drastically, and not in a way that would benefit the Democrats in the long term.

Losing by Winning

If conservatives had won by losing in 1964, they assuredly pulled off the reverse trick in 1968, with Richard Nixon. Conservatives consolidated in 1964 by taking over the Republican Party and showing that even with the most abrasive of candidates in the most unfavorable of circumstances, they could still garner 27 million votes and more than 38 percent of the electorate—quite a baseline for a ragtag group of newly coalesced dissenters rebelling against the country's liberal, bipartisan consensus. But the 1964 election gave conservatives another gift: an emboldened Lyndon Johnson. If anyone did more to unite conservatives in the 1960s than Barry Goldwater at the political level (and Frank Meyer at the theoretical level), it was LBJ.

With a boundless faith in the power of government to do good, Johnson set out to take the liberal project to new heights. His aim was nothing less than to end poverty and unemployment in the United States and to spontaneously heal the nation's painful racial past through voting-rights legislation and "affirmative action." He created the enormous Medicare and Medicaid programs, greatly increasing the federal government's role in health care. He created the Head Start program, getting the federal government into the business of running preschools. He created the National Endowment for the Arts and the National Endowment for the Humanities. At the same time, the liberal Warren Court went on a rampage: the Supreme Court had banned compulsory prayer from public schools in 1962; it created an expansive new class of rights for criminals at a time when crime was skyrocketing; it made obscenity harder to prosecute; and it recognized a constitutional right to privacy, which protected the use and sale of birth control products (and would eventually be expanded in *Roe v. Wade* in 1973 to include abortion).

In other words, Johnson gave the conservative coalition plenty to unite against. The problem was, they had no one good to unite behind. And that's where Nixon came in. Goldwater, of course, was off the stage. Reagan was where many conservatives' eyes turned, but a former actor who had been elected to his first political office only in 1966—be it the rather substantial office of governor of California—was simply not a candidate many people could take seriously. Thus, while Reagan would make a halfhearted push on the eve of the Republicans' 1968 national convention in Miami, the real primary contest was between Nixon and the hated eastern liberal Nelson Rockefeller. Nixon aggressively wooed conservatives, hiring a young editorial writer named Patrick Buchanan as his liaison to the movement. But they didn't need much convincing. Nixon was "conservative enough," the refrain went.[63] He may not have been much of a small-government guy, but at least he was as anti-communist as they came. Goldwater, for whom Nixon had campaigned aggressively in 1964, threw his full support behind the former vice president. As in 1960, *National Review* didn't give Nixon a formal endorsement, at the insistence of senior editors (including Meyer). But Buckley invited Nixon on his television show *Firing Line*, and arranged for a profile of him in the magazine.[64]

Nixon was the conservatives' candidate. But he would not be their president.

Nixon campaigned as a conservative in the general election, accepting a right-of-center platform, picking Governor Spiro Agnew of Maryland (who would become a conservative favorite) as his running mate, and promising to decentralize and privatize government. He positioned himself as the voice of the "silent majority" of Americans made resentful by things such as crime, drugs, forced busing, quotas, welfare, and draft dodging—what came to be known as "social issues."[65] With some help from Alabama's governor, George Wallace, a Democrat whose independent campaign that year siphoned off the votes of angry white northerners and southerners from the Democratic candidate, Hubert Humphrey, Nixon took the White House.

When it came time to govern, however, Nixon was the anticonservative. A few administration jobs went to conservatives, but the policy was all liberal. Federal spending and regulation grew faster under Nixon than they had under Johnson. Nixon signed the Clean

Air Act and the Endangered Species Act. He created the Environmental Protection Agency (EPA) and the Occupational Safety and
Health Administration (OSHA). Worst of all, Nixon shocked conservatives by bringing back wage and price controls—the greatest
government intrusion into the private sector since World War II. He
even flirted with guaranteeing every American a minimum income.

Hot-tempered conservatives boiled over in 1971 when Nixon
announced that he was going to China. Ever since Mao Zedong
had seized control of mainland China in 1949, America's support
for the Republic of China on Taiwan had been an article of faith
among conservatives. Now Nixon was consorting with the enemy.
Nixon announced his planned visit in mid-July. In August, a group
of twelve prominent conservatives—including Buckley, Meyer,
William Rusher, and others—issued a "Declaration" that they were
suspending their support of the Nixon administration. The piece
cited his "excessive taxation and inordinate welfarism at home"
and his "overtures to Red China" abroad, and it threatened "to
keep all options open" politically.[66] The Manhattan 12, as they
were known, would go on to endorse a primary challenge to Nixon
from Congressman John Ashbrook of Ohio, which failed to gain
any traction.

Nixon won reelection handily in 1972. With George McGovern,
the Democrats (not for the last time) aided a divided Republican
Party by putting up an ultraliberal who could unite the Right,
and much of the middle of the country, in revulsion. Conservatives, however, remained leery of the president at the beginning of
his second term. And the ones who stuck by him ended up being
dragged down by Watergate. When Nixon resigned on August 8,
1974, leaving the White House to Gerald Ford (Agnew had
resigned due to a tax-evasion scandal), the conservative movement
was in tatters. Ford promptly chose as his vice president Nelson
Rockefeller—the very man conservatives had backed Nixon to
keep as far away from the White House as possible.

Nixon, however, wasn't the only bump in the road for the conservative movement in the late 1960s and early 1970s. Frank
Meyer died of cancer in the spring of 1972, and the fortunes of

fusionism seemed almost to track his death. If anticommunism was the glue that held the conservative-libertarian marriage together, it would start to weaken as the quagmire in Vietnam deepened. The libertarians had always been the skittish faction when it came to the Cold War. War, they argued, always enhances the power of the state, and the draft, forcing men to kill and die, was the greatest imposition the state could ever perpetrate against the individual—a kind of slavery.

The more unpopular the war in Vietnam became, the more radicalized some libertarians became. Karl Hess, who had written Barry Goldwater's 1964 convention speech, declared that "conservatives like me" had for too long trusted Washington with enormous powers to fight communism. "Vietnam should remind all conservatives that whenever you put your faith in big government for *any* reason," he wrote, "sooner or later you wind up as an apologist for mass murder." Libertarian economist Murray Rothbard, long unhappy with the direction of the conservative movement under the Buckleyites, began to rail against *National Review* and its cohorts in various liberal magazines, openly cheering on a "burgeoning split" on the Right.[67]

While an all-out split was not to be, libertarians in this time did come to forge an identity separate from that of the conservative movement. One key incident came in August of 1969, with a confrontation between the "libs" and "trads" at a Young Americans for Freedom convention in St. Louis. Grabbing a microphone and declaring that every individual has the right to defend himself from violence, a libertarian YAF member set fire to his draft card and held it aloft for all to see. He was immediately mobbed by more conservative members of the group, while other libertarians formed a ring around him. Punches flew, the culprit escaped, and the rest of the convention was marked by jeering between the two camps. "Laissez-faire! Laissez-faire!" the libs chanted. "Lazy fairies! Lazy fairies!" the trads retorted.[68]

The Right, alas, has never had much of a flair for slogans.

By 1972, libertarianism had enough of a following to establish a Libertarian Party with a presidential candidate, John Hospers, chairman of the philosophy department at the University of Southern California.[69] By 1977, the libertarian Cato Institute was founded in the political wilderness of San Francisco. Perhaps it is of more than symbolic significance that in 1981, with the White House occupied by Ronald Reagan—the grand uniter of traditionalist and libertarian conservatives—Cato would come out of the cold and make the move to Washington, D.C.

A Rendezvous with Destiny

When Reagan ran in 1980, the liberal wing of the party expected a disaster. Instead, they got a revolution. Reagan carried forty-four states. Republicans picked up twelve seats in the Senate, giving the GOP its first majority in that body in a quarter century. They also picked up thirty-three seats in the House (though they wouldn't retake that body until another revolution, fourteen years in the future). How did Reagan do it? How did the Republicans go from Nixon's resignation in 1974—which some thought might actually end the Republicans' very existence as a party—to an overwhelming victory just six years later?

More weight than one might think can be attached to a proposed 1978 IRS ruling. In 1976, Jimmy Carter became the first presidential candidate to deliberately and successfully court Evangelical Christians, through the retelling of his own experience of being "born again." But the Christians he courted weren't organized into any particular groups or coalitions. That would all change when Carter's director of the IRS threatened to strip all private schools founded after 1953 of their tax-deductible status—based on the theory that, absent proof otherwise, such schools should be assumed to have been founded in an attempt to get around *Brown v. Board of Education*. The majority of these schools, especially in the South, were Christian.[70] The IRS received more than 200,000 letters, and the change was never enacted. Nonetheless, the incident spurred the Reverend Jerry Falwell and social-conservative strategist Paul Weyrich to form the Moral Majority in 1979. Over the next 10 years, it would register some 2.5 million new voters.[71]

These folks, the Religious Right, would become the foot soldiers of the conservative movement, in the way that labor unions had long been for the Democrats.

In the years before the organization of the Evangelicals, a related group of social conservatives, known as the New Right, had been seeking its political fortune. Led in part by direct-mail pioneer Richard Viguerie, this band became extremely dissatisfied with the Republican Party after Nixon's resignation and Ford's choice of Nelson Rockefeller as his vice president. They were so mad, in fact, that they agitated openly for a social-conservative alliance with the Democratic Party, or for conservative Democrats to join conservative Republicans in starting a third party. Their efforts failed, however, when Reagan, despite losing out on the 1976 GOP nomination, refused to be involved in any third-party politics.[72]

It's important to note that there is a distinction between what used to be called "traditionalist" conservatives and what are now broadly called "social" conservatives. Traditionalist conservatives were typically intellectual types, fomenting what they saw as a "revolt against the masses," against a culture that had grown crass and immoral due to the sins of the great unwashed. The social conservatives, on the other hand, *were* the masses, and they were revolting against what they saw as a liberal intellectual elite—an elite that banned prayer in schools, legalized abortion, dreamed up forced busing, and wanted to take their guns. Neither group, however, felt any great discomfort in using the state to enforce what they considered social norms, so they occupied (and continue to occupy) roughly the same space in the libertarian-conservative alliance.

And so Reagan, having refused to go the third-party route in 1976, set out in 1980 to unite the Religious Right, the New Right, the traditionalist Right, the libertarians, the economic conservatives, the anti-communists, even the neoconservatives (a group of ex-leftist intellectuals, primarily Jewish, who had drifted to the right)—all under the banner of the Republican Party. And it worked. It worked because Reagan himself was a fusion of all these elements; it worked because these groups had spent so many years in the wilderness, searching for a way to work together and for a leader to bring them to the promised land.

Conservatives, finally, after so many years in the wilderness, had one of their own in the White House. Reagan's presidency was far from perfect from the perspective of any of these factions. He didn't cut government enough for the libertarian conservatives, but he did reduce government spending as a percentage of the GDP and implement significant tax reform. He didn't pay the kind of attention to issues such as abortion and school prayer that the social conservatives would have liked, but he did appoint William Rehnquist chief justice and put Antonin Scalia on the Supreme Court. And, of course, he will always be credited by conservatives with having almost single-handedly tossed Soviet communism into the dustbin of history.

Reagan's ultimate triumph, however, only exacerbated his most serious failure of the conservative movement—his passing of the torch to George H. W. Bush. Bush had been put on the ticket in 1980 to "balance" it with an eastern liberal. As Cato Institute president Ed Crane would put it years later, "It was Reagan's duty to recognize that Bush didn't have an ideological bone in his body. All Reagan had to do was raise an eyebrow, and Bush's goose would have been cooked." Instead, Bush was elected with Reagan's blessing; some conservatives like to say Bush was never elected, Reagan was reelected for a third term.

Bush, however, turned out to be no Reagan, disappointing conservatives at every turn—most famously by breaking his "read my lips" no-new-taxes pledge. "If George Bush had pardoned Willie Horton or burned Old Glory on the lawn of the White House," Heritage Foundation staffer Daniel Mitchell wrote at the time, "it would hardly have rivaled the flip-flop he has committed on taxes."[73] Of course, when Nixon infuriated conservatives by going to China, he was handily reelected. He was, for whatever his faults, a warrior against communism and had been for his whole life. Bush was also a Cold Warrior, but by 1992, there was no Cold War.

With no enemy abroad to unite them, and unable to stomach uniting behind Bush, conservatives split. An eccentric Texan named

Ross Perot popped onto the scene and walked away with 19 percent of the popular vote, and a southern Democrat with some woman problems walked away with a plurality of the popular vote and the presidency. Bush captured only 37 percent of the popular vote in 1992—a smaller proportion than Barry Goldwater got in the disaster of 1964.

What a way for the conservative movement to come full circle. Having gone from the unifying disaster of Goldwater to the triumph of Reagan, they now found themselves adrift. And it wasn't just the 1992 election. Elections are won, and elections are lost. Parties survive such ups and downs all the time. The crisis here was a deeper one. The entire conservative movement Reagan represented had been built, at base and from its earliest days, on anticommunism as the glue that held together—that fused— libertarians and social conservatives. Without that glue, what would hold these factions together? Could these partners agree on a program, a new unifying principle, or only on a common enemy?

Having kept their rendezvous with destiny, were conservatives now doomed to shuffle through the 1990s without aim or purpose?

3

United against Clintonism

Conservatives were something short of crestfallen when George H. W. Bush failed to win reelection. Many of the economic conservatives he'd burned on his "no new taxes" pledge fled to Perot in the general election—or to Clinton after Perot started behaving erratically late in the campaign, dropping out and then reentering the race. From the social-conservative Right, Bush suffered the indignity of a primary challenge from television commentator Pat Buchanan, who garnered almost 40 percent of the vote in New Hampshire. When Bush lost that November, the sense of triumph among conservatives was almost as pronounced as that among Democrats. At the Heritage Foundation, a group of young staffers paraded through the halls with a mock-up of Bush's head on a platter.

After the dust settled, Republicans were naturally in a state of depression, having lost a national election. But there was also something more profound going on. With the Cold War over, the Republican coalition was left without a center of gravity. The pragmatic Bush wing of the party had wanted to muddle through without a clear philosophy—hoping to somehow convince social moderates and social conservatives that they could both find a home in the Republican Party. The Buchananites, however, wanted a war. Speaking in prime time on the third night of the Republican convention in Houston, Buchanan had declared that there was "a religious war going on in our country for the soul of America . . . as critical to the kind of nation we will one day be as was the Cold War itself." Amid attacks on the "militant homosexual rights movement" and "radical feminism," the TV talker conjured the image of the recent L.A. race riots, praising nineteen-year-old boys with M-16s and saying that "as they took back the streets of L.A., block by block, so we must take back our cities and take back our culture."

Neither the Buchanan nor the Bush vision would come to pass. There would be no cultural conflagration, but the status quo was doomed as well. Thrown from the White House and in the minority in Congress, Republicans would be forced to regroup. They'd be forced to find a purpose.

Clinton Unites the Right

Purpose can come in strange shapes and sizes. For Republicans in the 1990s, the shape and size was that of Bill Clinton, a pasty-white–thighed baby boomer with an overgrown faith in the power of government to feel and heal the American people's pain.

It would be difficult to overestimate the depth of Republicans' hatred for Bill Clinton. His very physical existence sent them into paroxysms of rage. His soft features and doughy physique betrayed a lack of character, a man with little control over his various appetites. His southern-slick voice yelled "Danger!" as he smooth-talked you right behind the wheel of a shiny new "preowned" vehicle. He bit his lip and Republicans bit their tongues as they felt a sudden urge to throw things at their TVs. He broke out his famous changing-the-channel thumbs-up, and conservatives broke into a cold sweat knowing that somewhere, someone had just bought Bill Clinton's bill of goods.

Yes, they hated him because he was good. He. Was. *Good.*

But it's worth remembering: he wasn't *that* good.

Clinton won the presidency twice not by forging a new Democratic majority, but by capturing the bigger minority. And in the process, he blundered so badly that he midwifed a Republican congressional majority that endures to this day. How did it happen? Simple. Fusion blew up in 1992, and Clinton was what was left when the smoke cleared. Perot split a Reagan coalition no longer held together by the Cold War and divided over economic policy; Perot voters preferred Clinton to Bush, but they were primarily disaffected Reagan voters answering Bush's "read my lips" with a bitter "kiss my . . ." well, let's just say "vote good-bye." Meanwhile, for all the "triangulation" and centrism Clinton would later learn from pollster Dick Morris, Clinton won in 1992 by holding together a slightly smaller base than Michael Dukakis had; while Clinton famously won with just 43 percent of the vote, Mr. Geek-in-a-Tank had captured 46 percent of the vote.

Clinton proved a masterful politician in many ways during his eight years in office—and he was especially good on defense. He earned his reputation as the Comeback Kid. But to come back, you have to fall behind, and Clinton displayed a peculiar talent for that as well. If it weren't for Clinton's disastrous first two years in office, and if it weren't for his weakness for women, a former history professor from Georgia would never have led a revolution in Congress and the presidency would never have been brought to its knees by an intern. Clinton, in his weakness, would prove to be the conservative movement's greatest friend in the 1990s, serving as its bête noire, its fund-raising engine, its stock villain. In his strength, however, Clinton would be the bane of conservatism, thwarting its advances, breaking its nerve, and twisting its heart and mind toward impotent rage and a lust for absolute power.

The Cold War made the conservative movement strong. Communism, by its nature, was an attack on both religion and capitalism. It was a fight worth fighting and worth winning. Uniting against Clinton, however, left conservatism angry and weak. Whatever his flaws as a person and as a president, opposition to a mere man was a cause unworthy of a great political movement—but it was the only cause on which conservatives could agree. Clinton was, in many ways, just a penny in the fuse box of a party ready to blow.

Talk radio, a resurgent Christian Right, small-business groups, magazines such as the *American Spectator*—all were united not around a single, affirmative conservative agenda, but around taking down Slick Willie. And he was all too ready to help, practically writing RNC fund-raising letters for them. With his 43 percent mandate in hand, Clinton set out to offend every variety of conservative in every way he could. In November of 1992, the president-elect declared, in response to a reporter's question, that he would follow through on his campaign promise to allow gays to serve openly in the military. After a revolt by the Pentagon establishment, he eventually had to settle for "don't ask, don't tell," but the draft-dodger president trying to remake the armed forces in the mold of liberal-elite sensibilities left a bad taste in blue-collar voters' mouths.

Then there was Janet Reno. In Clinton's comical quest to come up with "a cabinet that looks like America," a female attorney general was, for whatever reason, a must. His first nominee, Zoe Baird, was forced to withdraw her nomination over an illegal-alien-nanny problem. His second choice, U.S. District Court judge Kimba Wood, withdrew her name from consideration over a virtually identical issue. Upon confirmation to her post in March of 1993, the somewhat underqualified Reno inherited the standoff with the Branch Davidians in Waco, Texas. Reno took the bulk of the blame, in the eyes of the far Right, when she green-lighted a government assault on the compound that resulted in the deaths of some eighty of the cult's members, including children. Even to mainstream conservatives, Waco seemed to symbolize an overzealous federal government at best botching a legitimate law-enforcement action and at worst coming close to violating the First and Second Amendment rights of American citizens.

Further trouble came from Clinton's first U.S. surgeon general, Joycelyn Elders. An Arkansas transplant—in 1987, Clinton had made her head of the state's Department of Health—Elders quickly gained a reputation for courting controversy. She supported moving toward drug legalization and advocated various other liberal health-related ideas. But the incident that did her in was when, in 1994, she was asked at a U.N. AIDS conference whether it would be appropriate to promote masturbation to children to prevent them from engaging in unsafe sex. "I think that is part of human sexuality, and perhaps it should be taught," she responded.[1] That was pretty much that for Dr. Elders.

And when Clinton wasn't busy riling up the Religious Right, he—and his wife—were busy cooking up one of the largest proposed expansions of the federal government ever conceived. There are mitigated disasters and unmitigated ones. HillaryCare fell into the latter category. One of Clinton's first acts in office, before even his first week was through, was to set up a President's Task Force on National Health Care Reform, headed by his wife and presidential aide Ira Magaziner. Hillary's appointment was meant in part to symbolize the importance the president placed on the issue of health care, but it also reinforced the two-for-the-price-of-one image that had long irked the Right with regard to the Clintons. It also meant that no one would tell the first lady "no" as she went about trying to remake the nation's health-care system.

The 1,364-page plan, details of which leaked out before any formal legislation was introduced, was a monstrosity to conservatives. In an article in the *New Republic* in early 1994, Elizabeth McCaughey (a Republican who would go on to be elected lieutenant governor of New York) painted an alarming—if controversial—picture of the plan's outlines. "If you're not worried about the Clinton health bill, keep reading," McCaughey wrote. "You will have to settle for one of the low-budget health plans selected by the government. The law will prevent you from going outside the system. . . . To keep controls tight, the bill requires the doctor to report your visit to a national data bank containing the medical histories of all Americans."[2]

It was scary stuff. And while the administration fired back at McCaughey and other critics, it was impossible to get around the central fact that the president's wife was essentially trying to social-ize one-seventh of the nation's economy. The debate filtered down to the general public through radio hosts such as Rush Limbaugh blasting the first lady's "Soviet-style" health reform, and the famous "Harry and Louise" television ads, financed by the insur-ance industry and featuring a middle-aged, middle-class couple fretting about the president's plan. "Having choices we don't like is no choice at all," Louise said in one ad.[3] "What if our health plan runs out of money?" Harry asked in another.[4] Most of the ads ended with Louise declaring, with what the *New York Times* char-acterized at the time as "a Scarlett O'Hara glint of determination in her eyes": "There's got to be a better way."[5]

The American people seemed to agree—not just on health care, but also in response to the Clinton administration in general—and a reinvigorated conservative movement was ready to make the case that the Republicans were that better way.

The National Federation of Independent Business (NFIB), which today represents some six hundred thousand small businesses, was a potential convert to the Democratic side—Republicans are known to look out for *big* business, after all. But HillaryCare, with its bur-densome regulations and requirements for all employers, made a conservative stalwart out of the NFIB. The group would become particularly focused on tort reform—what, with two lawyers in the White House—at one point in 1995 generating some 265,000 letters a week in favor of a bill limiting lawsuits.[6]

The National Rifle Association also had a Clinton-fueled resur-gence in the 1990s. In 1991, hard-charging ideologue Wayne LaPierre took control of the organization from the by-comparison-milquetoast Warren Cassidy. Despite (or perhaps because of) inci-dents such as Waco, Oklahoma City, and the Columbine school shootings, the NRA saw a tremendous growth in its membership and fund-raising. Gun owners felt beleaguered and beset on all sides, so they began giving money and turning out in force. Clin-ton's 1994 crime bill became a particular call to arms. Not only did the bill contain a ban on "assault weapons," but it was also laden with ludicrous amounts of liberal pork, like $40 million for the infamous "midnight basketball" program, $630 million for arts and crafts and dance programs for kids, and tons of money for job training and public housing.[7] The NRA managed to slow the bill, but it got through the Democratic Congress largely in the shape Clinton wanted it—which gave the group all the more reason to spend big in 1994. In that election, seven out of ten gun owners voted Republican; over the course of the decade, the NRA went from giving 61 percent of its contributions to Republicans in 1990 to giving 92 percent to Republicans in 2000.[8]

Clinton didn't just fill the coffers of the conservative establishment, he also ushered in the golden age of conservative talk radio. The road was opened in 1987, when the Federal Communications Commission got rid of the anti-free-speech Fairness Doctrine, which held that all viewpoints must receive equal time on the public airwaves. When the cost of broadcasting opinionated commentary was that anyone and everyone had a claim to free airtime for rebuttal, stations did the logical thing: stick to music, traffic, and the weather. But with the Fairness Doctrine gone, daytime radio took a turn toward less rock and more talk. Between 1987 and 1993, more than a thousand stations switched to a talk-radio format. Leading the pack with a national show launched in 1988 was an ex-DJ named Rusty Sharpe, a.k.a. Jeff Christie, a.k.a. Rush Limbaugh, with—as he put it—"talent on loan from God." The bombastic Limbaugh was credited with saving daytime radio, with his mix of humor and populist outrage.

At the same time, even talkers whose names weren't Limbaugh were showing the potential political power of the medium. In 1988, the House of Representatives voted to increase its pay by 51 percent, to $135,000 from $89,500; a talk show host in Detroit, Roy Fox, launched a "tea-bag revolt" (the anniversary of the Boston Tea Party was coming up), where citizens sent tea bags to Congress as a protest, demanding that the pay hike be repealed. The protest worked, and as organizers dumped 160,000 tea bags in front of the White House, Congress withdrew the pay raise.[9]

But if talk radio got its sea legs between 1987 and 1993, it hit full stride as Bill Clinton began his first term. Clinton had aggressively courted talk radio during his campaign, and he made another push as he rolled out his health-care plan, inviting more than two hundred hosts from around the country to Washington for a briefing and to broadcast "direct from the White House." But things quickly headed south. *Talkers* magazine reported in October that "the initial infatuation with the health care plan is fading as a majority of those who choose to express themselves don't trust Clinton, don't trust government, and don't trust anything that smacks of socialism." Limbaugh led the on-air charge against HillaryCare. By the time it was all over, a survey of congressmen and their staffs found that 46 percent said talk radio had been the most influential media source during the health-care debate; only 15 percent mentioned the *New York Times*.[10]

The Clinton administration was, in many ways, simply ideal for talk radio. HillaryCare got the ball rolling, but the never-ending stream of scandals and get-you-up-in-arms policy proposals provided equally irresistible material. Just in Clinton's first two years, talk radio would glom onto: a Clinton proposal to make "lobbying" groups disclose the names and addresses of their volunteers, which Pat Robertson called a shocking attempt to "limit your freedom of speech and the rights of Christian people" (the bill was scrapped)[11]; a Democratic bill that religious conservatives feared would require parents educating their children at home to obtain federal certification (home schoolers won a specific exemption from the law)[12]; Clinton's crime bill (slowed down and revised); the plan to end the ban on gays in the military (scrapped); and the president's two failed candidates for attorney general (scrapped, scrapped). Having devoured all of this red meat, talk radio had strength to spare when the 1994 midterm elections rolled around. A growing base of conservative listeners were ticked off about what they came to perceive as a daily assault on their values and their freedoms, and they were ready to be mobilized—a fact for which the leaders of the Gingrich Revolution had Bill Clinton to thank.

Reedism as the New Fusionism

The early 1990s also saw the resurgence of the Religious Right. The 1980s had been a paradoxical decade for Christian conservatives. They'd had a president they saw as one of their own, yet their satisfaction bred complacency. Jerry Falwell's Moral Majority atrophied during the 1980s, partially because of a sense that with Reagan in the White House the political war had been won and partially because most Americans seemed unable to distinguish between Falwell and folks such as Jim Bakker and Jimmy Swaggart, whose financial shenanigans and sexcapades cast a pall of sleaze over the Religious Right.[13]

Christian conservatism needed a new face, and soon it got just that in the person of Ralph Reed, a rising-star Republican activist whose youthful looks have led far too many reporters to compare him to a choirboy. At a dinner during Bush's inaugural in 1989, Reed found himself seated with televangelist Pat Robertson, who had just run a failed primary campaign against Bush on an ultraconservative antiabortion, antipornography, pro-Bible-in-public-school platform. Falwell's Moral Majority was about to be shut down, and Robertson wanted to launch a new organization that could keep the activists who had mobilized for his presidential campaign involved in politics. Reed had supported fiscal conservative Jack Kemp for president in 1988, but after drafting a memo for Robertson on how such an organization might be structured, he decided to take its helm himself.[14]

Reed's Christian Coalition would be a smashing political success—but it would succeed on something much closer to Kemp Republicanism than Robertson Republicanism. At the end of 1990, the Christian Coalition had 125 chapters with 57,000 members; by the time Reed left the group in 1997, it had 2,000 chapters and 1.9 million members (not to mention a $27 million-a-year budget).[15] Why such phenomenal growth? While Robertson went merrily about his usual business of blaming feminism for encouraging women to "leave their husbands, kill their children, practice witchcraft, destroy capitalism, and become lesbians" and ranting about a "tightly knit cabal" of bankers (think: Jews) conspiring to do the work of Lucifer, Reed got serious.

Or perhaps it would be more accurate to say that he got fusionist.

The key insight that Reed brought to the resurgence of the Religious Right was that Christian conservatism could not survive by cultural extremism alone—it needed a strong economic message, one that inevitably corresponded with small-government principles. He laid out his thinking in a landmark article, "Casting a Wider Net," in the Summer 1993 issue of the Heritage Foundation's *Policy Review* magazine. "The profamily movement has limited its effectiveness by concentrating disproportionately on issues such as abortion and homosexuality," Reed wrote. "These are vital moral issues. . . . To win at the ballot box and in the court of public opinion, however, the profamily movement must speak to the concerns of average voters in the areas of taxes, crime, government waste, health care, and financial security." He backed up his thesis with polling. In 1992, only 12 percent of voters (and just 22 percent of born-again Evangelicals) indicated to pollsters that abortion was a key issue in their voting decision. Meanwhile, polling found that the issue that most united Evangelicals and fiscal conservatives was the deficit.[16]

"The reason is simple," Reed wrote. "Taxes fall heaviest on middle-class families with children, who must tighten their belts and balance their checkbooks. They wonder why government cannot do the same." Channeling Frank Meyer and updating him for the era of two-income families, Reed gave a rundown of the reasons why Christian conservatives should make a small-government, "profamily" agenda (yes, there are few people who are "anti-family," but such is the work of political message-making) their top priority: high taxes mean less time with the kids (and more mothers working out of the home); welfare policies contribute to the decline of the family (which in turn contributes to high crime); and school choice could give Christian parents an escape from chaotic, immoral public schools. Only with policies focused on the family, he argued, could Christian conservatives begin to win a wider following among Evangelicals and Catholics. "Their primary interest is not to legislate against the sins of others, but to protect the health, welfare, and financial security of their own families," he wrote. To appeal to them, the profamily movement would have to learn, like the Apostle Paul, to be "all things to all people."[17]

And it was no coincidence that Reed was making this new push in the summer of 1993, as Clinton was beginning to rile religious and economic conservatives—just as it is no coincidence that it was specifically the period between 1993 and 1995 that saw an explosion of the Religious Right as a force within the conservative movement. Marshall Wittmann, who was the legislative director of the Christian Coalition during that period, remembers the spirit of the time. "The day I started at the Christian Coalition was February 1, 1993," he recalled. "I can remember because on the front page of the *Washington Post* was an article on the gays in the military issue. It described followers of Pat Robertson and Jerry Falwell as 'largely poor, uneducated, and easy to command.' Didn't put it in quotation marks." The *Post* didn't use quotation marks, of course, because it was simply reporting what everyone in Clinton's Democrat-dominated Washington, D.C., knew to be the truth.

The poor-uneducated-easy-to-command story created a firestorm on the Right and did its part to fuel the growing discontent in the countryside. But it was just one of a thousand factors laying the groundwork for the Republican Party to run a campaign in 1994 as an insurgency, made up of a coalition of social and economic conservatives, out of power, ticked off and ready to turn Washington upside-down. A Democratic, liberal elite was running Washington, so the story line went. They were in charge, but out of touch and running roughshod over the values and pocketbooks of good-old-fashioned-mom-and-apple-pie Americans. Without such a monstrous threat, so offending and threatening to both freedom and morality, disunity may well have reigned for another four years on the Right. Another four years of drift like those during the first Bush administration might not have proved lethal to the conservative movement, but they certainly would have left it gasping for air. As it happened, Clinton united the Right as George H. W. Bush had never been able to.

But as he revived the beast, he also tamed it.

In the Ring with Ali

To conservatives, the Contract with America and the Gingrich Revolution were battles in a larger war against liberal big government. But while they won some stunning victories at first, conservatives quickly got bogged down in the swamps of Washington, D.C. The aftermath of the Gingrich Revolution has left conservatives with a number of questions. Was defeat inevitable? Were their ideas bad, or were their tactics bad? Or both? Could the war have been won if it had been fought differently, or was it always a fool's errand from which they were lucky to escape with their lives? And most importantly, going forward, was the lesson of the Gingrich years that attempts to reduce the size of government must be abandoned permanently, or that the Republican Party must learn to do a better job selling its policies and philosophy?

Without a doubt, the great majority of Republicans have taken the former lesson from that last question: They believe that any attempt to shrink government is political poison. While the American people may occasionally indicate that they want smaller government, through elections or through public-opinion polling, they're simply lying. When push comes to cut, they will turn on any politician foolish enough to try to slash spending on anything but the most outlandish of pork-barrel projects—and even there it's best to trim lightly.

But while taking such a lesson from the Gingrich years—particularly from the government shutdowns in 1995 and 1996—is understandable on the surface, a closer look at the revolution and its foundering tells a different story. Looking back at that time, one does not find any sweeping rejection of conservative ideas or affirmation of Americans' love of big government. Instead, one finds a massively botched public-relations campaign by the Republicans and masterful political gamesmanship by President Clinton and his chief political strategist, Dick Morris.

The Gingrich Revolution was sixteen years in the making. No sooner had Gingrich arrived in Congress in 1979 than he began pestering the National Republican Congressional Committee (NRCC) with plans for a Republican majority. Overwhelmed by the freshman congressman's brashness, the head of the NRCC, Guy Vander Jagt, skipped Gingrich over 155 sitting Republicans to head a committee on long-range planning.[18] Gingrich bombarded the committee with ideas. The joke at NRCC headquarters became that there was a wall of filing cabinets loaded down with "Newt's Ideas." Off in a corner was a much smaller cabinet of "Newt's Good Ideas."[19]

Gingrich spent the 1980s and early 1990s both building and destroying. He put together the so-called Conservative Opportunity Society, a small group of congressmen committed to a conservative Republican majority (they joked that the only two things standing in their way were the Democrats and the Republicans).[20] He trained state and local Republican troops through GOPAC, a national political action committee. At the same time, he set out to convince the American people that the Democratic Congress was corrupt and could not be trusted. His crowning achievement in that regard came when he forced the resignation of Speaker Jim Wright in 1989 over the particulars of a book deal.

For all the plotting and planning, however, the revolution practically snuck up on the Republicans. After all the years in the wilderness, it wasn't until the spring of 1994 that the goal of attaining power even entered the realm of the realistic. The first sign that something revolutionary was going on came on May 24, in a rural congressional district in Kentucky. The sitting congressman, Democrat William Natcher, had passed away two months earlier. The Second District was solidly Democratic; it had been held by a Democrat since 1865. But despite having an inexperienced candidate in the unknown Ron Lewis, the Republican Party pumped resources into the special election in the final weeks. They were encouraged by polling showing that only 30 percent of voters in the Second District believed Clinton deserved reelection and that 56 percent (including almost half of Democrats) believed that voting Republican was a good way to send a message to Clinton and Congress. The National Republican Congressional Committee cooked up an ad, using new computer technology, where the face of the Democratic candidate, Joe Prather, morphed into the face of Bubba himself. "If you like Bill Clinton," the announcer said, "you'll love Joe Prather." The ad closed by reading straight from the Republican polling: "Send a message to Bill Clinton. . . . Send Ron Lewis to Congress."[21]

The morph ad devastated Prather, who went from looking for real estate in Washington, D.C., to losing 55–45 in less than two weeks. "I wouldn't be surprised to see that ad in two hundred districts this fall," Gingrich told reporters shortly after the Lewis victory.[22] And indeed quite a few Democrats would find themselves morphing into Bill Clinton over the next six months. More broadly, however, the ad showed just how much Clinton had united and energized the Republican base.

After twelve years of Republican control of the White House, the party's direct-mail operation had atrophied. When Mississippian and longtime Republican operative Haley Barbour took over the Republican National Committee after Bush's defeat, he immediately quadrupled the number of direct-mail appeals, to 1.2 million a week. The message in those appeals was 100 percent anti-Clinton. Anything that wasn't about Clinton flopped. When they focused on Clinton, however, the money poured in. The responses to RNC fund-raising appeals built over the course of 1993 and 1994, reaching a crescendo about a month before the election, when 134,000 contribution letters were delivered to the RNC's offices in one day.[23]

At the same time, grassroots groups that had been well fertilized in 1993 took the fight door-to-door and person-to-person throughout 1994. In an Oklahoma special election, two weeks before the one in Kentucky, Republican rancher Frank Lucas was propelled into office by 50,000 pieces of mail from U.S. Term Limits,

$30,000 worth of radio ads by the Oklahoma Taxpayers' Union, and 80,000 "voter guides" from the Christian Coalition.[24] Nationwide in 1994, the Christian Coalition distributed some 33 million voter guides, the NRA spent $3.4 million in targeted congressional races,[25] and the RNC's anti-Clinton machine funneled a record-breaking total of $20.2 million into campaigns.[26]

Republicans, of course, didn't rely on anti-Clinton sentiment alone. Gingrich had somewhat grander ideas. Ever since helping set up a campaign event in 1980, where Ronald Reagan and Republican congressional candidates stood on the steps of the Capitol and promised to cut taxes and increase defense spending if elected, he'd wanted to re-create that event. The Bush campaign would have none of it in 1992. But now this was Gingrich's show, and he set to work. He put Dick Armey of Texas in charge of coming up with the substance of the Contract with America, and Armey's press secretary, Ed Gillespie, in charge of selling it. The only guidelines were that it would consist of ten items (because, hey, ten is a nice, round number), it would be made up of "60 percent" issues (issues that 60 percent or more of the public approved of), and it would be unveiled on September 27 (because a long-range weather forecaster in Georgia told Newt that it would be sunny that day).[27]

In retrospect, perhaps the most striking thing about the Contract with America, to those looking back on it from the vantage point of George W. Bush's Republican Party, is just how little focus it put on the issues important to the Religious Right. The lone plank of the Contract devoted to social conservatives was a provision for a $500-per-child tax credit. The idea was straight from Ralph Reed's new fusionist playbook—the one that said the Religious Right should refashion itself as a profamily movement concerned with small-government, dollars-and-cents issues—but it also was thin gruel when it came to feeding the base. The 60-percent rule took abortion off the table. There was a push for a school-prayer plank, but Gingrich blanched, fearing it would be a hook that would allow the press to paint the Contract as a tool of religious extremists. "[Liberal columnist] Al Hunt will go nuts," he supposedly said at the time.[28]

Agreeing on the rest of the items in the Contract was much easier. Term limits and a balanced-budget amendment to the Constitution, while unpopular with many Republican members, were seen as absolutely essential in the anti-Washington political climate of 1994. More natural fits for the GOP were items such as tougher measures on crime, welfare reform, and tort reform. There also were good-government measures, such as promising to make all laws that applied to the rest of the country also apply to Congress and to hire a "major, independent" auditing firm to conduct a comprehensive audit of Congress "for waste, fraud, and abuse."

Participants in the framing of the Contract with America insist that no polling was done to decide which issues to include. However, extensive polling and focus-group research were done to determine how best to sell the Contract to the American people. At the forefront of that effort was an ambitious young Republican pollster (who had worked for Perot in 1992) named Frank Luntz. Working under the supervision of an RNC war room set up to manage the Contract, Luntz conducted focus group after focus group to find out what language would get a response from voters—particularly Perot voters.

This was no easy task. The primary fact of the 1994 political season was that voters were in a rage. Republicans would later fume over ABC's Peter Jennings's postelection declaration that the voters had "had a temper tantrum," but there was a lot of truth to that analysis. In a Gallup poll right before the 1994 elections, 66 percent of Americans said they were dissatisfied with the way things were going in the United States at the time; in the same poll, roughly 70 percent of Americans rated the economy either "only fair" or "poor." The voters' wild, unfocused anger was certainly on display in Luntz's focus groups. These groups wanted lower taxes, tougher crime measures, welfare reform. They were against big government. They thought Washington squandered their hard-earned money. But they recoiled at any suggestion that voting Republican was the answer to their problems.

To deal with this, Luntz scrubbed the word "Republican" from the Contract, as well as all references to Clinton. The language of the Contract and all the materials surrounding it focused on "Washington"—not "Democrats" and not "government." Government, in and of itself, was not as unpopular with people as Washington. Government to many people meant local government, with which the public had little anger. And there was no reason to mention Democrats specifically. Anything with the slightest whiff of partisanship would turn off the Perot voters. The public would make the connection themselves that the problem in Washington was the Democrats, who controlled . . . well, everything.

In the end, the Republicans were tremendously successful at courting the Perotistas. In 1992, Perot supporters had split their votes for Congress roughly evenly between Democrats and Republicans, with a slight preference for the Democrats; in 1994, they voted two-to-one for the Republicans. An endorsement of the GOP by Perot in October on *Larry King Live*—where he urged Americans to "give the Republicans a majority in the House and the Senate and say, 'All right now, we're going to let you guys have a turn at bat'"[29]—didn't hurt. But the shift among working-class voters, who believed that the Democrats had come to care more about the welfare-collecting poor than blue-collar workers, was already a done deal, with or without Perot.

The dimensions of the Republican victory on November 8, 1994, were stunning. The Republicans gained 52 seats in the House, for a 230-seat majority. It was the biggest midterm gain by either party since 1946. Republicans captured 8 Senate seats by winning all 6 Democratic open seats and knocking off 2 Democratic incumbents. In the South, where voters had long supported Republican presidential candidates but held to the Democratic line when it came to Congress, Republican congressional candidates received 3.8 million more votes than in the 1990 midterm elections. In the states, they gained 11 governorships, for a total of 30. Republicans also picked up 484 legislative seats, giving them control of 50 state legislative chambers.[30]

A number of prominent Democrats also got swept out with the tsunami: Speaker Thomas Foley of Washington; House Ways and Means Committee chairman Dan Rostenkowski of Illinois, crippled by scandal; Governor Ann Richards of Texas was defeated by George W. Bush; Governor Mario Cuomo of New York was ousted by a charisma vacuum named George Pataki. Then there were those who simply switched sides. Senator Richard Shelby of Alabama switched to the Republican Party; he would be followed by Senator Ben Nighthorse Campbell of Colorado. Five southern Democrats in the House also switched parties in 1995.[31] The chairman of the Democratic National Committee, David Wilhelm, summed up the situation pretty succinctly on election night: "We got our butts kicked."[32]

And no one got his or her butt kicked more thoroughly than Bill Clinton. The story line from the Washington press corps after the 1994 elections was that Clinton, just two years into his first term, was a lame duck—left to while away the hours until his inevitable defeat in 1996. He was irrelevant. The power in Washington had now shifted to the other end of Pennsylvania Avenue, where Newt Gingrich would rule as a sort of Republican prime minister. And, for a time after the new Congress was sworn in on January 4, 1995, all this looked like it just might be the case. Gingrich held forth at daily press briefings. He ushered bills to the floor at a breakneck pace. The Contract had promised votes on the House floor on ten major items, and Gingrich delivered all those votes. The only measure that failed the House was a constitutional amendment to implement term limits. Things got stickier in the Senate, where Gingrich's old foe Bob Dole took his sweet time with numerous Contract objectives. But it was clearly Gingrich, not Clinton or Dole, who was driving the policy agenda in Washington.

Things got so bad for Clinton that at a press conference on April 18, 1995, he was forced to lamely react to charges that he was irrelevant by declaring, "the Constitution gives me relevance." Clinton's press conference, an attempt to seize back the spotlight from the Republicans after months in the shadows, was carried live only by CBS. ABC went with *Home Improvement* and *Roseanne*, while NBC showed *Frasier* and *Friends*.[33]

While Clinton was reeling, however, the Republicans had already set themselves on the path to self-destruction. The first step was massively misinterpreting the meaning of their 1994 landslide. Frank Luntz remembered election night in an interview—and not fondly. It was on that night that Gingrich first began to talk about the vote in terms of its having been a revolution. "When I first heard Newt use the word 'revolution,' frankly, I freaked," Luntz recalled. "I knew that the public didn't see their vote as a revolution." Even in that overwhelmingly Republican election, voters had split only roughly 54–46 in the GOP's favor. As Luntz said, "doesn't sound like a revolution to me."

"This is the secret of '94," Luntz said. "It's not that the public embraced the Republican Party, but they rejected the Democratic Party, and the Republicans were there to pick up the votes." For all the attention paid to the Contract, even Luntz, whose reputation has been tied tightly to the document's success, admits that it was not the central factor behind the Republicans' victory. "It wasn't really an embracing of the Contract, even though the Contract was perceived very favorably," Luntz said. Others might take the argument even further, noting that even after the election a Gallup poll showed that only about one-third of voters had ever heard of the Contract.[34]

What's clear, however, is that assuming that the American people had embraced the Republican agenda, specifically a small-government agenda, led to disastrous missteps by the new Republican majority. Luntz recalled that shortly after the election, Gingrich wrote him a letter—a beautiful letter that Newt typed himself and Luntz framed—discussing the importance of communication going forward. The Republicans would have to be careful not to go native, not to seek the approval of the Washington press corps, he wrote. They would have to watch their words and their language, making sure to keep the favor of Main Street America. The letter was destroyed ten years later, when Luntz's house was flooded. Much sooner, however, Newt's words would be washed away by the daily waves of Washington politics and by the new

Speaker's own uncontrollable verbal outflow. "Funny," said Luntz, "that it ended up being Newt who had some of the most inflammatory rhetoric in the end."

If not for the inflammatory rhetoric—always talking about "revolution" and smashing the welfare state—it would have been that much harder for Clinton to ever take the first step out of hell. As it was, Clinton's road to recovery began the very day after his Constitution-gives-me-relevance embarrassment. On April 19, 1995, Timothy McVeigh blew up the Alfred P. Murrah Federal Building in Oklahoma City, using a Ryder truck full of fertilizer and motor-racing fuel, killing 168 people. As in any national crisis, the people rallied around the president. And Clinton's empathetic gifts served him as they always have.

What's more, Clinton couldn't help but use the Oklahoma City tragedy as a weapon against the Republicans. Not a week later, on April 23, Clinton got up before a meeting of the American Association of Community Colleges in Minneapolis and launched an attack on talk radio. "I am sure you are now seeing the reports of some things that are regularly said over the airwaves in America today," he told the crowd. "They leave the impression that, by their very words, that violence is acceptable."[35] Shortly thereafter, in a commencement speech at Michigan State University, Clinton attacked "the militias and all those who believe that the greatest threat to freedom comes from government." The Republicans in Congress, you see, were an orienteering course away from joining the Michigan Militia. He continued: "There is nothing patriotic about hating your country, or pretending that you love your country but despise your government."[36]

Clinton's tactics were ugly, but they worked. For the first time since the election, the Republicans were thrown on the defensive—and the president's political genius began to shine through. Gingrich and most of the Republican House leadership had been in Washington longer than Clinton, but the truth was that they were amateurs up against a professional. A natural. When the Republicans thought they might win Congress in the summer of 1994, a staffer was tasked with putting together a black book on . . . well, how the hell Congress is run.[37] They had a plan for the first hundred days—pass the Contract—but nothing much beyond that. Clinton was back on his heels for a bit, but once he summoned to the White House Dick Morris, who'd helped him win so many gubernatorial elections back in Arkansas, he quickly got back on his stride. The Republicans, meanwhile, would never quite regain their footing.

The biggest mistake the Republicans made was taking on Medicare during the first year of their majority and shutting down the government. There was a tremendous amount of hubris to the Republicans' approach. Gingrich seemed to believe that if the Republicans could just get a handle on the language of Medicare reform, they could control the debate. He hired a pollster, Linda DiVall, who said to stay away from words such as "change," "cap," "cut," and "freeze," and instead go with terms such as "preserve" and "protect."[38] It was a little bit like the Washington Generals preparing to play the Harlem Globetrotters. While the GOP was practicing free throws, Clinton was getting ready for a slam dunk.

The Republicans had denied Clinton and the Democrats any traction by taking Social Security off the table in 1994, defending themselves against Republicans-hate-the-poor-type attacks. But moving on Medicare threw the floodgates open. At the end of April, Gingrich gave his first speech about "preserving" and "protecting" Medicare. By early July, the Clinton White House had begun an advertising bombardment that would not cease until Election Day 1996.[39] In one ad, an EKG machine monitored a patient's heartbeat; as the announcer described the premium increases and benefit cuts the Republican plan would bring, the line went flat, and all that was left was the continuous monotone signaling Medicare's death. The ads worked. Clinton's job approval rating climbed continuously, and voters came to trust him to balance the budget "in a way that is fair to all" over the Republicans by 12 to 15 percentage points.[40]

Despite the direction the political winds were blowing, the Republicans—remarkably enough—decided to shut down the government. With or without a balanced-budget amendment to the Constitution, the Republicans committed themselves to the goal of erasing the federal deficit in seven years. That couldn't be done without reducing Medicare's rate of growth, so they headed into the fall on a collision course with Clinton.

Dick Morris later wrote that he had "underestimated the capacity of Gingrich and Dole for political suicide."[41] But, in truth, Dole wasn't the one on the kamikaze mission. It was Gingrich who was after a showdown with Clinton—partly out of pique, partly out of hubris, but mostly out of a monumental strategic miscalculation. Gingrich's calculus was very simple and very wrong. His assumption was that Clinton would simply have no choice but to give in to all of the Republicans' demands. He couldn't risk a government shutdown because presidents get blamed for shutdowns. Gingrich based this assumption on the fact that President Reagan had taken the blame for government shutdowns in the 1980s. What Gingrich didn't understand until the polls were upon him was that, in actuality, *Republicans* get blamed for government shutdowns. They're the ones who hate government, they're the ones who want to slash government—the public knows this and assigns the blame accordingly. What's more, the Republicans couldn't very well blame Clinton for the shutdown when Gingrich and House Budget Committee chairman John Kasich had been out publicly threatening to shut down the government for the better part of the year. It sort of gave away the game.

Aside from the who-would-be-blamed problem, the Republicans made another fundamental miscalculation in forcing a dramatic showdown with Clinton. Bill Clinton thrives on drama. Former majority leader Dick Armey, looking back on the shutdown a decade later in an interview at his Washington, D.C., office, compared Clinton to Muhammad Ali. "If you take me out in the back street with Muhammad Ali and give me a gun, I'll shoot him, right, and nobody will notice," Armey said. "But if you let me get in the ring with him, he's gonna kick the tar outta me."

Gingrich was desperate to climb in that ring and prove he could take on the greatest of all time, but once he got in there, he found that Clinton floated like a butterfly and stung like a bee. In meetings between the White House and the congressional leadership, Clinton consistently outwitted and outmaneuvered the Republicans, stringing them along and stringing them along—making them think he was ready to give far more than he ever would—all the while clobbering them in the press and with paid ads. He got them to make real concessions, offering nothing more in return than slippery platitudes.

The Republicans didn't do themselves any favors, either. Shortly before the first government shutdown, which ran from November 14 through November 19, Gingrich made a comment in a speech about wanting to let Medicare "wither on the vine." The very same day, Dole told a meeting of the American Conservative Union that he was proud to have voted against Medicare in 1965 because "we knew it wouldn't work."[42] The Democrats ran ads featuring Gingrich's quote (but not Dole's; they wanted to make sure to have him as an opponent in 1996) all through November in roughly 40 percent of the country.[43] Then, two days into the first shutdown, Gingrich told a group of reporters that Clinton had snubbed him on the plane ride to and from the funeral of the assassinated Israeli prime minister, Yitzhak Rabin, and that this had played a part in his decision to shut down the government. The next day's New York *Daily News* carried the front-page headline, CRY BABY, next to a caricature of Gingrich in a diaper.

Gingrich's fraying nerves also would play a role behind the scenes in ending the second, much more drawn-out government shutdown, which lasted from December 17 to January 6. The breaking point came at a Saturday meeting on December 30 in Bob Dole's office. Dole, Armey, and Gingrich got into a heated confrontation on the phone with Clinton. The president had called to ask if the three Republican leaders would be coming to the White House for more budget talks, but the conversation turned to a picture that had appeared recently in *Time* magazine. The picture showed Clinton gesturing at an easel with budget figures on it, lecturing the Republican leaders. They felt it made them look like a bunch of schoolkids.

Suddenly Gingrich grabbed the receiver. "Newt got on the phone, and he was frustrated and angry and very, very profane," Armey recalled. "I mean, shockingly so." It was apparently quite something. "Hey, I'm an old country boy, I'm not easily shocked," said Armey. "But Newt's language was really startling to me. . . . Given an old gentleman like Bob Dole, if I was stunned by it, Bob must have been horrified." The demeanor of it all was so shocking, Armey believes, that Dole decided to pull the plug then and there. The meeting broke up and Armey was heading home. As Armey left, Dole asked Gingrich to stay behind. Armey headed home to Leesburg, Virginia. The next thing he heard was that they were giving up the whole thing.

Days later, Dole broke with Gingrich publicly, passing a resolution in the Senate to end the shutdown. The House would soon follow, paying government workers and then reopening the federal government—all without any solid balanced-budget commitment from Clinton. Less than three weeks after that, Clinton would announce in his State of the Union address that "the era of big government is over." But, he added, "we cannot go back to the time when our citizens were left to fend for themselves."

The Syndrome Sets In

There are those who argue that the Republicans withdrew too quickly from the government-shutdown quagmire, particularly from the first shutdown, during which, it's clear from the after-the-fact accounts of various Clinton staffers, the president was close to making significant concessions. And if rats had bushy tails they'd be called squirrels. The fact is the Republicans were outmatched by the White House political operation six ways from Sunday, and they made decisions based on what little information they had. What's certain is that Republicans quickly came to view the entire engagement as a mistake. Just as the United States suffered from a "Vietnam syndrome" after that conflict, so the Republicans would live for the next five years holding significant power yet being deathly afraid to wield it.

Disunity and disarray reigned among conservatives in 1996. In the primaries, economic conservatives flocked to Steve Forbes and his call for a flat tax. Social conservatives looked to Pat Buchanan. *National Review* endorsed Senator Phil Gramm of Texas; he got in the race late and finished nearly last. When the nomination fell to Dole—few people's first choice, but a man even fewer could deny was next in line—the contest was over before it began. Dole had not only to run against Clinton, but also away from the Republican Congress that had shut down the government. Dole's base didn't care for him, the center was happy with a strong economy, and the Left was looking for revenge. Dole didn't offer much in terms of bold vision, especially in the eyes of conservatives, only toward the end of the campaign calling for a 15 percent across-the-board tax cut and suddenly hitting on key social issues such as affirmative action and immigration. Clinton hammered the final nail in Dole's coffin in August of 1996, when he signed the Republicans' welfare-reform bill, complete with time limits on how long people could receive welfare, and sending the administration of welfare programs to the states. He made it look like a Democrat was perfectly capable of shrinking government in the places it mattered—even if he never would have reformed welfare in the absence of a Republican Congress.

That November, the tax collector for the welfare state lost to the man who had just ended welfare as we know it by 49 percent to 41 percent. How surprising that the former was the Republican and the latter the Democrat. The Republicans lost a number of seats in the House but narrowly held on to control; they gained seats in the Senate. Gingrich, also, was narrowly reelected as Speaker. This time he took office a chastened man, with no talk of revolution, but instead relief at simply having survived. "We're in a situation where we survived all the ads, we survived all the campaigning, we survived a very strong showing by their nominee for president," Gingrich told the *Washington Post* the day after the election. "I don't start this new process automatically expecting us to have to get into a confrontation," he said. Instead, Republicans were looking for "common ground."[44]

The problem for the Republicans politically was that all that common ground had already been staked out by Clinton. NAFTA? Clinton was for it. Welfare reform? What took you Republicans so long?! A balanced budget? Just call him Bill "Balanced Budget" Clinton. With no new agenda and no greater objective than to keep Clinton's spending in check as best they could—though without any credible threat that they might shut down the government—the Republicans grew increasingly restless and bitter.

Anger over their political impotence, and sheer rage that Clinton seemed to be able to get away with anything and everything led the Republicans to pursue impeachment after the president's affair with intern Monica Lewinsky came to light in January of 1998. Impeachment, however, would gain them absolutely no purchase with the public. Clinton's job approval rating remained sky-high, even as the public's personal opinion of him plummeted appropriately. In the 1998 midterm elections, the Republicans ran an intensely personal campaign focused on Clinton, and it backfired big time. Pollster David Winston, who was Gingrich's director of planning at the time, said in an interview that the Republicans were "absolutely 100 percent successful" at what they were trying to do, pumping up Clinton's negative personal ratings; and the Democrats were 100 percent successful at pumping up his job approval. "Basic assumptions behind the two plans: ours were flawed, theirs were right on the money," he said. "We lost five seats as opposed to picking up thirty."

The problem for Gingrich was that he'd promised a pickup of thirty. The GOP may have held on to Congress, but the 1998 midterms were a huge defeat for the Speaker. He resigned days later, on the evening of Friday, November 6. He was eventually succeeded by Representative Dennis Hastert of Illinois, a man who wouldn't know a vision if you slipped him a tab of LSD.

The achievements of the 1994 Republican Revolution are nothing conservatives should sneeze at. Gingrich's minions put the brakes on a government takeover of the health-care industry. They gave Clinton the proper incentives to sign welfare reform. They even, in 1997, balanced the budget. At the broadest level, as Fox

News reporter Major Garrett argues in his book *The Enduring Revolution* the Republican Revolution and the 1995–1996 government shutdowns "dramatically changed the trajectory of the federal government" for the rest of the 1990s, putting the country in a far better position to make use of the prosperity of the late 1990s than would have been the case if Clinton had been left unchecked.[45]

At the same time, however, the extent to which the Republicans lost their nerve in the 1990s was unnerving. Mike Franc, who was the Heritage Foundation's director of congressional relations during 1994 and 1995, remembers one forum he moderated where there were four freshmen from the class of 1994. Each had a bill to close down a cabinet-level agency. "It all sounds so nice and quaint right now," he said more than a decade later. That spunk died out pretty quickly after the government shutdowns ended. And, yes, the budget was balanced, but even the Republicans who worked hardest toward that goal admit that half or more of the work there was done by the economy itself, which churned out tremendous tax revenues in 1996, 1997, and 1998, fueled by the Internet boom. The Republicans certainly held the line on entitlement spending, whereas a Democratic Congress likely would have embarked with Clinton on new spending programs. But even the Republicans' discipline started breaking down after 1997, when the House appropriators rebelled and refused to work anymore with hard-nosed Dick Armey. In 1998, the Republicans caved like a house of cards and acquiesced to $20 billion extra in domestic spending that Clinton wanted, simply to avoid even the word "shutdown" being mentioned too close to Election Day.[46]

It was quite the fall from grace. But it is crucial to remember just how much of the problem was with style, as opposed to substance. After all, Clinton made himself a pretty popular president by co-opting the bulk of the GOP's substance. "Clinton was quick to move to the center and push us off to the right," said Luntz. "On Election Day '94, Clinton was a liberal, and we were moderate conservatives. By Election Day '96, we were conservatives, and Clinton was a moderate," he said. "By Election Day '98, we were strong conservatives, and Clinton was just persecuted." When it comes down to it, said Luntz, "At a time when we wanted to become mainstream, we came across as extreme."

"A lot of it was naiveté on our part; we'd never been there before," Dick Armey said. "Quite frankly, I look back at it, we did a remarkable job for people who'd never been in control of anything. . . . But the idea that we could meet Clinton on his ground and beat him, I just think was naive on our part." Instead, Armey said, the Republicans should have employed the "quiet no"—the one thing Clinton couldn't deal with. "Just keep our mouth shut, go through the year, stick to our guns, stand quietly on the ground that we had, live by continuing resolutions until we break them," that would have been the way to go, Armey said. Instead: "What we did was we precipitated a political confrontation, and we got our butts kicked."

The last word, of course, must go to Gingrich himself. "This is a city that talks in sound bites, but history actually occurs in volumes," he told a forum at the Cato Institute before the 2004 election. Responding to a question from the audience, Gingrich told the story that in 1986, during one budget fight or another, he was down at the White House yelling at Reagan for not taking a hard enough line. Afterward, Gingrich said, Reagan put his hand on his shoulder and told him, "It took us seventy years to get into this mess, I'm the first eight on the way out. . . . Maybe you guys will have to do some heavy lifting on your own." In truth, Gingrich said, Goldwater had been Part One. Reagan was Part Two. The Republican Revolution in 1994 was Part Three.

"I think the Bush presidency in some ways is Part Four, and in some ways isn't Part Four," Gingrich said.

More than a year into George W. Bush's second term, it looks like Part Four may be on hold indefinitely.

4

The Breaking Apart

Representative Mike Pence, Republican of Indiana, said he felt like a Minuteman who showed up late for the Revolution. Sitting in the Capitol dining room in October of 2005, the House conservative leader was in the middle of a rebellion against the Bush administration—sparked by its massive spending requests in the wake of Hurricane Katrina. The revolution he'd wanted to be a part of, the Gingrich Revolution, had passed him by. Gone now, as his BlackBerry periodically interrupted his Cobb salad, was any sense that the Republican Party's purpose was still to change Washington; here to stay was the sinking feeling that the conservative movement's permanent revolution had slowly mutated into a permanent reelection campaign, willing to spend whatever it cost and do whatever it took to hold on to power.

That was not what Pence had signed up for.

The midwesterner, who looks something like a cross between Howard Dean and John McCain, but who might have to punch a person in the mouth for comparing him to such a couple of lefties, got into politics for a simple reason: to shrink government. And he'd waited a long time to get his shot. Though he arrived in the capital in 2001, along with President Bush, he'd made his first run for Congress in 1988. He recalled that first campaign with some relish, running through memories of driving all over east-central Indiana in a Chevy Impala with GOPAC tapes all over the floor of his car and speeches by Ronald Reagan and Newt Gingrich on the stereo. He lost that race and went on to lose another in 1990, both to Democrat Phil Sharp. Pence spent the 1990s out of politics proper, instead going into the pundit business, running a conservative think tank and then broadcasting the *Mike Pence Show* on eighteen radio stations in the Hoosier State. So when Pence—who describes himself as "a Christian, a conservative, and a Republican, in that order"—won the congressional seat being vacated by Republican representative David McIntosh in 2000, it was a long-awaited moment for the Rip van Winkle revolutionary.

In fact, it wouldn't be too much of a stretch to say that Pence's fortunes over the twelve years leading up to his election had pretty well mirrored those of the conservative movement as a whole. Having faced disappointment after disappointment ever since Reagan left the White House, and having looked on as Bill Clinton thwarted the Republican Congress's lofty goals, Pence now arrived in a city where the possibilities for conservative Republicans looked limitless: They had the House. They had the Senate. And now they finally had the White House, too. It was time to pick up where the class of '94 had left off.

Yet it was not to be.

"I'm elected, I arrive for my first session of Congress. Here I am, I'm finally suited up. General Washington, I'm here," Pence said, mimicking the excitement he felt at the time. But excitement would quickly yield to deflation. "Instead of the end of the Department of Education, they hand me H.R. 1 [House Resolution 1, the top legislative priority], which is the largest expansion of the federal Department of Education since Jimmy Carter." Congress ends up passing No Child Left Behind. "They tell me don't worry about it, it's an anomaly."

Not so.

"I fight for reelection, I'm reelected in 2002, I show up, they hand me the next H.R. 1: the prescription-drug entitlement," he recalled. Pence had been one of a handful of Republicans to vote against NCLB, and he would be one of a handful to vote against the $1.2 trillion Medicare prescription-drug giveaway. "I don't try to be all holier than thou," Pence said. "But you want to create a new entitlement, you want the federal government to do national testing in my local school? Wrong answer. Not what I came here to do."

The Elephant in the Room

It wasn't what a lot of conservatives in Washington had come there to do. Pence started speaking out against the direction in which President Bush was leading the Republican Party when he delivered the keynote address at CPAC in January of 2004. "Picture, if you will," he exhorted the crowd, "a ship at sea." Modern conservatism, he said, was like a tall ship "veering off course into the dangerous and uncharted waters of big-government Republicanism."

But Pence wasn't ready to jump ship just yet (in fact, to this day, he takes great pains never to attack the president or the congressional leadership directly). And, by and large, even the most committed small-government conservatives stood by their man in 2004. Pat Buchanan—primary challenger to Bush Sr. in 1992 and fourth-party opponent of Bush Jr. in 2000—ended up endorsing the incumbent, explaining that, "while Bush and Kerry are both wrong on Iraq, Sharon, NAFTA, the WTO, open borders, affirmative action, amnesty, free trade, foreign aid, and big government, Bush is right on taxes, judges, sovereignty, and values. Kerry is right on nothing." What's more, he added (echoing, no doubt, millions of Americans trying to balance their disappointment in Bush with their detestation of people who have the time and disposable income to go around protesting things), "I cannot endorse the candidate of Michael Moore, George Soros, and Barbra Streisand."[1]

A few conservative pundits of the libertarian variety jumped ship publicly. Andrew Sullivan, former editor of the *New Republic* and a libertarianish, hawkish conservative, reluctantly endorsed Kerry on the grounds that Bush was botching the war in Iraq and was a "theocon" who had corrupted conservatism. Robert George, an editorial writer for the *New York Post* (and a former colleague of the author), wrote a cover story for the *New Republic* titled "Conscientious Objector," arguing that Bush's embrace of big government and failure to demand any form of accountability from members of his administration constituted "a betrayal of conservative values."[2] Not many conservatives, however, seemed to heed these calls when Election Day rolled around; and very few others—pundit, politician or otherwise—declared against Bush.

A public reassessment of the state and direction of the conservative movement simply wasn't in the offing in a year when an incumbent Republican president faced a tough reelection campaign. That was especially the case in an election when, after 9/11, security was still at the top of the national agenda. There was a growing sense of disquietude on the Right, but for the duration of 2004 it was sublimated into angry rumblings in back rooms.

It took a hurricane to blow the doors to those back rooms open.

Katrina hit the Gulf Coast at the end of August 2005 and immediately tore up America's political landscape. Why hadn't New Orleans' levees been built stronger? Where was the federal government with aid? Why hasn't the president visited? Who's this "Brownie" guy, and what exactly counts in this administration as "a heckuva job"? *This* is "compassionate conservatism"?

As Bush's poll numbers sunk in the New Orleans floodwaters, he sent his staff scrambling to spend money at a pace that might dispel the notion, expressed most memorably by rapper Kanye West in an NBC telethon after the disaster, that "George Bush doesn't care about black people." He preemptively waved off the concerns of fiscal conservatives, saying that rebuilding was going to "cost whatever it costs." And he rushed down to do a televised national address from the French Quarter, pledging $60 billion as a first installment of federal recovery aid (New York City, by way of contrast, had gotten $20 billion in federal aid after 9/11). When the conservative Republican Study Committee, which Pence chairs, began pushing for budget cuts to pay for the Katrina cleanup, then majority leader Tom DeLay declared that there was simply no fat left in government to cut: "Yes, after eleven years of Republican majority we've pared it down pretty good," he told the *Washington Times*.[3]

There was, in other words, a sudden moment of clarity. All at once, it became impossible to ignore the elephant in the room. The conservative revolution of 1964, 1980, and 1994 had come to a end. In its place was some new, mutant ideology—or anti-ideology—that, after more than a decade of controlling Congress and more than four years of dominating the entire federal government, had lost all touch with its former self. It might occasionally make noises about small government (though it rarely did even that anymore), but it did so more out of habit than conviction.

In some ways this moment wasn't such a shock after a first Bush term that had included NCLB, the prescription-drug giveaway, farm subsidies, steel tariffs, and a 33 percent jump in federal spending. But it was nonetheless jolting to those conservatives who still took the idea of small government seriously and hadn't yet reconciled themselves to the fact that the majority of their friends and colleagues no longer did.

If nothing else, the moment—with Bush safely reelected but foundering at the start of his second term—was cathartic. Finally, thoughts could turn to a time after Bush and a real debate could begin. Echoing Goldwater's indictment of Eisenhower's presidency as a "dime-store New Deal," Pence said over that lunch in October that he no longer saw why his party deserved to hold on to the White House in 2008 if all they stood for was "what the Democrats will do minus 10 percent." Or, as Reagan speechwriter Peggy Noonan put it in a column for the *Wall Street Journal*'s Web site at about the same time, "If we are going to spend like the romantics and operators of Lyndon Johnson's Great Society; If we are thereby going to change the very meaning and nature of conservatism; If we are going to increase spending and the debt every year; If we are going to become a movement that supports big government . . . shouldn't we perhaps at least discuss it?"[4]

Of course, to other conservatives, Bush's reckless spending and abandonment of traditional conservatism were exciting, even exhilarating—a welcome departure from the cramped, small-government philosophy of the Gingrich years. In a practically giddy column after Katrina, *New York Times* columnist David Brooks celebrated the aftermath of the storm as a chance to set up a "Bushian Laboratory" to experiment with the president's fabled compassionate conservatism. Bush, Brooks admitted, had "never resolved the conflict between his compassionate spending policy and his small-government tax policy." Nonetheless, he argued, the president had "muddled his way toward something important, a positive use of government that is neither big government liberalism nor antigovernment libertarianism."[5]

There, in a few ebullient sentences, Brooks laid out the basics of the mass of contradictions, non sequiturs, and elisions that make up what has come to be known as big-government conservatism. The flat-out impossibility of increasing spending by breathtaking leaps and bounds, year after year after year, without ever increasing the burden on the American taxpayer? A niggling detail, that. The assumption that the cure for what ails America must always entail more government, not less? That, apparently, goes without saying. And the idea that conservatism can have meaning stripped of any commitment to limiting the size of government, despite the fact that its modern form has been defined by such a commitment for more than fifty years? To believe otherwise, it seems, is to give in to foolish nostalgia.

However, for all the flaws in this new conservatism—being pushed by the likes of Brooks, the *Weekly Standard*, Karl Rove, and the president himself, and perfectly acceptable to career politicians who find lower taxes and ever-expanding government entitlements surprisingly easy to sell to their constituents—one thing is undeniably clear: it is winning. The crisis in the Republican Party is real. The crisis in conservatism is real. And if the people who built the conservative movement and then took over the GOP don't want to lose everything many have worked a lifetime for, they need to wake up.

Since the close of the Cold War, there has been the ever-present danger that the fusionist marriage between small-government conservatives and social conservatives described by Frank Meyer would fail—no longer held together, as it had been since its beginning, by a common commitment to anticommunism. In 1992, the coalition frayed, but it quickly regrouped to fend off the scourge of Clintonism, a horror to social conservatives, economic conservatives, paleoconservatives, and neoconservatives alike. In 2000, still smarting from the defeats of the Gingrich years, conservatism's factions set aside their pet issues—and, well, principles—and came together in their quest for complete dominance of the federal government. And in 2004, the War on Terror and the impulse not to cut and run from Iraq were enough to quell most conservative defections and keep Bush in office for a second term.

Now, with all three branches of the federal government under its control, the GOP has arrived (to summon Reagan) at another time for choosing. If the Republican Party cannot renew its core commitment to the cause of small government now, at the height of its power, then it can never do so. And if limited government is no longer at the center of conservatism, then conservatism—at least as it has been known since libertarianism and traditionalism fused in the pages of *National Review* in the 1950s and in the Goldwater campaign of 1964—has ceased to exist. Conservatives concerned primarily with issues such as abortion, school prayer, gay marriage, and the like—that is, social conservatives—may well decide that the Republican Party remains their logical home for the foreseeable future. But conservatives who care about low taxes, less regulation of business, less regulation of political speech, school choice, free trade, fiscal responsibility, and reforming massive entitlements such as Medicare and Social Security, whose costs threaten to crush the rising generation, can no longer assume anything.

Certainly there have been false alarms about fissures in conservatism before. With the tensions that have always existed between small-government conservatives and traditionalists, between libertarians and social conservatives, it is all too easy to confuse a spat for World War III. But what's happening within conservatism now isn't a blowup, big or small.

It's a slow but sure breaking apart.

The problem can be hard to see. Sometimes it's misdiagnosed as simple financial corruption. But that's far too easy an answer—especially for the Left, which is most comfortable when it can paint Republicans as Thomas Nast caricatures of plutocrats, complete with top hats and beanbag-chair-size bellies. The truth is that lobbyist money will flow to those in power like water down a hill. Corrupt politicians of either party deserve the scandals they bring upon themselves and their colleagues, but the GOP's troubles can't be blamed on the fact that its members' ethics conform to the laws of gravity and human nature.

Likewise, it would be a tremendous oversimplification to look at the emerging split as one that breaks down neatly along economic-conservative versus social-conservative lines. Any observer of the current Congress will quickly recognize that many of the most socially conservative members are among the most economically conservative, and vice versa. That, however, is not to say that the split is one between, say, conservative Republicans and moderate Republicans. The moderate Republicans are most likely to take the lead in betraying the GOP's small-government principles on economic issues; the conservative Republicans are most likely to take the lead in betraying the GOP's small-government principles on social issues.

The process under way is more along the lines of plate tectonics, the sliding and movement and cracking of two masses of rock and dirt that have long been fused together. As the Republican Party has moderated its rhetoric and its policies on size-of-government issues, and amped up its rhetoric on "values" issues to draw in and turn out more Evangelicals and Catholics in the South and the Midwest, the base on which the party sits has shifted.

Since 1987, the Pew Research Center for the People and the Press has tracked American voters not just based on traditional breakdowns among liberals, conservatives, and moderates, but also has divided them further, into political "typologies" based on values, political beliefs, and party affiliation. In May of 2005, it released its latest political typology, breaking Americans down into nine discrete categories: three on the Left, three in the center, three on the Right.[6] What's interesting, right off the bat, is the third category on the Right. While in 1987 and 1994, when the first two surveys were conducted, the Republican Party was basically split between social conservatives and economic conservatives, the 1999 Pew survey picked up on a major new segment in the Republican coalition: in 1999, Pew called them Populists; in 2005, Pew dubbed them Pro-Government Conservatives. Economic conservatives— what Pew calls Enterprisers—make up 11 percent of registered voters, Social Conservatives make up 13 percent, and Pro-Government Conservatives weigh in at 10 percent.

According to the report, the Pro-Government Conservative group "agrees fully with the religious values of Social Conservatives" but favors "greater government action in assisting the poor and in regulating business to improve the environment, as well as to protect morality." In fact, the Social Conservatives and the Pro-Government Conservatives look an awful lot like each other, in most respects. Both groups are largely female and southern. Both support teaching creationism alongside evolution in public schools (62 percent and 64 percent, respectively). And both believe government should guarantee health insurance for all citizens (59 percent and 63 percent). The main differences are that Pro-Government Conservatives are younger, less economically secure, less educated, and slightly more diverse racially; they're also much more interested in seeing government intervene in the economy on behalf of the poor.

Enterprisers are the odd men out—literally. Predominantly white (91 percent) and male (76 percent), they believe corporations mostly play fair, environmental laws are too costly, and people should basically improve their own lot in life without handouts from anyone. They're religious and socially conservative, but far less extreme in their views and their desire to impose their views on others than their fellow conservatives. And they're by far the most enthusiastic about tax cuts, private Social Security accounts, and cutting spending to reduce the deficit.

Nothing's to say that the way Pew slices the pie is the only way it could be sliced, but the analysis certainly seems to get at an essential truth of what's going on in the Republican Party as it becomes more southern, more religious, and more working-class, and all the time more friendly toward expanding the size and scope of the state. What's more, it paints a fairly clear picture of just how it is that small-government conservatives and libertarians have ended up marginalized within their own party and movement—and how they will continue to be marginalized unless the party changes course.

One could argue that the American people have spoken, and they just don't want small government. In fact, that's the exact argument that *Weekly Standard* executive editor Fred Barnes—the reputed originator of, and only known self-confessed adherent to, the term "big-government conservatism"—makes in his recent book about George W. Bush, *Rebel-in-Chief*. Writes Barnes: "The possibility of smaller government has been tested twice in the past quarter-century, first with the Reagan Revolution following the 1980 election, then with the Gingrich Revolution after 1994. Both revolutions led to a single year of meaningful spending cuts, then a return to sizable annual increases, with departments and agencies targeted for extinction still intact. Reagan and Gingrich failed for lack of public support."[7]

Now, this isn't quite the full story. According to the Heritage Foundation, Reagan reduced domestic discretionary spending from 4.5 percent of GDP in 1981 to 3.1 percent of GDP in 1989. That's nothing to sneeze at. Clinton pulled off a similar feat during his first term, under the duress of the Gingrich Congress, reducing domestic discretionary spending from 3.4 percent to 3.1 percent of GDP.[8] And, let's not forget, at the end of his first term Clinton ended welfare as we knew it, one of the most significant conservative reforms in a generation—and another thing for which to thank Newt Gingrich.

(George W. Bush, meanwhile, by fiscal year 2005 had let domestic discretionary spending shoot up to 3.5 percent of GDP.[9] The Katrina cleanup will only send spending higher.)

Sure, neither Reagan nor Gingrich could quite get rid of the Department of Education, and fiscal restraint was shot to hell in Clinton's second term as the surpluses rolled in and the Republican Congress lost its backbone. But did that mean conservatives had to stop even trying in 2000? And just what dividends has the Bush approach paid that are in any way superior to, or even within spitting distance of, the records of Reagan and Gingrich?

So instead of blaming the public—which, by its very nature, will always want a million contradictory things, chief among them low taxes, a strong defense, and gobs of government services, all at the same time—those responsible for the direction of the Republican Party should be looking inward. The American people have their virtues, but knowing what they want from the government and setting sensible long-term priorities in the absence of principled political leadership are not among them. If the Republican Party has found itself with a constituency that does not value, or perhaps won't even tolerate, small government, it is because that is the coalition party leaders have built. In other words, they are living in a prison of their own construction.

That neoconservatives such as Brooks and Barnes, from an intellectual tradition that has long been hostile to the conservative movement's commitment to small government, would cheer this turn of events is no great surprise. But for the rest of the conservative movement, it's time to acknowledge that big, grayish, wrinkly thing with the long trunk and the big, floppy ears over in the corner: George W. Bush has been a tremendous mistake for the Republican Party; and if the GOP hopes to remain the party of limited government, its next presidential nominee will have to repudiate, not extend, the Bush legacy.

How the party stumbled into this mistake is understandable, if regrettable. But not to correct it, after witnessing five years now of the failure of the Bush approach to conservatism, would be unforgivable.

Betting on Bush

To understand the long-shot bet conservatives placed on Bush back in 1999 and 2000, it's important to remember where the Republican Party was at the tail end of the Clinton administration. The Republicans had held on to the House, but just barely, in November of 1998. Gingrich stepped down. A month later they impeached Clinton. And two months after that, the Senate acquitted the president on all charges. Republicans were thoroughly dispirited. Taking over Congress had gotten them only so far in advancing a conservative agenda, as they found themselves thwarted year after year by a Teflon-slick Democratic president. They wanted the White House, and they wanted it badly.

One of the more amusing aspects of the post-Katrina debate on the Right was that it centered around the question of not whether, but precisely to what extent, conservatives had sold their souls back in 1999 by falling in line so early behind Bush in the primaries. Had they been duped half-willingly into believing that "compassionate conservatism" was nothing more than a fig leaf for the same old Gingrichite agenda? Or had Bush not even done conservatives the courtesy of lying to them and worn his big-government-loving heart on his sleeve?

In a *New York Times* op-ed during the Harriet Miers Supreme Court nomination debacle—which came smack after Hurricane Katrina—*National Review* senior editor Ramesh Ponnuru made the case for the latter scenario.[10] "Conservatives who were paying attention in 2000 knew that Mr. Bush would not be a budget-cutter," Ponnuru wrote. But they calculated that Bush could be counted on "to make the nation more secure, to appoint 'strict constructionist' judges in the mold of Antonin Scalia and Clarence Thomas, to cut taxes and to reform entitlements." What's more, according to Ponnuru's theory, conservatives gambled that Bush could be counted on to do the right thing even when his heart and head were in the wrong place. Bush was too amenable to racial preferences? His judicial picks would undo the damage. Bush was bad on spending? His tax cuts would prevent him from blowing the budget. With the nomination of Miers, Ponnuru said, conservatives were rethinking their wager. But it was never much of a plan to begin with. And it's far too complex a set of calculations to represent the thinking of anyone but a few conservative intellectuals; rank-and-file primary voters decided on other grounds.

The reality was a bit less convoluted. Essentially, Bush talked out of both sides of his mouth, and people heard what they chose to hear.

Bush and those around him certainly went out of their way to distance the new Republican Party from that of the bad-old Gingrich-Dole years. In late September of 1999, already enjoying a towering lead in the GOP primaries, both in terms of polls and fund-raising, Bush began his tack to the center with a blistering sneak attack on the Republican Congress and its new leader, Representative Dennis Hastert of Illinois. His staff having been briefed only days before on a Republican plan to adjust how the Earned Income Tax Credit was distributed, Bush laid into the plan at a campaign news conference, saying: "I don't think they ought to balance their budget on the backs of the poor." Nobody in the House leadership would have been mistaken for Sister Souljah in a police lineup, but this was surely Bush's Sister Souljah moment, when he separated himself politically from what he perceived to be the least attractive elements of his party. The line was so thoroughly Clintonian that Speaker Hastert mistakenly attributed the swipe to President Clinton himself at a press conference and had to be corrected by a reporter.[11]

A few days later in New York, Bush followed up his "backs of the poor" slam, declaring, "Too often, my party has confused the need for limited government with a disdain for government itself." Instead, he said, government should be "focused, effective and energetic . . . doing a few things and doing them well."[12] Bush's advisers described it this way to the press: conservatism with a frown versus conservatism with a smile. Like Reagan, they said, Bush would give America the latter.[13]

But unlike with Reagan, who had been a hero of the conservative movement for well over a decade when he ran in 1980, voters had no idea what was behind Bush's smile. He did his best to give small-government conservatives reason to hope. "Big government is not the answer," he said in his acceptance speech at the Republicans' Philadelphia convention. But, he couched that by adding that "the alternative to bureaucracy is not indifference."

His performance at the three presidential debates with Vice President Al Gore was more telling. In the first debate, Bush accused Gore of wanting a "big, exploding federal government" and wanting to "grow the federal government in the largest increase since Lyndon Baines Johnson in 1965." In the second debate, in his closing statement, Bush said: "I don't believe, like the vice president does, in huge government. I believe in limited government. . . . By having a limited government and a focused government, we can send some of the money back to the people who pay the bills. I want to have tax relief for all people who pay the bills in America, because I think you can spend your money more wisely than the federal government can." In the third and final debate, at Washington University in St. Louis, he declared: "If this were a spending contest, I would come in second. I readily admit I'm not going to grow the size of the federal government like he is."

Since those debates, of course, Bush has surpassed Johnson's record—and the Republicans in Congress have challenged the president to a spending contest every year. Both sides consider themselves winners.

Summing up small-government-conservative disappointment in how things have turned out, former majority leader Dick Armey remembered back to 1999. He is, he said, probably as good a test as anyone as to whether conservatives really knew what they were getting with Bush. "When Bush wanted to run as president, he called me and we met in a hotel room in Dallas," Armey recalled. "He said, 'I'm more like Ronald Reagan than my father.' And that's true, but to a far lesser degree than I'd hoped." He explained it this way: "In politics you're either a pleasant surprise or a bitter disappointment." Reagan was a pleasant surprise. Bush 41 was a bitter disappointment. "Right now Bush 43 has a better chance of ending up a bitter disappointment than he does a pleasant surprise."

So why were conservatives so eager to believe the best about George W. Bush? Certainly not out of any magnetic attraction to the man. As one July 1999 *National Review* editorial put it: "He has avoided providing an overarching reason why voters should entrust him with the presidency. Bush cannot run to get the country moving, as Kennedy did in 1960, or to make America stronger than an adversary, as Reagan did in 1980. Nor can infusing government with effective compassion be the basis for a winning Republican presidential campaign. The most important W. question is 'Why?'"[14] Standards fell quickly, however—call it the soft bigotry of low expectations—as the inevitability of a Bush nomination quickly solidified into fact. More than a year later, reporting on the Philadelphia convention, the magazine noted wryly that "Given the Republican Party's hunger to win the presidential race this year, George W. Bush could probably have elicited cheers from the audience with a call to nationalize the banks."[15]

The notion that it didn't matter what Bush said, at the convention or anywhere else, had more than a slight ring of truth to it. There was an overwhelming sense during the 2000 election that, at base, like *Seinfeld*, it was about nothing. ("What's the deal with Social Security?") There were policy disagreements, of course, but little was at stake in terms of big ideas. Both candidates had plans for Social Security and Medicare. Both candidates pledged, in their different ways, to give the public a break from the embarrassing scandals of the Clinton years. And both candidates (though especially Bush) gave short shrift to foreign policy, seeing no new foreign threat in need of immediate attention. This was not, the assumption seemed to be, an election that would define any new era in American politics. Whoever was elected would be little more than a place holder until some more inspiring figure came along—hopefully in four, not eight, years.

No, this election had more to do with simple power. There were eleven candidates of varying degrees of seriousness in the Republican primary: Lamar Alexander, Gary Bauer, Bush, Elizabeth Dole, Steve Forbes, former Representative John Kasich, Senator Orrin Hatch of Utah, Alan Keyes, Senator John McCain, Dan Quayle, and Senator Robert Smith of New Hampshire. Yet by June of 1999—more than seven months out from the New Hampshire primary—more than half of GOP House members and a nice-sized gaggle of GOP senators had already closed ranks behind Bush. The Democrats were following a similar strategy, with House minority leader Richard Gephardt endorsing Gore early to help head off a challenge from the Left by former New Jersey senator Bill Bradley. With the presidency in the balance, both houses of Congress hinging on six-seat margins, and the Supreme Court's ideological balance presumed to be up for grabs as well, neither party wanted to take any chances. "This is as big as it gets," the chairman of the Democratic National Committee, Joe Andrew, told the *Washington Post*. "It's certainly the biggest election of my lifetime."[16]

Few voters, it's safe to say, felt that way when they went to the polls on November 7.

Cataclysm and Drift

Two events in the next year would make Americans quickly reconsider the importance of their votes. During thirty-six excruciating days, the Florida election controversy split the country into Red and Blue camps, much more interested in the outcome of the dispute and much more attached to their respective candidates than either of them had been during the campaign itself. The second event, however, quickly overshadowed the Florida farce, rendering it an almost nostalgia-worthy symbol of a time when politics may have been rancorous but at least the stakes were low: 9/11.

It's become a cliché to say everything changed on 9/11—but that doesn't mean it isn't at least half true. It brought the country together (at least temporarily) and sent Bush's approval ratings through the roof (again, temporarily) as he proved an able leader in a time of crisis. More than that, it created a new category of security-minded voter, heavily inclined to trust the GOP over the Democrats to manage the new War on Terror. "Soccer moms" turned into "security moms," as it were; and by the time the 2004 election cycle rolled around, GOP pollster David Winston esti-mated that these voters made up 11 to 14 percent of the electorate.

The War on Terror, in effect, quickly became not just the defin-ing conflict of a generation but also a cudgel with which the Repub-lican Party could bludgeon the Democrats over and over again. In the 2002 midterm elections, the Republicans retook the Senate (after the Jeffords defection) and gained seats in the House—reversing the trend where the party in the White House usually loses seats in the off-year—partly by blasting the Democrats for holding up the bill to create the Department of Homeland Security. The Democrats wanted a rider that would have given the agency's workers extensive civil-service protections; Republicans insisted that the department should be able to fire employees quickly in case of security concerns or incompetence. The White House also pushed for a congressional resolution authorizing the use of force in Iraq ahead of the midterms, forcing Democrats to disappoint their antiwar base lest the GOP be given another excuse to call them soft on terror. In 2004, of course, Senator John Kerry would be subjected to much the same treatment, accused by the GOP of wanting to treat terrorism as a "law enforcement" matter and said to have a long history of turning against America in tough times.

But if the Republicans have exploited 9/11 oftentimes, Democ-rats have found themselves chained to a cast of fringe-Left clowns so repugnant as to do more damage to the liberal cause than a mil-lion Swift Boat Veterans for Truth ads. While most of the dissent from the War on Terror on the Left is well within the bounds of rational discourse, the harsh gets lumped in with the bat-scat insane—and Democratic candidates pay the price.

With Democrats taking a beating about the head over terrorism, and shooting themselves in the feet regularly to boot, it might seem like the Republican Party should have had a relatively easy time pushing through the bulk of the agenda that had eluded it during the Gingrich years. But if 9/11 was a cataclysm that remade the American political landscape, there were significant things that didn't change, especially within the Republican Party and the conservative movement. The drift away from small-government conservatism that began after the failure of the government shut-downs only accelerated under Bush. And any pretense that Bush's increases in the size of government somehow served broader conservative goals falls apart immediately upon inspection. What's more, while there's been a concerted effort among Bush's defenders to blame much of this drift on 9/11 and War on Terror–related spending, the truth is that the outlines of Bushian big-government conservatism were visible from day one.

Nothing, perhaps, could be a clearer illustration of the effort to recast the Right than the No Child Left Behind bill, Bush's first legislative priority when he took office. The broader failings of this bill will be discussed in more depth in the next chapter, but essentially it followed the outlines of Bush's much-heralded project to remake conservatism: it twisted a gloomy Republican idea to cut the size of government (i.e., to eliminate the Department of Education and send the money back to the states) into a sunny idea for using the power of the federal government to pursue conservative ends. In this case, those conservative ends were defined as making schools accountable for performance. Unfortunately, all NCLB does is label some schools failing and then subject them to the most negligible of penalties, the bulk of which go unenforced in the nation's most troubled school systems. Not much of a conservative victory, that. And the price? A more than doubling of the federal education budget.

The rest of the Bush record is even less impressive. In fact, the number of crimes against conservatism committed by Republicans during the Bush administration is almost too many to list. But perhaps it's worth a shot.

To start, there are the simple raw numbers. As of the fall of 2005, when Pence and his colleagues were launching their rebellion, federal spending had increased 33 percent since Bush took office in 2001, from $1.8 trillion to $2.4 trillion a year. By comparison, the rate at which federal spending grew under Bush during that period was twice the rate at which it had grown under President Clinton. According to the Heritage Foundation, federal spending neared $22,000 per household (in 2005, inflation-adjusted dollars), the highest level since World War II; the deficit swelled to more than $2,800 per household.[17]

While the Bush administration and its defenders point to 9/11, the War on Terror, and the war in Iraq to justify those numbers, the fact is that the bulk of the increase in new federal spending is completely unrelated to defense or homeland security. What's more, the idea that emergency spending doesn't need to be offset by reductions in discretionary spending is a relatively new and unconservative one. Presidents Roosevelt and Truman actually decreased nondefense spending during World War II and the Korean War. Likewise, major disasters during the Clinton years—such as the Oklahoma City federal-building bombing and the 1994 Los Angeles earthquake—were met with billions of dollars of cuts in discretionary spending.

So what are the big-ticket items behind the surge in domestic spending?

Education, as mentioned above, has shot up to about $83 billion in 2006 from $35 billion in 2001. In 2002, Congress passed and Bush signed a massive farm bill that will cost $180 billion over ten years, doling out fat subsidies to commercial farms and reversing the progress the Gingrich Congress had made in the landmark 1996 Freedom to Farm law, which moved toward reducing farm subsidies. And in 2003, the Republicans moved to take the issue of prescription-drug costs off the table for the 2004 election by passing a massive new middle-class entitlement to prescription drugs through Medicare—not just for low-income citizens, but for everyone. The bill did next to nothing to reform Medicare or bring market mechanisms into the program, though the importance of the Health Savings Accounts it created remains to be seen.

Of course, to look at spending alone would be to take a rather cramped view of the ways Bush has grown the size and scope of government. In March of 2002 he signed the most expansive infringement on Americans' First Amendment rights since the Alien and Sedition Acts of 1798: the Bipartisan Campaign Reform Act, a.k.a. McCain-Feingold. Looking to get his onetime primary rival

Senator John McCain off his back on campaign-finance reform (and perhaps realizing that the bill would hurt the Democrats more than the Republicans), Bush signed a law that he admitted he believed was unconstitutional. Specifically, in a signing statement, he wrote that he had "reservations about the constitutionality of the broad ban on issue advertising, which restrains the speech of a wide variety of groups on issues of public import in the months closest to an election." No worry though, he said; the Supreme Court (remember, those activist judges he's always complaining about) would "resolve these legitimate legal questions as appropriate under the law." It didn't.

Abrogating your oath of office to "preserve, protect, and defend the Constitution" and delegating it to another branch of government? There's only one word for that: leadership.

Other offenses?

There was the Sarbanes-Oxley bill, passed in a panic after the Enron and WorldCom collapses. The bill did little to address the actual causes of those calamities, while at the same time adding a significant extra burden to American businesses. It now costs millions of dollars more for U.S. companies to comply with Securities and Exchange Commission rules; some U.S. companies are going private to avoid the cost, and some foreign companies are delisting from U.S. stock exchanges for the same reason.

Then there were Bush's steel tariffs. In 2002, ahead of the midterm elections, Bush imposed tariffs of 8 to 30 percent on most steel imports from Europe, Asia, and South America, a move designed to curry favor in steel-producing states in the Rust Belt, such as Pennsylvania, Ohio, and West Virginia. (The move also was aimed at getting the necessary votes from congressmen in those same states to win fast-track trade authority; but the usefulness of that authority was severely diminished, as former Reagan administration official Bruce Bartlett points out, because the U.S. tariffs made other nations more reluctant to give up their own protectionist measures during the crucial Doha Round of multilateral trade negotiations.[18]) The tariffs were dropped in 2003—earlier than Bush would have liked, as he faced reelection the next year—when the European Union threatened retaliatory action. The Bush administration also has slapped politically expedient tariffs on shrimp and soft lumber.

And—oh, yeah, just sort of out of nowhere—shortly before his 2004 State of the Union address, the president proposed a manned mission to Mars that could cost anywhere from $500 billion to $1 trillion to infinity. There's also supposed to be some sort of space base on the moon. For some reason.

The one defense the Bush administration and its defenders will make time and again boils down to two words: tax cuts. And cut taxes the Bush administration has. It doubled the child tax credit to $1,000 per child from $500 per child. It eliminated the marriage penalty. It reduced the top marginal tax rate to 35 percent from 39.6 percent. It created a 10 percent tax bracket for low-income workers. It reduced taxes on dividends and long-term capital gains. And it eliminated the death tax (at least until it springs back to life in 2011).[19] But an administration can cut taxes until it's blue in the face—if spending is exploding, if entitlements are exploding, and if the deficit is exploding, all that's been accomplished is to put off a significant tax hike for another day.

So how has the drift in the Republican Party's commitment to small-government gotten so bad—drifting off, as it were, into space?

A look at virtually any budget chart will tell you that as bad as Bush has been on spending, the problem predates the 2000 election. Spending was held flat after the Gingrich Revolution in 1995. The line starts to creep up after 1998. And then it takes off starting in 2001. The upward drift began in the late '90s, when the federal government was flush with cash from the dot-com boom and looking at surpluses as far as the eye could see. As Heritage's Mike Franc recounted it, Dick Armey and Senator Phil Gramm were coming over to Heritage and delivering lectures about what would happen if the entire federal debt were paid down. Suddenly the perceived need to keep spending down just evaporated, and the Republicans didn't want any big budget fights with Clinton coming into the 1998 midterms and then the 2000 presidential election.

Also, the Republican majority was, shall we say, maturing. "You had your first wave of staff and ex-members leaving Congress and going into the lobbying world, setting up their own shop, attracting very senior people," Franc recalled. It changed the face of lobbying in about the third or fourth year after the Gingrich Revolution. "When it started to happen it picked up momentum, and it's very strong these days," he said. In part, what that's meant is an explosion in so-called earmarks—a.k.a. pork. It used to be that Congress funded a program and then federal and state agencies determined who got the money. Now Congress "earmarks" funds to specific recipients. And, no surprise, those earmarks tend to go to the highest bidder, and lobbyists can do a pretty good trade running the auction.

Between 1995 and 2005, the number of earmarks in appropriations bills has increased roughly tenfold, to 14,000 from 1,400. Recent earmarks, according to Heritage, have included the Rock & Roll Hall of Fame in Cleveland, Ohio; a therapeutic horseback riding program; a grant to combat teen "goth" culture in Blue Springs, Missouri; an indoor rain forest in Iowa; and, of course, Alaska's now-(in)famous "Bridge to Nowhere," the star earmark— out of 6,400—of 2005's $300 billion highway bill. (Under intense scrutiny from blogs and other media outlets, the bridge earmark was removed from the bill, but the same amount of money will still be sent to Alaska, and, as of this writing, Governor Frank Murkowski, a Republican, wants to use it to . . . build the damn thing anyway.) As the columnist George F. Will noted in a *Newsweek* column at the time, whereas President Reagan vetoed a highway bill in 1987 because it included 152 earmarks, costing $1.4 billion, Bush signed the 2005 bill despite $24 billion in pure pork.[20]

And, in fact, Bush has never issued a veto. "He's completely abrogated one of the most important powers given to him by the Constitution," said Bartlett, whose new book, *Impostor*, accuses Bush of betraying Reagan's legacy. The president, he said in an interview, "just signs any goddamn piece of crap legislation that crosses his desk." A single veto of a spending bill early on, he contended, could have saved taxpayers tens of billions of dollars down the road, as Congress would have been chastened into showing more restraint.

Beyond all of these mechanical reasons, however, there's something to be said for the simple but subtle corruption of one-party government—where everyone in power is on the same team and saying "no" to anything is simply bad etiquette among friends. "When I used to stand up and say 'hell no' to Bill Clinton, I was always applauded by all the people I love," recalled Dick Armey. "When I stood up and said 'hell no' to George Bush, I was berated by all the people I love."

Pondering the Pachyderm

Perhaps sick of the acrimony, and of sticking up for conservative principles against supposed conservatives, Armey announced at the end of 2001 that he would not run for reelection. Armey's great friend and fellow Texan, Senator Phil Gramm, retired at the same time, marking something of an end to the Gingrich-era, small-government old guard in Congress. But by 2005, Armey was around to start serving as an unofficial adviser to Mike Pence and his fellow rebels, advising them on how to operate as an insurgent force within their own party—much as Gingrich and Armey had been forced to do against the status-quo Republicans they needed to displace as they engineered the GOP takeover of Congress in 1994. Armey even went so far as to pen an op-ed for the *Wall Street Journal* in November of 2005 stating that there needed to be "another Republican takeover of Congress."

That takeover wasn't to be, at least not immediately. While Pence and his colleagues threw a lot of ideas at the wall as to how to slash the budget—delaying the prescription-drug benefit for a year, a 1 or 2 percent across-the-board budget cut in all nondefense discretionary spending, reopening the highway bill, and carving out the pork—almost none of it stuck. As *National Journal* columnist Jonathan Rauch put it, the House conservatives showed after months of sweating and haggling and maneuvering that "Spending is not completely uncuttable. It is, rather, 99.5 percent uncuttable."[21] They won some minuscule cuts and declared victory, but it would all immediately be overrun by spending on Katrina cleanup, bird flu, and the Iraq war.

Pence may well be back, fighting to keep the flame of small government burning. In fact, it's something to count on. And that's a good thing, because right now there's the small matter of a very large pachyderm sitting in the Republican Party's living room.

The leaders of the GOP aren't going to deal with it. In fact, they're the ones who snuck the damn thing in through the window. In August of 2004, during the heated reelection campaign, the then-chairman of the Republican National Committee, Ed Gillespie, stopped by the offices of the *Manchester Union Leader* to discuss the state of the Republican Party. The paper's staunchly conservative editorial page described the basic message as such: "The party's new chairman, energetic and full of vigor, said in no uncertain terms that the days of Reaganesque Republican railings against the expansion of federal government are over. . . . No longer does the Republican Party stand for shrinking the federal government, for scaling back its encroachment into the lives of Americans, or for carrying the banner of federalism into the political battles of the day. . . . No, today the Republican Party stands for giving the American people whatever the latest polls say they want. . . . The party's unofficial but clear message to conservatives is: Where else are you going to go? To the Democrats? To the Libertarians? They don't think so."[22]

It was a harsh takedown of the state of the modern Republican Party, and it generated enough outrage against Gillespie that he had to go on Rush Limbaugh's show a week later to backpedal furiously—but there was no running away from Bush's record. Ultimately there can never be any way to defend a president as conservative who dismisses a commitment to limited government as a "destructive mind-set" and "an approach with no higher goal, no nobler purpose, than 'Leave us alone.'"

Our country was founded on "Leave us alone."

Proponents of big-government conservatism say they want to transform the Republican Party's program into a positive one, as opposed to a negative one. But there once was a time when Republican presidents and politicians realized that small government *is* a positive vision, not a negative one. Freedom is a positive vision, not a negative one. Low taxes, based on low spending as opposed to high deficits, are a positive vision. Giving parents a choice where to send their kids to school, as opposed to federal testing, is a positive vision. Deregulating the health-insurance market is a positive vision. Keeping trade free and lowering the cost of living is a positive vision.

Pence, though definitely both a social and a small-government conservative, understood the problem of where the Republican Party was drifting clearly that October day. And looking back on the first four-plus years of the Bush administration, he saw big problems ahead. "Many Washington, D.C., Republicans have changed their philosophy," he said. "But the millions of people who get up on Election Day, who go put out yard signs, who work phone banks, who pick up shut-ins and take them to the polls . . . let me say this as eloquently as I can: They ain't changed." These conservatives, he said, understand that "freedom is tied up with the size of government," that as government expands, freedom contracts. Predicting that 2006 would be the most difficult year for the Republican majority since it was minted in 1994, he warned that "to the extent that we walk away from our reasons for being as a majority, we do so at our peril."

The question, then, is will the Republicans keep walking, keep drifting, keep trying to ignore the elephant in the room? And what exactly would it take to make them stop? The most dangerous thing right now is that many Republicans still think the elephant might be their friend. It's a sure way to get trampled.

5

The Ownership Society and Its Discontents

If you can't beat 'em, join 'em.

That's at least half the logic behind the loose amalgam of programs, approaches, ideas, theories, buzzwords, and catchphrases that has come to be known, during the course of the Bush administration, as the Ownership Society. Many conservatives have concluded that the size of government can never be cut and that the growth of government can hardly even be slowed. This new paradigm holds then—conveniently enough—that it's okay for the state to keep expanding, as long as it's Republicans in charge of the expansion.

In other words, it's not the size of government that matters, but what you do with it.

Yeah, we never heard that one before.

The other half of the logic behind the idea of an Ownership Society, however, is something a bit less cynical. It is the understanding, central to modern conservatism, that individuals should make the most important decisions in their lives—that parents know best what schools are most likely to allow their children to thrive; that patients and their doctors know better than government or HMO bureaucrats what courses of treatment are right for them; that most workers are planning their retirements based on their own 401(k) statements and not the Social Security Administration's troubling promises. Choice, in other words, would become the central organizing principle in how citizens interact with the government in an Ownership Society: choice of schools, choice of health plans, choice of retirement plans.

Choice is an appealing concept politically. And that's why it's at the heart of President Bush's and Karl Rove's attempt to bring *everyone* inside the Republican tent. People who are happy with the government just the size it is shouldn't be spooked; the Republicans aren't trying to take anything away, they just want to give people more choices. Libertarian types shouldn't be spooked either, and maybe they should even be excited; Republicans are finally dismantling the New Deal and replacing it with (at least a Rube Goldberg approximation of) the free market. And if policies regarding expanded home and small-business ownership can be tied in (because, hey, the word *ownership* is in there) as part of an attempt to appeal to African Americans and Hispanics, all the better. A Republican Party organized around the concept of an Ownership Society can, it would seem, be all things to all people.

This leaves conservatives who care about small government with a dilemma: Do they take the idea of an Ownership Society seriously, despite the fact that it comes from a group of people in the Bush administration who have proven beyond the shadow of a doubt that they are comfortable not just increasing but ballooning the size of the federal government? Or do they cast it aside, despite the fact that as a political formulation the Ownership Society offers perhaps the most promising path toward the expansion of individual freedom in a generation?

At the risk of giving the Bush administration the benefit of the doubt just this once, small-government conservatives, libertarians, paleoconservatives, anarchocapitalists, and all other natural skeptics of the president and his policy shop should take a step back, take a deep breath, and take the concept of creating an Ownership Society very seriously. The neoconservatives, the big-government conservatives, the progovernment conservatives—whatever one wants to call them—are right about one thing: Republicans are never going to roll back the New Deal. But they can shape what takes its place as America moves past the framework of its old industrial-era economy, to which the New Deal is inextricably tied.

At the same time, however, the Ownership Society can't be judged in a vacuum. The president has had five-plus years to push forward his bold new approach to conservatism under some of the most favorable political conditions imaginable, and—at least at first glance—it doesn't look like he has much to show for it. What's more, the small steps he has taken toward realizing his vision seem to have come at great expense in sheer dollars and cents, as well as in greatly expanding the role of the federal government in areas it had previously left relatively unmolested.

If the Ownership Society is going to be advanced as the best political means to achieve conservative ends—as the realistic alternative to the paint-fume-huffing delusions of committed libertarians—then it only makes sense to judge its performance in the real world, without pulling any punches or granting any points for effort. If the current administration has arrived at the end point of fifty years of ideological evolution and happened upon the mutation that brings conservatism to the next level, then even Bush bashers should be forced to acknowledge success when it stares them in the face. But if the Ownership Society is an evolutionary dead end, synonymous with or indistinguishable from big-government conservatism, then it is all the more important that the error be detected immediately.

The Evolution of Ownership

It was Milton Friedman, hero to libertarians and small-government conservatives everywhere, who pioneered at least two of the ideas central to the Ownership Society: education vouchers and private accounts for Social Security. In the 1955 article where he first proposed school vouchers, Friedman wrote that their creation would "bring a healthy increase in the variety of educational institutions available." Private initiative and enterprise, he wrote, "would quicken the pace of progress in this area as it has in so many others. Government would serve its proper function of improving the operation of the invisible hand without substituting the dead hand of bureaucracy."[1] A more concise and eloquent description of how government should behave when it is forced to interfere with the private sector can hardly be imagined. In the 1970s, conservative think tankers would expand on Friedman's ideas in areas such as health care, coming up with the idea of health savings accounts, tax-free savings accounts from which people could pay for medical treatment or health insurance.

The notion of ownership closest to that being pushed by the Bush administration today, however—that of ownership being linked to better citizenship—was actually pioneered by British prime minister Margaret Thatcher. Along with Thatcher's efforts to privatize government-run industries, her administration sold 1.5 million public-housing units to their occupants, transforming 1.5 million families from tenants to homeowners. The idea was that the housing would be better taken care of, residents would behave more responsibly, and, just maybe, Thatcher's Conservative Party would mint some new voters.[2] "The Thatcherite argues that being one's own master—in the sense of owning one's own home or disposing of one's own property—provides an incentive to think differently about the world," wrote political philosopher Shirley Robin Letwin in *The Anatomy of Thatcherism*. "A Thatcherite . . . sees in wider individual ownership a useful means of promoting the moral attitudes that Thatcherism seeks to cultivate."

Just how closely does this Thatcherite thinking match the project that the Bush administration is currently undertaking? The above passage was actually cited at length by the director of the Office of Strategic Initiatives at the White House, Peter Wehner, in a speech at the beginning of 2005 to the conservative Hudson Institute. In his own words, Wehner told the crowd that the president, like Thatcher, was seeking "to provide Americans with a path to greater opportunity, more freedom and more control over their own lives. . . . Government's default position should not be to view citizens as wards of the state, but rather as responsible and independent, self-sufficient and upright."

Though Bush had used the phrase on occasion before, it wasn't until his reelection campaign, and more specifically his 2004 Republican National Convention speech, that he brought under the umbrella of the Ownership Society a number of preexisting administration policies and goals that turned out (more by happenstance than by design) to tie together thematically. "Another priority for a new term is to build an Ownership Society, because ownership brings security, and dignity, and independence," Bush told the crowd at New York City's Madison Square Garden. "In an Ownership Society, more people will own their health-care plans, and have the confidence of owning a piece of their retirement." Bush extolled the fact that home ownership was at an all-time high in America, and he promised that more Americans would own their own homes. He said that his administration was transforming America's schools by raising standards, and he promised that it would keep insisting on accountability and empowering parents and teachers. "In all these proposals," he said, "we seek to provide not just a government program, but a path—a path to greater opportunity, more freedom, and more control over your own life."

A fine vision, that. But Bush's words didn't flesh out exactly what an Ownership Society *is* at the end of the day or how far along his administration might be in creating one after a full term in office. In fact, Bush didn't make a single speech during the 2004 campaign or in the year after his reelection giving significant depth or detail to the idea. Still, upon examination, it's possible to map out a constellation of programs and proposals that, taken together, form something of a coherent picture. Bush's so-far-stalled proposal for private Social Security accounts? Definitely part of the Ownership Society. The tiny health savings accounts tacked onto the humungous Medicare prescription-drug bill? Also part of the Ownership Society. Setting targets for increased minority home ownership? Sure; why not? Proposed job-training accounts? What the hell. A prospective overhaul of the federal tax code? Somewhat inexplicably, Bush aides also consider this idea part of the Ownership Society. The president's No Child Left Behind law? Passed in 2001, it predates the newfangled slogan, but Bush administration officials acknowledge that giving parents more control over their kids' education is central to the notion of an Ownership Society.

What's remarkable, then, on the face of it, is just how short a distance Bush has traveled with this idea in five-plus years. Even the president's greatest defenders are left praising achievements his administration hasn't . . . well, achieved. "Imagine if the president had won the fight for private accounts in Social Security," Fred Barnes wrote in his book, released at the beginning of 2006. "And imagine if he had expanded consumer-driven health care. . . . Achieving it would have been an epic feat. And Bush, having succeeded in creating an ownership society, would be the most important and consequential domestic policy president since FDR."[3]

Too bad it didn't work out that way.

Barnes still says he thinks the Ownership Society has a shot at going down in history next to the New Deal and the Great Society (some company) as one of the great leaps forward in American history. Bush's conservatism, Barnes and others argue, breaks daring new ground because it is not aimed at reducing the *supply* of government, as in the Gingrich years. Instead, it aims to reduce the *demand* for government, by making people more self-sufficient and less dependent on handouts. Even if many of Bush's bolder proposals haven't yet been enacted into law, they argue, his pilot programs and half measures will whet Americans' appetites for choice, and his reorientation of the political debate will set the course for future Republican presidents and congresses.

Critics of the Ownership Society, however, see things a bit differently. Liberal critics see the idea as a simple ploy to "soak the poor"—shifting the burden of paying for government programs off of the wealthy and onto the middle and lower classes. In this, they simultaneously overestimate Republican cynicism and underestimate the Bush administration's contempt for fiscal responsibility. Republicans, contrary to popular belief, don't actually sit up nights thinking of ways to stick it to the middle class or the poor or grandmothers or puppies; Bush is perfectly content to cut taxes and grow government spending at the same time. Liberals also object to the idea of giving Americans more choices in some areas because—not to put too fine a point on it—the American people are stupid, and they might choose wrong. What if people don't pick the right investments with their private Social Security accounts? What if they don't buy the right health insurance? What if they send their kids to Big Bob's Edutorium and Pet Grooming Salon instead of good ol' P.S. 101? More than one liberal critic of the Ownership Society has cited a book by Swarthmore social theorist Barry Schwartz, *The Paradox of Choice*, which argues that having too many choices stresses people out and leaves them not wanting to make any choice at all. The public, these critics are fairly certain, is bound to reject Bush's risky, overly complicated new schemes.

This is the mirror image of the objection raised on the Right that the Ownership Society is merely big government by another name, providing only the faintest illusion of choice. The government would still be taking people's money and forcing them to spend it on schooling, or saving for retirement or purchasing health insurance; but, adding insult to injury, it would then allow (force?) citizens to choose from a menu of preapproved, government-sanctioned options as to how precisely they would like to receive the required services. Meanwhile, government's growth would continue unabated, and the liberal welfare state would hum along virtually untouched.

These alternate views of the Ownership Society—bold innovation, half-baked conservative ideological crusade, and mealy-mouthed sellout of conservative principle—each have their elements of truth to them. But the only way to judge Bush's success at creating a new conservatism is by looking at the results so far. The Republicans have held the presidency, the House, and the

Senate (except for two years) since 2001. The Democrats have been knocked on their heels most of this time. There may never be political circumstances so amenable to conservative reform again in any of our lifetimes. How content, then, should conservatives of all stripes be with the progress that's been made to date?

Owning Education

In January of 2003, a little over a year after President Bush signed the No Child Left Behind Act with a beaming Senator Ted Kennedy by his side, Harlem mother Eunice Staton filed suit against the New York City public school system. Staton and a group of parents from New York City and Albany were suing for their right, under the new federal law, to transfer their children from the failing public schools they were in to more successful ones. The school district had neglected to notify them that their children's schools were failing and that they had the right to transfer, but once they found out, they wanted to take control of their kids' destinies. "I feel like a prisoner," said Staton, who had three boys in two of the city's three hundred failing public schools, Matthew and Jermaine at P.S. 30 and Christopher at I.S. 172. "I want them to have a much better life than I have, and a good education is key to that."[4]

The suit, however, was thrown out—making Staton and her fellow plaintiffs just a few of the millions of parents let down by the promise of a bold new approach to federal education reform.

NCLB was the first test of Bush's attempt to remake conservatism in his own sunny image. Fred Barnes calls it "a perfect example" of the president's redefinition of conservatism "to fit the times and to come to grips with political reality."[5] But if that's true, then Bush's conservatism is in worse shape than almost anybody could have imagined. While NCLB was enacted with the noble goal of holding America's public schools accountable for their performance, it has been essentially worthless in terms of giving parents ownership over their children's education. In an effort to seem less dour and less mean-spirited, the Bush administration settled for meaningless platitudes, coupled with massive new spending, rather than any attempt to implement real reforms.

Bush and his team were certainly right during the 2000 campaign and when they arrived in Washington to do away with the old Republican answer to education reform: closing down the federal Department of Education. While it's still not such a bad idea (the money would be better spent at the state level), it could hardly make for worse politics. As Republican pollster David Winston put it, "Getting rid of the Department of Education doesn't explain anything to me about how my child's going to be better educated."

What Bush came up with instead, however, wasn't a way to devolve power to the states in a more politically acceptable way—though House Republicans had been working on that track, with President Clinton as their main obstacle, for years—or a way to give parents more control. Rather, the Bush administration came in and said: we can tame the federal behemoth better than the last guys; we can be the ones to finally make it accountable.

The administration's initial plan was ambitious. Bush's "blueprint," released not long after he took office, included two fairly radical proposals: one, kids in failing schools could take their share of federal funds to a more successful school, public or private—that is, use those funds as a voucher; and two, states that agreed to strict accountability timetables could get all their federal money as essentially a block grant, instead of being bound by strict federal allocation formulas that tend to steer funds to special interests.

The problem was how quickly the Bush administration abandoned real reform in favor of getting a bill, any bill, through Congress. On March 22, 2001, Representative John Boehner (R-Ohio) introduced the No Child Left Behind Act, which essentially followed the president's blueprint: vouchers of up to about $1,500 and flexibility for the states. By May 2, the House Education and the Workforce Committee had stripped the voucher provisions from the bill (on a 27–20 committee vote where 5 Republicans sided with all of the panel's Democrats) and significantly watered down the flexibility provisions. It was a nice month while it lasted.

Conservatives were crestfallen. At the time, Representative Jim

DeMint (R-S.C.) summed up the feelings of many of his colleagues, saying, "When the president talked about reform, we didn't realize he intended to 'Leave No Democrats Behind.'" The White House, however, couldn't have cared less about conservative discontent. *National Review* recounted a White House education aide explaining that conservatives should have done more to lobby lawmakers on school choice instead of expecting the White House to do it. The aide said that the issue was "never central to the president."[6]

What was central to the president was changing the politics of the education issue from favoring the Democrats overwhelmingly to favoring the Republicans—at least narrowly. Internal GOP polling in May of 1999 showed the Republicans trailing Democrats by a full 21 percentage points on education, 29 percent to 50 percent. When Bush entered the race, however, he changed how Republicans talked about education. He talked about closing the "achievement gap." He talked about ending "the soft bigotry of low expectations." And, of course, he talked about leaving no child behind. By August of 2000 the Republicans had closed their education gap with the Democrats to ten points. By March of 2001, when NCLB was introduced in Congress, Republicans were *leading* the Democrats by five points on the issue.[7]

There's no question that Bush pulled off an astounding turnaround on education, eliminating one of the party's most glaring weaknesses, a feat that has paid dividends in the elections since, especially with minority voters. But having come so far during the 2000 campaign, Bush chose not to spend any of that political capital on a worthwhile bill. "The president wanted a bill," said Krista Kafer, a former House education committee staffer who also did a stint as an education analyst for the Heritage Foundation. "It didn't bother him that it was a significantly flawed bill."

In the end, Bush got pretty small potatoes. The price of getting a bill that could pass 340–81 in the House and 87–10 in the Senate (with Senator Kennedy part of that 87) was high: no vouchers, almost no more flexibility for states, a large across-the-board spending increase, a program combating hate crimes, a program promoting "gender equity," and a "cultural exchange" for "Alaska

Natives, Native Hawaiians, and Their Historical Whaling and Trading Partners in Massachusetts."[8] All that NCLB amounted to, really, was the strengthening of certain federal accountability requirements that were already in place, plus the president's Reading First initiative, which helps states and schools adopt research-based reading programs. Representative Bob Schaffer (R-Colo.) put it succinctly at the time: If President Clinton had sent Congress a bill with federal testing, a huge increase in spending and no private school choice, Republicans would have shot it down in an instant. "Not only would we have killed it," he said, "but we would have had a press conference celebrating."[9]

Now, the president's defenders argue that even without school vouchers, NCLB's toughening of federal accountability standards is a worthy conservative achievement in and of itself. After all, that's what Republicans are all about, isn't it? Getting tough. No excuses. No exceptions. Get the job done or get out of town. But a closer look at what NCLB's "accountability" consists of makes it difficult to say the word while keeping a straight face.

Under NCLB, states have to test students and report on their progress, and they also have to break student performance down by subgroups, such as white, black, Hispanic, Asian, special education, low income, etc. The idea is that high performance by some groups of students at particular schools shouldn't mask low performance by others. Leave *no* child behind. All of these groups must make progress toward meeting standards. When schools don't make what's called "adequate yearly progress" (or AYP), they're subject to certain sanctions. After two years of a school failing to make AYP, students are supposed to be allowed to transfer to a nonfailing school in their district. Students are also supposed to be allowed to transfer if their school is "unsafe." After three years, the school has to offer free tutoring. After five years, the school district is supposed to significantly restructure the school, perhaps turning it over to a private education-management company or turning it into a privately run charter school.

Sanctions only matter, however, if they're enforced and if they're free of gaping loopholes. Unfortunately, NCLB is pretty much just one big loophole. Take the unsafe-schools provision. Most states got around that simply by claiming that none of their schools are unsafe. In 2003, New York City claimed it had two unsafe schools—*two* out of some twelve hundred schools in one of the toughest public school systems in America, where kids regularly have to walk through metal detectors just to get to class.

School districts have done everything they can to avoid granting kids transfers out of failing schools, preferring not to deal with the expense and hassle. In particularly troubled districts, administrators will deny kids transfers because there's nowhere for them to go; there are simply few or no spots at adequately performing schools into which to transfer. Other districts do what they can to thwart parents from ever even seeking a transfer. They don't inform parents of their rights. They give them extremely small windows of time to act. They even send letters home meant to confuse or mislead parents. A researcher in Colorado found that a district there had sent parents home a letter with the good news that their school had been selected for "School Improvement" under federal law. "We are excited by this opportunity to focus on increasing student achievement," the letter said, making it sound as if the school had won a grant, as opposed to having just gotten a slap on the wrist.[10] No wonder then that in the 2004–2005 school year, according to the Center on Education Policy, just *1 percent* of students eligible for choice under NCLB actually transferred schools.[11]

The public-school choice provisions are the only thing approximating "ownership" in the No Child Left Behind law, and yet they have been an utter failure because of resistance from local bureaucrats—resistance that NCLB does nothing to uproot. The demand for choice is small but growing. One study of 47 states and 137 districts by the Citizens' Commission on Civil Rights found that 2.3 percent of eligible students requested transfers in the 2002–2003 school year; that percentage more than doubled, to 5.6 percent requesting transfers in the 2003–2004 school year.[12] But as Heritage's Kafer points out, as long as the parties with the least to gain from granting transfers and tutoring—the districts—have a choke hold on the information and options available to families, the education shell game will continue.[13]

The results of NCLB's testing regime are equally unimpressive. The basic problem: there's no way to tell if states are simply watering down their tests to make it look like they're making better progress than they are. "There's no clear and simple way to do it," Fred Hess, director of education policy studies at the American Enterprise Institute, said. Since states conduct the testing, they can make the test questions easier or they can reduce the number of questions kids have to get right to pass. States have also successfully petitioned the federal Department of Education to let them: monkey with statistics to boost their scores, get "partial credit" for the performance of failing students, retest kids over and over again until they pass, and ignore the scores of various subgroups of kids if there aren't that many of them in a given school (apparently it's okay to leave a few kids behind). Most egregiously, states have been allowed to "backload" their performance goals, promising huge gains in test scores, but not until six years from now, at the end of the next presidential administration—when the goalposts, as always in education reform, will have moved again.

"In a lot of ways," said Hess, "it's a stupid law." His words, not mine. Okay, I'll say it, too: it's a stupid law.

As with many of Bush's Ownership Society projects, the claim is sometimes made by the administration and its defenders that their reforms simply need time to work—that right now they're just planting seeds of accountability and choice and personal responsibility. They say they're changing the way Americans relate to their government, conditioning them to expect to have more say in the big decisions that affect their lives. In a sense, they're right. It will take some time to get parents in the inner cities used to the idea that they might actually get to choose their children's schools. But change can happen only so slowly, and the Bush administration is testing the lower limit every day with its timid education reforms. It's a shame, because as Eunice Staton said of her three sons, trapped in failing schools in Harlem, "They need help now. . . .

They needed the help last year." And she wasn't just talking about her own kids.

Owning Health Care

If Bush's Ownership Society has been an unmitigated disaster when it comes to education, its record when it comes to health care might be termed a mitigated disaster. Specifically, the disaster of the $1.2 trillion Medicare prescription-drug entitlement is mitigated by the significant expansion of health savings accounts that was won in the same bill, the first major free-market health-care reform in a generation. The question for conservatives, ever since the bill began to take shape in the summer of 2003, has remained the same: Is the trade-off worth it? Is it worth significantly (and permanently) expanding the size and scope of the welfare state as long as the expansion is tied to measures that will give Americans a degree of ownership over benefits that have typically been controlled by the government?

The choice has certainly not been an easy one for many Republicans, as the final House vote on the Medicare Prescription Drug Improvement and Modernization Act of 2003 made clear. When critics of the bill say it was passed "in the dead of night," they're not exaggerating. The vote opened at 3:00 A.M. on Saturday, November 22, and instead of lasting the originally scheduled 15 minutes, it was held open until just before 6:00 A.M. to buy time for the House leadership to turn a 216–218 rejection of the bill into a 220–215 victory. The length of the vote was more than double the previous record in the House, as the Republican leadership took unprecedented actions to cajole, browbeat, and even attempt to bribe reluctant conservative House members. Who says our legislators don't work hard enough?

A hard-core group of about two dozen House conservatives, including Representative Mike Pence, huddled in the back rows and withstood the pressure. But others crumbled. Health and Human Services secretary Tommy Thompson defied custom and lobbied members on the floor of the House. Thompson and Speaker Dennis

Hastert cornered "no" voters sitting alone, such as Representatives John Shadegg of Arizona and Nick Smith of Michigan, though they couldn't get them to budge. At about 5:00 A.M., Bush was brought in, just back from a trip to Britain, to call House members personally. The breakthrough came when the White House legislative liaison and House leaders convinced two conservative Republican members that the Democrats would have the votes to pass their own Medicare measure if Republicans didn't stick together. Such a scenario was highly unlikely, but the prospect was enough to make the members switch their votes, guaranteeing a Republican victory.[14]

The fallout from the vote was ugly. Conservatives were furious. Pence marks that vote as the moment he began speaking out about the Republican Party's ideological corruption. Almost a year later, the House Ethics Committee admonished then majority leader Tom DeLay for offering to endorse Smith's son in a congressional primary if he would support the Medicare bill. It also came out that the Bush administration had withheld key budget estimates, with Medicare administrator Tom Scully threatening to fire Medicare's actuary, Richard Foster, if he released figures to members of Congress showing that the bill would cost $130 billion more over ten years than the White House had let on. (Scully was also, at the time the bill was being hammered out, pursuing jobs representing the pharmaceutical and insurance industries; a little more than a week after the president signed the bill, Scully left the White House and took a job at Alston & Bird, a firm that represents numerous drug companies.)

Why did the Bush administration have to fight so dirty to get its bill through? If it were really so loaded up with important free-market reforms, shouldn't more Republicans have been eager to swallow the pill, knowing it would ultimately be good for them?

Well, it was a big pill to swallow. There was certainly a logic to adding a prescription-drug benefit to Medicare; in short, it made little sense to say the government would pay for open-heart surgery but not for the drugs that might make such surgery unnecessary. But most seniors already had some form of drug coverage. In 2002, the year before the benefit was passed, some 70 percent of seniors spent less than $500 out of pocket for prescriptions.[15] A relatively small, targeted drug benefit, aimed at the 22 percent of seniors who didn't have drug coverage, could have caught those who were falling through the cracks at much less expense.[16] But why be efficient when you can be popular for only a few hundred billion dollars more? The Bush administration and congressional leaders, with their eyes on the 2004 election, were set on creating a universal benefit for more than forty million elderly and disabled Americans. So they created Medicare Part D, the Medicare prescription-drug benefit.

The expense of all this is tremendous. Not only is the government crowding out private insurance that individuals were paying for themselves (such as Medicare supplemental plans), but it's also having to write checks to corporations to discourage them from dropping retirees' drug coverage and leaving the federal government to pick up the tab. In 2003, the Congressional Budget Office said the drug benefit would cost $400 billion over ten years, and the White House accepted that number. The president's first budget after the bill was signed bumped that number up to $511 billion (essentially the $100 billion-plus increase Scully had tried to suppress). But neither of those numbers was a real ten-year figure; both counted two years, 2004 and 2005, when the new benefit wouldn't even be on line yet. The real ten-year cost, for 2006–2015, is closer to $1.2 trillion—though Bush administration officials estimate that various forms of savings will bring that down, closer to $720 billion.

With Medicare, however, it's never been a good idea to accept the more modest cost estimates. While there has been some early evidence of cost savings from drug plans competing against one another, it's unlikely to make a serious dent in the program's cost. And even going with the most modest of estimates, the prescription-drug benefit will increase the financial burden of Medicare by roughly a third, bringing its expenditures up from 2.6 percent of gross domestic product in 2003 to 3.4 percent in 2006. As seventy-eight million baby boomers head toward retirement and Medicare eligibility, things will only get much, much worse.[17]

All of this, to many conservatives, seemed like a high price to pay for an expansion of health savings accounts (HSAs) and a few minor tweaks to Medicare. But it would be a mistake to underestimate just how radical a reform HSAs represent. "They were the first market-based health-care reform really in over sixty years," said Michael Cannon, director of health policy studies at the Cato Institute. "They're potentially revolutionary."

An HSA is essentially a 401(k), but for medical expenses instead of retirement savings. Individuals and their employers can make contributions tax-free. But, unlike with a 401(k), funds withdrawn to pay for medical expenses before age sixty-five are *never* taxed. HSAs can only be set up in conjunction with qualifying high-deductible health insurance (so that catastrophic expenses will be covered). According to supporters, they allow younger and healthier workers to save money on premiums while building up assets they can tap into when they're older and need more health care; this encourages HSA owners to be more price-conscious when tending to their everyday health-care needs.[18]

HSAs became available under the new law at the beginning of 2004. Interest in them gained momentum quickly. In the first fifteen months they were available, one million people had purchased the high-deductible health insurance to qualify for opening the accounts; in the next ten months, another two million people signed up. What's more, HSAs seem to be fulfilling their purpose: making health care affordable to the uninsured and containing costs. According to separate estimates from America's Health Insurance Plans, a trade group that represents some thirteen hundred health-insurance providers, and the health company Assurant, as many as 40 percent of HSA applicants were previously uninsured.[19] And a survey from Deloitte Consulting shows that the cost of consumer-driven health plans, such as HSAs and less-flexible health reimbursement arrangements, increased by only 2.8 percent from 2004 to 2005, as opposed to an average of 7.3 percent for all other types of plans.

Building on this success, Bush proposed in his 2006 State of the Union address expanding the amount of money individuals can put in HSAs and making them more accessible to individuals and employees of small businesses. His prescription-drug plan, one of the signature "accomplishments" of his first term and a key campaign issue in 2002 and 2004, which was just going into effect and enrolling millions of seniors that January? He didn't even mention it.

Coming up on three years out from the signing of the 2003 Medicare bill, the politics and the political trade-offs behind it still rankle conservatives of all stripes. And the question remains the same as from the beginning: were health savings accounts, and the long-term political boost from getting behind the idea of a prescription-drug benefit, worth the cost?

On the political side of things, there can be little doubt that the prescription-drug bill has been a disaster. A Gallup poll taken in the month the bill was passed found that 73 percent of seniors thought the drug benefit wouldn't go far enough. Their perception didn't seem to change much throughout 2004. As the election neared, columnist Robert Novak reported that privately, senior administration officials were admitting that the bill had been "a disaster substantively and politically."[20] Another Gallup poll, in March of 2005, found only 41 percent of Americans supporting the prescription-drug plan—and only 36 percent of those over age sixty-five. Subsequent polls haven't shown much improvement.

Once the benefit's implementation got under way in January of 2006, anger over the bill heated up even more as seniors came into contact with its complex machinery and as hostile news stories flooded the media. An AP poll in January found that two-thirds of those who signed up found the plan confusing. As the midterm campaign season got under way, it was clear that the Democrats would use the prescription-drug plan as a weapon going into November, harping on its alleged stinginess, its complexity, and the Bush administration's refusal to allow Americans to buy price-controlled prescription drugs from Canada and Europe. The AARP, meanwhile—which had been brought into the fold to support the 2003 Medicare bill—in January launched a push to "fix" the program by making it even more generous and moving the government toward instituting price controls.[21] It's enough to remind one of Ted Kennedy's admonition to liberals when the Medicare bill was hammered out. This is just a "down payment," he told them. "When we get this as a down payment, we're going to come back again and again and again to fight to make sure that we have a good program."

Boy, will they ever.

With so little short-term or long-term political benefit having accrued to Republicans from the prescription-drug bill, all that's left is the question of whether it was a wise policy trade-off. Grace-Marie Turner, president of the Galen Institute, a free-market-oriented health-care think tank, in an interview ran through her logic when she decided to support the bill back in 2003. "It's real clear that somebody is going to pass a prescription drug benefit for Medicare. . . . It's either going to be Republicans or Democrats," she said. "If it costs $400 billion, then I'm sorry, but it's saving the private health sector, and I think it's worth it." What's more, she said, she is absolutely certain that HSAs could never have been passed into law any other way. "I cannot believe the naiveté of those who ask why couldn't we have just passed HSAs on their own."

One such naive soul is Cato's Michael Cannon—though he has a bit more than wide-eyed innocence behind his assertion that HSAs could have been won another way. He described the prescription-drug bill as "sending a Scud missile to destroy the children's ward of a hospital and then sending a Patriot missile up after the Scud and crossing our fingers." We may hope that HSAs intercept some of the fiscal damage that will be done by the drug benefit, but we didn't need to take such a big risk in the first place.

Cannon, who formerly served as a domestic policy analyst at the U.S. Senate Republican Policy Committee, under Senator Larry E. Craig (R-Idaho), thinks HSAs could easily have been added to a tax or budget bill. In particular, he points to a roll call vote in the Senate in 2001 that showed that support for lifting the restrictions on Medical Savings Accounts (the forerunners of HSAs) was only a few votes short of a majority—and the 2002 elections resulted in the net gain of one new HSA supporter. "You had two stinking votes to get, you could have bought that for less than $400 billion," Cannon said. But since HSAs were more of an afterthought designed to keep conservatives in line than a central part of the president's agenda, a push to pass them on their own was never made. "The president never really lifted a finger to get HSAs passed," Cannon said. Conversations with congressional staffers who were close to the hammering out of the Medicare bill confirmed what Cannon was saying.

Whatever one's view of such hypotheticals, however, one of the corroding effects of the Ownership Society was clearly on display in the process that brought about the Medicare bill: its underlying assumption that the growth of government can never be stopped, or even slowed. In the third year of Bush's presidency, and with the Republicans having just reestablished control of the Senate and increased their margin in the House in the 2002 midterms, those underlying assumptions expanded to include not just that government will stay the same size, not just that it will get bigger, but rather that *it will explode catastrophically no matter who is in power*—and there's nothing anyone can do about it, so it might as well be Republicans doing the exploding.

This was, in truth, a remarkable step down a road at the end of which lies a very simple and very alluring philosophy of government: anything goes, as long as we stay. It's not a principled philosophy, certainly. It's not a politically effective one, as the public's contemptuous response has shown. And it's not a fiscally prudent one, as the most cursory glance at the federal budget shows. A drop, or perhaps even a bucketful, of good was extracted—but from an ocean of harm.

Owning Retirement

If the 2003 Medicare bill was wildly cynical and crassly political, it needs to be said that Bush's advocacy of Social Security privatization over the years has been consistent, principled and, yes, even bold—if not at all times well articulated (despite Bush's well-known articulateness).

While Bush, Rove, and other Republican strategists inside and outside the White House see Social Security reform as part of a larger plan to—how to put this gently?—destroy the Democratic Party, the president also has long understood that the federal retirement system is unsustainable in its current form, short of massive tax hikes or benefit cuts. Fred Barnes traces Bush's advocacy of private accounts back to his first, unsuccessful campaign for Congress in 1978. During that race out in West Texas, Bush told a group of realtors at the Midland Country Club that "the ideal option would be for Social Security to be made sound and people be given the chance to invest the money the way they feel."[22] The issue wasn't a big one in the campaign, but the idea would remain the same twenty-two years later.

Bush hit Social Security privatization hard during the 2000 campaign, and Al Gore and his allies hit back even harder. In the presidential debates, Gore labeled Bush's plan "Social Security minus" and said that Bush would cut benefits and leave seniors eating cat food. The AARP and the labor unions weighed in with millions of dollars spent on phone banks, mailings, and ads. There were even recorded calls by Ed Asner made to scare old folks out of their homes and into the voting booth. But ultimately Bush had the politics of the issue right. In exit polls, 57 percent of voters said they supported Bush's vision of private accounts—including one-third of those who'd voted for Al "Lock Box" Gore.[23] In Florida, seniors split fairly evenly between Bush and Gore. Social Security was no longer the third rail of American politics. The new president might not quite have mustered the momentum for reform, but he demonstrated that it was no longer suicidal to try.

Once in office, Bush appointed a commission, chaired by the late Senator Daniel Patrick Moynihan and AOL/Time Warner COO Richard Parsons, to consider how to "modernize" Social Security. The panel was heavily tilted toward privatization proponents, but it had the unique disadvantage of releasing its final report on December 11, 2001—when the nation was in no mood to start worrying about an issue that fell well short of life or death. After that, the spring and summer of 2002 just got worse and worse for the prospects of private accounts as the names Enron, Ken Lay, and WorldCom became household names and late-night punch lines and the stock market sank to five-year lows. Reform was off the table for the rest of Bush's first term.

Social Security was far from the biggest issue in the 2004 campaign, but when Bush won reelection, he decided it was time to take his big gamble. "Let me put it to you this way," Bush told a reporter at a White House press conference who had asked him if he felt more free now that he'd been reelected. "I earned capital in the campaign, political capital, and now I intend to spend it." And spend it he did, dedicating a twelve-hundred-word section of his 2005 State of the Union address to a call for reforming Social Security with personal accounts, before embarking on a barnstorming tour of America, including sixty stops in sixty days in March and April. "Social Security was a great moral success of the twentieth century, and we must honor its great purposes in this new century," Bush said, addressing the nation. "The system, however, on its current path, is headed toward bankruptcy. And so we must join together to strengthen and save Social Security."

The White House certainly considered the stakes in the Social Security fight of the highest order. "I don't need to tell you that this will be one of the most important conservative undertakings of modern times," the White House's Peter Wehner wrote in a memo to conservative activists that was leaked to the press. "If we succeed in reforming Social Security, it will rank as one of the most significant conservative achievements ever. The scope and scale of this endeavor are hard to overestimate." And this wasn't just about retirement security. "We have it within our grasp to move away from dependency on government and toward giving greater power and responsibility to individuals." The Democrats, Wehner wrote, could be consigned to the status of "the Party of the Past."

But for all the focus, all the commitment, all the rhetoric, and all the political capital spent, the push fell flat. By late spring of 2005 it was clear reform was going nowhere. As early as March, Bush's personal approval rating began to dip. Support for his Social Security proposal also dropped. A report from the Pew Research

Center for the People and the Press found that support for private accounts dropped among those considered most likely to support them, younger Americans, between February and March, from 66 percent in favor down to 49 percent. Opposition among older Americans was much higher. The Pew poll also found that among all Americans, the more they heard about the plan, the less likely they were to support it. And when the public's support wavered, Republicans in Congress got squirrelly and ran for cover.

Why did Bush's Social Security reform push fail?

One fairly simple answer presents itself. While Bush succeeded in convincing Americans that Social Security needs to be reformed—building off of years of such warnings from Republicans and even some moderate Democrats—he didn't convince them there was any particularly good reason to reform it *right then*. A Gallup poll taken toward the end of Bush's barnstorming tour found that while 81 percent of Americans believed major changes were needed in Social Security in the foreseeable future, only 45 percent thought those changes were needed in the next year or two. While Americans were pretty evenly split over whether they'd prefer to see a Republican or a Democratic plan to reform Social Security (27 percent versus 22 percent, respectively), a solid plurality (46 percent) just wanted to leave things alone. The Democrats didn't particularly convince people that Bush wanted to "dismantle" Social Security, but the burden to prove reform was necessary was on the president.

Some, however, such as the folks at the Cato Institute, who have been working for Social Security reform for decades, think Bush botched one of the clearest shots at reform that may come along for some time. Rove's thinking, said Cato president Ed Crane in an interview, is that "the best strategy is to scare the shit out of people . . . that's how they got the war started." In April of 2005, while Bush was storming barns, Crane penned a piece for the *Wall Street Journal* called a "Memo to Karl Rove." In it he blasted the president and his strategists for pushing the solvency issue above all others. "Solvency discussions are boring," Crane wrote. "Ownership and inheritability are inspiring."

Crane's deputy David Boaz said that when Cato expressed its concern, the White House just didn't get it. "You just ought to be able to go out to people and say, 'Would you like to have money in an account with your name on it, money that could never be taken away?'" Boaz said. But that's not how the administration sold reform. "When we point this out to them, they send over seventeen pages of quotes where the president has said that, but it is buried in speeches about medicine," Boaz said. "Right after Karl Rove said he does too talk about ownership, we checked [Bush's] speech in Orlando. . . . It was a twenty-five-page transcript, and on page seventeen there's a reference to ownership." In the end, said Boaz, "Bush is a strikingly inarticulate advocate of political ideas. . . . If we thought Gingrich was inarticulate, Bush is off the charts."

Crane and Boaz probably aren't being entirely fair in their assessment. Creating a consensus that Social Security needs to be changed and creating broad familiarity with the concept of private accounts among the public were two nontrivial accomplishments. And it's hard to see how anything short of political miracle-working would have brought a nervous public charging headfirst into the most radical reform of the New Deal ever undertaken.

But it's also worth pause to recognize that while the ownership pushed by Bush is in some ways more politically palatable than the austerity pushed during the Gingrich years, it is also no political palliative. Tough choices are still tough choices, and the public isn't likely to believe that it can get something for nothing. Social Security may be the key to creating an Ownership Society, but no one's yet found a way to make it click.

Failing, but Not Irredeemable

On balance, it's hard to escape the conclusion that Bush's Ownership Society has been a monumental failure as a political means toward achieving conservative policy ends. And instead of uniting conservatives, it's driving them further apart. On education, it's increased the federal bureaucracy without winning any form of choice or ownership for parents—a step backward. On health care, it's given us a massive new entitlement, poorly designed and poorly administered, in exchange for seedlings of reform that might have been won at far less cost—call it a half step forward. On Social Security, it may have advanced the debate incrementally, but it also reinforced the sense of inertia and political impossibility surrounding any attempt to remake this centerpiece of the New Deal—call it stuck in neutral.

The problem, at base, seems to be that by accepting the premises behind so much of the liberal federal edifice, conservatives have left themselves with precious little room to maneuver. If a Republican president comes into office set on education reform but accepts off the bat that the Department of Education's role should increase, not decrease, and that vouchers are off the table lest Teddy Kennedy not sign off on the final bill, he's going to end up with a meaningless clump of sod like NCLB. The same with health care, where a lack of conservative confidence and imagination—not to mention a routine triumph of politics over principle—prevented Republicans from even attempting to win free-market innovations like HSAs on their own before tying them to a massive expansion of the welfare state.

Still, there is a kernel at the heart of the Ownership Society that is worth saving. There is no reason to think that Bush's version is the only version imaginable. Bush may be many things, but a committed and effective conservative reformer is not one of them. Time and again he's decided that getting any bill is more important than getting a *good* bill. A more principled conservative president and/or Congress might yet do some real good with the ideas Bush has clumsily (and carelessly) groped his way toward.

For now, however, all Bush's Ownership Society has done is prove a timeless law of politics: once you've written yourself a permission slip to bend on principle in the service of a higher good, you end up looking like a pretzel.

6

Dancing with an Elephant

In July of 2005, two of America's most polarizing politicians—Senator Hillary Clinton (D-N.Y.) and Senator Rick Santorum (R-Pa.)—passed in a Senate hallway.

"It takes a village," Senator Clinton fired off, citing the African proverb that served as the inspiration for the title of her best-selling 1996 book of the same name, which makes the case that the federal government must expand to serve as an extended village to look out for the well-being of the nation's children.

"It takes a family," Senator Santorum fired back, citing the title of *his* best-selling 2005 book, which cheekily rebuts the former first lady's tome and which makes the case that the federal government must expand to serve as an incubator of healthy families for the well-being of the nation's children.

"Of course," came the rejoinder from Clinton, "a family is part of a village!"[1]

Whether Senators Clinton and Santorum will ever pick up their hallway debate in a more civilized forum looks in doubt. Rhetorically, Santorum has set up the former first lady as his bête noire, the unwitting star of countless tales told before the conservative faithful of how he has taken New York's junior senator on and fought to lay waste to her "radical feminist" ideas. Clinton, for her part, has avoided controversy like the plague in her first Senate term, doing what she can to ignore the Religious Right's favorite son.

What's certain, however, is this: when it comes to the proper size and role of government, there's far less daylight between Clinton and Santorum than either of them would care to admit.

Sure, each would use the power of the government for different purposes. Clinton would use it to institute national health care, government-funded child care, and government-mandated family and medical leave. Santorum would use it to create government-funded savings accounts for every child born in America, to sneak Intelligent Design into public-school curricula, and to implement state-mandated marriage counseling for all couples with minor children who want to get a divorce. But neither has any qualms about the underlying use of government power to bring into being his or her preferred vision of the perfect society. Clinton declaims against "antigovernment extremism" on the Right, Santorum against "radical individualism" on both the Left and the Right. Neither, it would seem, has much regard for individual liberty or limited government as ends in and of themselves.

Clinton says it takes a village; Santorum says it takes a family. But neither puts the individual at the center of political thought.

For the Left, views like Clinton's are nothing new; it was in response to just such paternalism that the modern conservative movement took shape in the first place some fifty-plus years ago. But for the Right, views such as Santorum's represent a distinct evolutionary step, decisively away from the tradition of Goldwater and Reagan and the fusionism described by Frank Meyer and toward something new and distinctly different. That something different is a form of big-government conservatism that holds that socially conservative ends—stronger families, stronger churches, stronger communities—can be achieved through traditionally liberal means.

Social conservatives have been asked to swallow this line of thinking—much as libertarians have been asked to swallow the idea of the Ownership Society—as the Republican Party executes its general drift away from small-government principles. And it is a tempting idea for many on the Right. The social-conservative half of the conservative movement has always been more concerned with morality than with individual liberty for its own sake. Their alliance with the small-government true believers was always premised on the idea that traditionalist ends could best be achieved through libertarian means—the idea that scaling back government makes room for civil society to grow and thrive.

But what if, instead, social conservatives could pursue their own ends more directly? Fifty years ago, when it looked like liberalism would always be the dominant creed of the governing class and Democrats always the natural stewards of government, it made sense to try to limit the power of Washington, D.C. But if Republicans are now running things in the nation's capital, perhaps it's finally time for the gloves to come off and for morally motivated conservatives to start pushing their views forcefully, backed by the power of the state—just as liberals hostile to their values have been doing for decades. An eye for an eye, so to speak.

The idea is tempting, but it's dangerous. In flirting with the notion of bending the federal government to its own ends, the Religious Right is dancing with an elephant. The proximity to power may be enticing, but the chance of getting trampled is high.

Expansive government is an inherently unconservative institution. It seeks standardization, centralization, and bureaucratization of everything it touches, displacing the efforts of churches, schools, families, nonprofits, and other local groups. Every time the welfare state steps in with a handout where a church or community group used to offer a hand up, every time failing urban public schools outspend successful urban Catholic schools into oblivion, every time parents rely on the federal government to monitor what their kids watch on TV instead of spending more time with them, the government tears away at America's social fabric. The federal government can't get more powerful and less intrusive at the same time; it can't get bigger and simultaneously foster less dependence. What's more, any piece of the federal machinery under supposedly efficient Republican control today will be under reckless Democratic control tomorrow—nothing in politics can be more certain.

Social conservatives should be wary of the path down which the current leaders of the Republican Party seek to direct them. Some of the leaders of the social Right are already waking up to the danger and trying to sound the alarm to their flocks. But others are still asleep. It's worth recalling, then, just why social conservatives held for so long to their side of the fusionist bargain and why now they are so close to breaking it and throwing the conservative coalition into disarray.

Leviathan

Economic conservatives and religious conservatives, of course, have disagreed about the proper role of government since the modern conservative movement began to take shape in the 1950s. In an era ripe with fears of Communist subversion and much gnashing of teeth over the decline of morality in the West, their quarrels ranged from the limits of freedom of speech to the state's right to enforce virtue.

In truth, however, as sharp as the philosophical differences were on some level between traditionalists and small-government conservatives, there was also more than a fair bit of common ground. Traditionalist Russell Kirk, for all his panegyrics to authority, was still a hearty skeptic of the federal behemoth—or Leviathan, as he so often called it. "Power is full of danger; therefore the good state is one in which power is checked and balanced, restricted by sound constitutions and customs," Kirk wrote in a 1957 essay. "So far as possible, political power ought to be kept in the hands of private persons and local institutions."[2]

What's more, as conservatism became more and more politically viable, there were better things for conservatives to do than to constantly tear each other apart. There was the Republican Party to take over, and there was a candidate, pleasing to traditionalists and libertarians alike, ready to lead the way: Barry Goldwater.

The rise of Goldwater as the hero of the early conservative movement is instructive in a number of ways. In particular, it may seem a bit of a mystery today how a man who in his later career and in death would ultimately become an icon of the libertarian Right commanded such loyalty from the forerunners of today's Religious Right. While some modern-day social conservatives have tried to wrest the Goldwater legacy away from the libertarians, looking to make the case that the Goldwater of 1964's race against Lyndon Johnson was actually in line with the Religious Right he would come to disdain in his later years, the charge simply doesn't stick. Goldwater's views on a few social issues (most notably abortion) evolved toward the end of his Senate career and after he retired, but for the most part it was the Religious Right that drifted away from him, not the reverse.

More than anything else, the fact that Goldwater appealed so strongly to voters concerned with "moral" issues in 1964, and in the Republican nominating process leading up to the general election, said more about the state of the conservative movement of the time than about the Arizona senator himself. While there was a traditionalist intellectual wing of the conservative movement, there was no Religious Right in the sense that we mean the term today. There was no Moral Majority, there was no Christian Coalition, no army of churchgoers ready to storm the voting booths. Instead there was simply what Richard Nixon would come to call a "silent majority" of Americans who felt that their values were under attack—often by the federal government.

Goldwater came to prominence in the conservative movement, after all, not by preaching about moral decay but by blasting big government and by attacking those in power whom he perceived as having gone soft on communism. In one of the more memorable incidents on his way to becoming the leader of the conservative movement, in 1957 Goldwater took to the floor of the Senate and blasted Eisenhower for being lulled by "the siren song of socialism" and attacked the president's budget as "bloated" and "squander-bust." He was going to take a stand, he said, against the notion (which more and more Republicans were accepting) that Americans should be "federally born, federally housed, federally clothed, federally educated, federally supported in their occupations, and die a federal death, thereafter to be buried in a federal box in a federal cemetery."[3] The row ended up with his being profiled in *Time*, pictured in the cockpit of a fighter plane. Thereafter, as Goldwater biographer Rick Perlstein put it, "mentions of the dashing Arizona senator's name began cropping up in the press like dandelions."[4]

In the 1964 campaign itself, Goldwater did take late to the "moral issue," which had been largely absent from his rhetoric until then. He touched on it in his convention speech in San Francisco, decrying "violence in our streets, corruption in our highest offices, aimlessness amongst our youth, anxiety among our elders," and "despair among the many who look beyond material success for the inner meaning of their lives." But only one speech during the campaign focused exclusively on the issue, given at the Mormon Tabernacle in Salt Lake City, where Goldwater decried how "the moral fiber of the American people is beset by rot and decay." The speech was broadcast on TV and drew high ratings.[5] Trying to capitalize on a theme that seemed to have struck a nerve, the RNC also ran some TV ads on the topic. "Graft! Swindle! Juvenile delinquency! Crime! Riots!" the titles in one ad shouted, intercut with images of kids running around and fighting with cops, before Goldwater came on the screen to proclaim: "The leadership of this nation has a clear and immediate challenge . . . to restore law and order in the land."[6]

None of this, of course, was enough to turn the tide. But what's interesting is that Goldwater's version of the moral issue had far less to do with God than with government. While Goldwater certainly didn't shy away from any reference to God or "Divine Will," he also wasn't ostentatiously religious. In fact, just the opposite. Not a regular churchgoer, he rebuffed the entreaties of his campaign staff to become one for the cameras. Goldwater's view of moral decay was that it started at the top, with corruption in the Johnson administration, and it filtered down through the government and on down to the American people. It was the federal government, specifically the Supreme Court, that had just outlawed school prayer. It was the federal government that was fostering an atmosphere that was soft on crime and inducive to social chaos. It was the federal government whose "urban renewal" had turned American cities into urban jungles. And it was the federal government that had long been sapping the American spirit of rugged self-reliance and replacing it with self-indulgence and dependence on Uncle Sam.

The social conservatism of the Goldwater era and earlier, then, was one concerned primarily with the growth and corrupting influence of Leviathan. Many of the hot-button issues that would come to define the Religious Right—such as abortion, feminism, gay rights, criminal rights, an out-of-control counterculture—had simply not yet emerged (or were just barely emerging) on the national stage. The fusion described by Frank Meyer was not a perfect framework, but with such broad agreement among conservatives on the Cold War, the dangerous growth of the federal government, and the sense of moral decline, the peace was easy enough to keep.

The Moral Minority

More than forty years after Goldwater broached the moral issue in national politics as something of an afterthought in the first ever conservative general-election campaign for the presidency, it may look to outside observers as if the social Right has conquered the world—or at least Washington, D.C.—as the string-pullers of the Republican Party. Nothing could be further from the truth; and much of the social Right could hardly be more despondent. A "silent majority" may have put Nixon in office, a Moral Majority may have ridden into the nation's capital behind Ronald Reagan, and a Christian Coalition may have fought alongside Newt Gingrich's Republican revolutionaries in 1994, but three-branch Republican rule hasn't brought the Religious Right to the promised land. Instead, it's left Christian conservatives increasingly coming to see themselves as an embattled minority. What's more, it's left this minority aiding and abetting a big-government agenda that would have been anathema to it three decades ago.

The chief strategist of the Religious Right in the nation's capital, Paul Weyrich—a working-class German Catholic who came up with the name for Jerry Falwell's Moral Majority in 1979—laid it all out in a fairly stunning letter to his fellow conservatives in February of 1999. "Politics itself has failed," Weyrich declared. It had failed, he wrote, because of the collapse of American culture. "Conservatives have learned to succeed in politics. That is, we got our people elected," he wrote. "But that did not result in the adoption of our agenda."

What was keeping them from true success? The American people weren't on the conservatives' side. "Let me be perfectly frank about it," he wrote, "If there really were a moral majority out there, Bill Clinton would have been driven out of office months ago." It was time for conservatives to face some unpleasant facts: "I no longer believe there is a moral majority. I do not believe that a majority of Americans share our values."

Seven years later to the month, speaking from his home office in Virginia, with George W. Bush in the White House and John Roberts and Samuel Alito having recently taken their seats on the Supreme Court, Weyrich confirmed that he still believes politics is failing—despite the widespread assumption that Bush has been the savior of the Religious Right. "We've actually slipped further back," Weyrich said. "Culturally, and with the attack on religion and with the idea of nontraditional marriage advancing and so on, it's actually worse than it was in 1999."

As for the Bush administration, he says values voters are "not thrilled," but not angry either. Bush hasn't done enough on abortion in their eyes. And after paying "appropriate lip service" during the 2004 campaign, he hasn't pushed hard enough for an anti-gay marriage amendment to the Constitution. While Bush's judicial picks have been solid—"Roberts and Alito are big boosts in our community," Weyrich said—that's pretty much the only area where the Religious Right is content. "I don't think they have deliberately tried to swindle us," Weyrich said. "We've got a White House that is not appropriately focused when it comes to big-ticket issues."

At base, Weyrich said, he's come to believe that conservatives fighting the decline of American culture simply can't depend on electoral politics to get the job done—a conclusion he came to as he watched the Gingrich years unfold (and unravel). "Here we had, in 1994, this extraordinary election," he said. "If anybody should have been ready to do something"—on abortion and other social issues, that is—"it would have been this class. They really ran on that and got a mandate for doing it. And yet they behaved the same way as previous classes did. . . . At that point, I just said, this is not only not working, it's not going to work."

In Weyrich's view, while social conservatives can't leave politics (imagine how the liberals would run riot!), they must look first to change the culture. "People want to use the legislature as a substitute for tackling the culture," he said. "These guys [politicians] are never going to stand up to the pornographers, the abortionists, and the homosexual lobby and the whole nine yards." But "Turn the culture around, and politics will follow."

Regardless of one's view of Weyrich's choice of enemies, his thinking does at least partially get at one of the great dilemmas of the modern Religious Right: a movement that started out looking for little more than benign neglect from the federal government (or, as they say, "leave us alone") now spends its time cultivating, imploring, and disciplining skittish politicians who seek the favor of social conservative leaders while simultaneously fearing the wrath of the general electorate if they make the mistake of appearing to be pandering too much to the Bible-thumping crowd. In other words, the Religious Right has become a moral *minority*— not able to count on the broad appeal of its ideas to win over the American public, but instead forced to play bare-knuckle, coalition-building, nose-counting, pressure-group politics.

As discussed in chapter 2, the modern Religious Right grew up initially from a grassroots rebellion by Christians, revolting against interference from the federal government. Jimmy Carter had been the first president to mobilize Evangelical Christians in his 1976 presidential campaign, where he won a majority of their votes. But when his IRS went after Christian schools two years later, threatening to remove their tax-exempt status if they didn't enroll enough minorities—regardless of whether the schools were actually engaging in discrimination—pastors around the country woke up to the fact that bureaucrats in the nation's capital could swoop in at any moment and wreak havoc with their most cherished institutions.

The IRS kerfuffle was the galvanizing incident for many Christian conservatives, but the other issues that had been riling them for years shared a similar theme: overbearing government, usually federal. The Supreme Court's 1973 decision in *Roe v. Wade* (which turned abortion, formerly a state issue, into a bitterly divisive national issue), the push for an Equal Rights Amendment to the Constitution (which social conservatives feared could lead to women being drafted and special protections for women in the law being invalidated), court-mandated school busing, gun control, quotas, out-of-control local taxes—all of these issues saw do-gooder liberals and busybody government bureaucrats interfering in the lives of everyday American citizens.

How different this largely small-government agenda, which brought the Religious Right into existence, is from the agenda the leaders of the Religious Right are pushing today. Whereas conservative Christian parents once thought it was inappropriate for public schools to teach their kids about sex, now they want the schools to preach abstinence to children. Whereas conservative Christians used to be unhappy with evolution being taught in public schools, now they want Intelligent Design taught instead (or at least in addition). Whereas conservative Christians used to want the federal government to leave them alone, now they demand that more and more federal funds be directed to local churches and religious groups through Bush's faith-based initiatives program. Whereas conservative Christians used to bemoan the creation of "no fault" divorce, now many cheer as the Bush administration spends nearly $1 billion on federally funded marriage counseling and fatherhood initiatives. And whereas an unborn child's right to life used to be the key issue for Christian conservatives, now they have added to their agenda the overriding of state laws that allow chronically ill patients to choose to end their own lives with the assistance of a physician.

This isn't to say that all of the Religious Right's goals were exactly libertarian back in the day. Their long-standing opposition to gay rights has carried forward quite logically to their opposition to gay marriage (even if it means amending the Constitution to overrule states that might democratically adopt gay-marriage or civil-union laws). And the crusade against pornography and other forms of indecency—whether at the Super Bowl halftime show, in a video game, on TV, or anywhere else in the universe—is a theme likely to carry over until the end of days.

But it is instructive to note just to what extent the Religious Right, in becoming further and further entangled with the Republican Party, has moved away from its raison d'être. In coming to grips with the realization that it is, in fact, a minority, the Religious Right has increasingly adopted the mind-set of an embattled, persecuted sect (roughly a quarter of Protestants—both black and white—consider themselves to be members of a minority group because of their strongly held religious beliefs, according to a 2001 Pew survey). That mind-set, in turn, has left Christian conservatives more amenable to seeking alliances, convenient or otherwise, that have left them at the whim of their coalition partners, begging (but sometimes loudly demanding) scraps from the table.

When the Christian Coalition's Ralph Reed proposed in his landmark *Policy Review* article in 1993 that social conservatives hitch their wagon more tightly to the economic conservatives' star, it was an admission of weakness by the Religious Right. In essence Reed was attempting to decontaminate a part of the party that had come to be considered radioactive. The fusionist marriage between these two groups had been on the rocks after the fall of communism; the disappointments (for both sides) of the George H. W. Bush administration, and especially the disastrous 1992 Republican National

Convention in Houston, where Pat Buchanan preached holy war in prime time. *The Religious Right isn't just a bunch of wackos shouting about fire and brimstone and holding up placards with pictures of aborted fetuses and looking for gay people to picket,* Reed seemed to be saying, *we like tax cuts just as much as the next guy!*

In truth, it was probably less the change of message than the threat to Western civilization posed by Bill and Hillary Clinton that drove the Christian Coalition's surge in membership and fundraising during the 1990s, but Reed's resort to reviving fusionism made it possible for the Republican Party to mobilize the Religious Right in 1994 without putting forward a divisive message on cultural issues at the national level. As noted in chapter 3, the Contract with America had nary a word to say about social-conservative policies, with Newt demanding "60 percent" issues only, and Reed was perfectly happy to see school prayer left out while his Christian Coalition distributed tens of millions of voter guides that helped elect the first Republican House in forty years.

According to former Christian Coalition legislative director Marshall Wittmann—who left not just the Religious Right but also the Republican Party in 2002 (for the moderate, Clintonite wing of the Democratic Party)—Reed largely succeeded in what he was trying to do. "His goal was to make the Religious Right as mainstream as the labor movement, so that the Religious Right would be to the Republican Party what the labor movement once was to the Democratic Party," Wittmann said. "The Christian Coalition did not become the AFL-CIO," Wittmann said (it waned in influence significantly after Reed left in 1997), "but yes, Christian conservatives became a critical component of the Republican coalition."

As a "critical component," the Religious Right got a seat at all the finest tables in Washington, D.C., one it has held on to tenaciously to this day. But it didn't necessarily get much else—at least not during the Gingrich years, during which the Republican Congress focused first on passing the Contract with America and then ended up in a prolonged budget fight with the president. During the 1996 election season, social conservatives did get the Defense of Marriage Act, defining marriage as between one man and one woman (to head off a court decision in Hawaii that made it look for a time like the state might be the first to legalize gay marriage). However, the bill passed both houses of Congress overwhelmingly and Clinton eagerly signed it, making it less a Republican triumph than an expression of bipartisan opposition to the idea of redefining marriage. The Republican Congress also passed various versions of a partial-birth abortion ban, but Clinton vetoed each one.

All this left many leaders of the Religious Right exasperated. Weyrich wrote his famous letter to social conservatives. Even more searing was a tirade delivered by Dr. James Dobson, head of Focus on the Family, in February of 1998 to the Council for National Policy (a somewhat secretive far-right forum). Gingrich's Republican Congress had been spitting in religious folks' faces almost since the second they took power, Dobson said, starting with the decision to have New Jersey's governor Christine Todd Whitman—a pro-homosexual, procondom, proabortion "symbol of the immoral, amoral constituency"—give the 1995 State of the Union response. They had failed to pass parental-consent or parental-notification laws for minors seeking abortions. They had given hundreds of millions of dollars to Planned Parenthood for overseas programs. They hadn't gotten rid of the National Endowment for the Arts. They hadn't passed a school-prayer amendment to the Constitution. They'd funded "safe sex" programs. They hadn't called for the prosecution of pornographers. Bob Dole's 1996 presidential campaign had given them the cold shoulder.

"Now I've been waiting to say this for a long time and you guys are the ones that are gonna get it," Dobson told the crowd. "Does the Republican Party want our votes—no strings attached—to court us every two years, and then to say, 'Don't call me. I'll call you.' And to not care about the moral law of the universe. Is that what they want? Is that what the plan is? Is that the way the system works? And if so, is it going to stay that way? Is this the way it's going to be? If it is, I'm gone, and if I go—I'm not trying to threaten anybody because I don't influence the world—but if I go, I will do everything I can to take as many people with me as possible."

But, of course, Dobson was issuing a threat. Weyrich and Dobson both were: Evangelicals and their Christian Right compatriots revolting against the Republican Party, pursuing third-party politics, or even simply staying home would spell disaster for the modern GOP. More than any other group on the Right, they've got the numbers and they've got the cohesion. In 1994, nine million more people turned out to vote Republican than had in the last midterm elections, in 1990, and an awful lot of them were, as Dobson pointed out in his speech, "conservative, Evangelical, and pro-life" (though the huge influx of anti-Washington Perot voters can't be ignored, either). In the South alone, the home turf of the Religious Right, the GOP received 3.8 million more votes in 1994 than in 1990.[7]

And the importance of the Religious Right certainly hasn't waned in recent years. John Micklethwait's and Adrian Wooldridge's 2004 book *The Right Nation* notes that in the 2000 election, the best predictor of how a white American would vote was not income, but how often the voter went to church; Bush won 79 percent of white voters who went to church more than once a week, as opposed to 54 percent of Americans who earned more than $100,000 a year.[8] Even in that election, however, the Bush team found that 4 million Christian conservatives who had voted in 1996 failed to vote for George W. Bush. When those voters returned to the polls in 2002, it helped the Republicans increase their margin in the House and pick up Senate seats in Georgia and Missouri.[9] In 2004, Pew found that four out of five white Evangelical Christians supported Bush, constituting more than a third (36 percent) of the ballots cast for him. And the influence of Evangelicals isn't likely to wane anytime soon: in 2005, Gallup found that 41 percent of Americans classified themselves as "born again" or Evangelical Christians; 59 percent of Americans said that "religion can solve all or most of today's problems."

What's more, on top of this broad-based demographic clout, the leaders of the Religious Right themselves command vast private armies. The Christian Coalition, even with its influence having dropped off, still has about half a million members. Dobson's Focus on the Family, now the most important Christian group in the country, sits on an eighty-one-acre campus in Colorado Springs, Colorado, with its own zip code and entrance off the highway. The formerly obscure academic, who has written a series of popular books on child rearing, reaches an audience of twenty-two million in America with his radio broadcasts, books, and other media endeavors. Dobson also helped found the Family Research Council in 1983 to lobby for "traditional family values" in Washington, D.C.; it has some 450,000 members.

Less than 10 percent of Focus's $130 million annual budget officially goes to public policy—it's a 501(c)(3) nonprofit organization and is restrained by IRS regulations—but Dobson throws his weight around in the national political arena regularly. For instance, according to the *Washington Post*, he gave the White House the green light to nominate Harriet Miers when Karl Rove was afraid she might not pass muster with conservatives (oops).[10] In another instance, in 2002, Focus managed to kill a bankruptcy reform bill when Senator Chuck Schumer (D-N.Y.) added language that Dobson didn't like, cracking down on abortion protesters.[11]

(Dobson is, however, extremely touchy about his political activism. Before his 1998 tirade against the Gingrich Congress, he made it explicitly clear that he was not speaking on behalf of Focus and that he'd paid his own way to the talk. When contacted with a request for an interview with Dobson for this book, a Focus vice president wrote back, "Over 90% of what Focus is and does pertains to the nurturing of the family. . . . A small percentage of our activities pertain to public policy issues, but not to endorsing or rendering commentary on candidates or parties.")

Yet for all this clout, whether wielded openly or behind the scenes, it is still the clout of a minority—constantly crying for the attention of the Republican Party and constantly pouting when it doesn't get its way. After the Dobson tantrum in 1998, Republican leaders holed themselves up in a room for two hours with profamily leaders and vowed to do better by them. They established the "Values Action Team," headed to this day by Representative Joseph Pitts (R-Pa.), to plan "real action" in support of the

Religious Right's legislative agenda. Many Christian leaders after the meeting felt they'd been "listened to for the first time."[12]

And yet, fewer than six years later, the Religious Right found itself shafted once again, as a president who'd campaigned for reelection heavily on the idea of "defending marriage" put that aside once the votes had been cast and focused instead on Social Security. "We couldn't help but notice the contrast between how the president is approaching the difficult issue of Social Security privatization . . . and the marriage issue," a group of social conservatives, including Weyrich, Dobson, and Jerry Falwell, wrote in a letter to Karl Rove in January of 2005. "Is he prepared to spend significant political capital on privatization but reluctant to devote the same energy to preserving traditional marriage? If so, it would create outrage with countless voters who stood with him just a few weeks ago."[13] They threatened to withhold their support on Social Security reform, but it didn't get them any action on a marriage amendment (nor were social conservatives much of a factor in the sinking of Bush's private-accounts plan).

Locked into such a dysfunctional relationship with the GOP, social conservatives might start asking themselves just why they're treated the way they are. Part of it is no doubt because they've earned themselves a tremendous amount of enmity from the politicians whom they are trying to influence through their constant threats and badgering. Dick Armey, for one, had to work with the Religious Right throughout his time in Congress, especially as majority leader, but from the outside now he has no qualms about saying what he thinks about that crowd. "Dobson and his gang of thugs are real nasty bullies," Armey said, asked about the growing influence of the Religious Right. "I pray devoutly every day," he said, "but being a Christian is no excuse for being stupid." Issues such as school prayer have a "high demagoguery coefficient," he said, because they're "shallow as water on a plate. . . . There ain't no thinking."

What's more, he thinks that the current Religious Right leadership's "ugly disposition" is antithetical to the kind of party that Ronald Reagan once presided over. "There is no more beloved conservative in America today than Ronald Reagan, and he never said an unkind word in all his public life . . . these guys want noise." All of the noise, however, Armey fears will drive off moderates. "Amo Houghton"—a former moderate Republican congressman from upstate New York—"has to be able to go to a cocktail party at the Arts League and be comfortable and not embarrassed about his party, or Amo doesn't get reelected," Armey said. "We can say to hell with Amo. . . . Well, you can say that fifteen times, then you're in the minority."

The general public is also—despite its own religiosity and general sympathy with the idea that our culture could use a moral revival—imbued with a profoundly American skepticism of mixing religion and politics. An overwhelming majority of voters want the president to be a person of faith, yet half of Americans become uncomfortable when a politicians talks about his or her own religiosity.[14] And a majority of voters (including 60 percent of Democrats and 54 percent of independents) felt at the start of the second Bush term that government is getting too involved in morality.[15]

Barry Goldwater perhaps put it best in remarks to the Senate back in 1981. "One of the great strengths of our political system always has been our tendency to keep religious issues in the background," Goldwater said. "Can any of us refute the wisdom of Madison and the other framers? Can anyone look at the carnage in Iran, the bloodshed in Northern Ireland or the bombs bursting in Lebanon and yet question the dangers of injecting religious issues into the affairs of state? . . . I'm frankly sick and tired of the political preachers across this country telling me as a citizen that if I want to be a moral person, I must believe in A, B, C, and D. Just who do they think they are? And from where do they presume to claim the right to dictate their moral beliefs to me?"[16] (Goldwater also said, at about the same time, that "Every good Christian ought to kick Falwell right in the ass." Also eloquent, if in a different way.)

Still, despite facing such skepticism about its agenda from politicians and a large part of the public—and despite a constant stream of disappointments and sellouts and rank ingratitude from the

Republican Party—the moral minority keeps on shutting its eyes, keeps on hoping, keeps on praying that organization can outweigh the unpopularity of much of its agenda and the inborn skittishness of elected officials.

Checkbook Compassion

As the Religious Right goes casting about for the best way to manipulate the Republican Party, the reverse just as surely happens as well. And the professional politicians have so far proven the better puppetmasters. No one example, perhaps, could better illustrate the skills of Bush, Rove, and Company as manipulators of the moral minority than the policy disappointment/political coup that has been the president's faith-based initiative.

Conservatives had every reason to get the willies about Bush's faith-based plans when he ran in 2000. They were part of his squishy "compassionate conservatism" platform and reeked of big government entangling itself where it ought not—into the midst of religiously affiliated community organizations and churches doing what they see as the Lord's work. But if conservatives didn't get the willies in 2000, they might well have in January of 2005, when New York's junior senator threw her arms around the president's controversial policy. "There is no contradiction between support for faith-based initiatives and upholding our constitutional principles," Hillary Clinton told the crowd at a fund-raiser for a Boston-based charity. In a speech where she invoked God more than half a dozen times—throwing in that "I've always been a praying person"—she said that there has been a "false division" between pursuing faith-based approaches to social problems and respecting the separation of church and state.[17]

Clinton's speech was noted far and wide as sop to the Religious Right. *Time* magazine pegged her as one of a pack of Democrats trying to affect, as the title of the article put it, "A More Soulful Tone."[18] In truth, however, Clinton wasn't paying homage to the political clout of the Religious Right; she was paying attention to the political smarts of the Bush White House. Clinton's support of faith-based programs was, in fact, nothing new. Bill Clinton had taken the first steps toward opening up more government grants to religious groups back in 1996, under an initiative known as "charitable choice," which allowed religious charities to compete for federal funds to provide social services on an equal footing with secular groups.

In fact, in 2000, both campaigns had plans to expand charitable choice. Speaking at a Salvation Army drug treatment center in Atlanta, Al Gore declared that faith-based groups, in "partnership with government," can "weave a resilient web of life support under the most helpless among us." On July 22, 1999, speaking at a black church in Indianapolis, Bush said that it "is not enough to call for volunteerism. . . . Without more support, public and private, we are asking them to make bricks without straw. . . . Government cannot be replaced by charities, but it can welcome them as partners, not resent them as rivals."[19]

At that 1999 speech in Indianapolis—the first major policy address of his presidential campaign—Bush laid out a very aggressive agenda for his faith-based project, which was in many ways at the center of this strange compassionate conservatism he was pushing. Along with expanded charitable choice, there would be more than $6 billion set aside to expand tax incentives for charitable giving. Another $1.7 billion would go to faith-based and nonfaith-based groups caring for drug addicts, the children of inmates, and teenage mothers. Some $200 million would be used to establish a Compassion Capital Fund to expand and replicate successful local programs.

What actually happened when Bush got into office, however, was a case study in how economic-conservative concerns tend to dominate when Republicans run things, and how the GOP nonetheless manages to pull the Religious Right's strings *just right* to keep them in line.

First off, in June of 2001, the $6 billion in expanded tax incentives for charitable giving—in dollars-and-cents terms the only substantial part of the entire initiative—was thrown out the window right off the bat. Why? To make room in the $1.6 trillion tax cut bill for the repeal of the estate tax, which (whatever its merits as policy) benefits the heirs of the wealthiest 1.9 percent of Americans who die each year. The rest of Bush's faith-based plan met a similarly ignominious fate in Congress in the summer of 2001. Essentially, hard-line social conservatives in the House insisted on a bill that would allow religious groups to proselytize with federal funds and exercise an almost unlimited right to discriminate against employees on the basis of religion; the bill was dead on arrival in the Senate.

Bush, however, did manage to implement a portion of his plan through the power of the executive branch. Shortly after his inauguration, Bush set up an Office of Faith-Based and Community Initiatives. The office's official duties involved ensuring that "faith-based programs have equal opportunity to compete for federal funding" and coordinating "public education and outreach activities to mobilize public support for charitable organizations." But what this really ended up meaning, after the president's plan failed in Congress, was a mandate to use the idea of faith-based initiatives and the enticement of federal money to begin aggressively courting black churches and black clergy members.

As Bush political adviser Matthew Dowd put it, "The minister is the No. 1 influencer in the African American community."[20]

In September of 2002, the *Washington Post* reported on Republican efforts to use the faith-based initiative to boost support for GOP candidates, especially among black voters in states and districts with tight congressional races. In South Carolina, the state Republican Party hosted a seminar to which about sixteen hundred black ministers were invited. The keynote speaker was Jeremy White, director of outreach for the faith-based initiative. Attendees received follow-up letters, on GOP stationery, with instructions on how churches could apply for federal grant money. Over the summer, the director of the faith-based initiative, Jim Towey, appeared with several Republicans in tight races in states such as Kentucky, West Virginia, Connecticut, Illinois, and Arkansas, visiting largely black neighborhoods and black churches—sometimes with a check in hand, but always with the hint that one might be coming later.[21]

The Bush administration, of course, has consistently denied that the faith-based initiative has anything to do with politics. But those who have left the administration have told a somewhat different story. John DiIulio, widely considered the father of the faith-based initiative idea (and called by Bush "one of the most influential social entrepreneurs in America"), offered a scathing criticism of the White House after stepping down as the head of the newly created faith-based office. In an interview published shortly after the 2002 midterm elections, DiIulio told *Esquire* magazine, "What you've got is everything—and I mean everything—being run by the political arm. It's the reign of the Mayberry Machiavellis." (Facing the wrath of the Bush White House, DiIulio issued a series of bizarre apologies after the article ran, but he never disputed the substance of what he had said.)

Still, the political use of faith-based initiative only increased as the president geared up for his own reelection campaign. In their recent book *One Party Country*, *Los Angeles Times* reporters Tom Hamburger and Peter Wallsten recount a speech Bush delivered in Philadelphia, shortly after the 2002 midterms, before fourteen hundred religious leaders at a White House–sponsored conference on private, religious charities fighting poverty, drug abuse, and crime. "I'm here today to stop unfair treatment of religious charities by the federal government," Bush told the crowd. And, indeed, onstage he signed the second of two executive orders he would sign that day—one creating faith-based centers in the Department of Agriculture and the U.S. Agency for International Development, and one ordering all government agencies to treat religious charities just like any secular social service organization. "The days of discrimination against religious groups—just because they're religious—are coming to an end," Bush said, both forwarding the idea that religious believers in America are somehow an oppressed minority and tying the struggle of that minority to the civil rights movement.[22]

There would be plenty more along these lines, leading up to the 2004 campaign. "I asked Congress to not fear faith," Bush told a crowd of black religious leaders in New Orleans in January of

2004. "I called on Congress to join me in passing laws that would . . . open up the federal treasury to faith-based programs, and they balked."[23] And of at least twenty publicly financed trips taken by faith-based office head Jim Towey between the 2002 and 2004 elections, sixteen were to battleground states.[24] "Look at where they planned their large-scale meetings," Robert Wineburg, a professor of social work at the University of North Carolina at Greensboro, told the *Los Angeles Times*. "A grant-writing workshop in St. Louis in September before Missouri was a lock, in Miami in October before Florida was sealed. I wouldn't call it honest technical assistance based on communities that needed that assistance most at that specific time. I'd call it honest American, or maybe old-style Chicago, politics."[25]

When it comes to the role that money has played in the faith-based initiative, however—whether grants have been used to buy votes—that's where things get tricky. It's easy to point to grants going to swing states, and particularly to Evangelical Christian groups, many of them African American. But there are a lot of grants, and Evangelical Christian groups run a lot of social-service organizations. Even one of the biggest critics of how the Bush administration has politicized its faith-based initiative, and someone in a position to know the inner workings of the program, doesn't think the grants have been used as bribes. "There was none of that," said David Kuo, who quit as the deputy director of the Office of Faith-Based and Community Initiatives in December of 2003. "The White House didn't control the process."

As Kuo put it in an impassioned article he wrote for the Web site *Beliefnet* in 2005, explaining why he left the Bush administration: "Some liberal leaders have been quoted as saying the administration was looking to 'buy minority votes.' Nothing could be further from the truth. There wasn't enough money around to buy anyone." In Kuo's view, the White House was never very interested in funding, as he put it, "the poor people stuff." Instead, the faith-based initiative was just "the cross around the White House's neck," little more than a symbol of Bush's own faith. The sad thing, in Kuo's view, was that urban faith leaders had been so neglected for so long that "simple attention drew them in." Liberals, in turn, played right into the White House's hands by playing to type and hyperventilating about the separation of church and state—yet one more confirmation to the faithful that the Democratic Party was worse than indifferent to believers.[26]

It's virtually impossible to calculate the exact value of what Bush has spent on faith-based initiatives—the numbers released by the administration include both grants to groups that may not be faith-based and grants that significantly predate the president—but it's clear that new spending on initiatives he has hyped is in the hundreds of millions after five years, not the billions originally promised.[27] What's more, the administration hasn't been shy about cutting social programs, even when they provide money to faith-based groups. A President Gore or a President Hillary Clinton, either of whom would have supported a program similar to Bush's, might well have spent more generously.

It turns out, then, that whether it is campaigning against gay marriage and then forgetting about it after the election or promising big bucks to religious charities and then giving them lip service instead, the Republican Party has found the moral minority to be a cheap date.

"Holy Means Set Apart"

In a 2000 collection of essays on religion in American politics and government, Peter Wehner, who would go on to be director of the Office of Strategic Initiatives at the White House, penned a warning to religious conservatives. He did so in what he called "A Screwtape Letter for the Twenty-First Century"—an allusion to C. S. Lewis's famous work *The Screwtape Letters*, in which a senior devil, Screwtape, instructs a junior devil, Wormwood, in the art of temptation. "The good news for us," Screwtape writes in Wehner's version, "is that being actively involved in politics without being seduced by it can be difficult. . . . Your task is to so thoroughly twist your patients' understanding of Christ's kingdom that they actually come to believe that by forming coalitions, networking among the politically powerful, writing laws to advance His 'social agenda,' and securing 'a place at the table,' they are following in His footsteps."[28]

Whether or not they truly believe they are following in His footsteps, such is the path that much of the Religious Right in America has chosen to walk. How far it can lead them in the political realm is limited, as many have learned from bitter experience. The Republican Party will always have to balance the demands of the Religious Right against the squeamishness of moderates and centrists, no matter how organized and disciplined the moral minority manages to be. What's more, they will always live on the precipice of political catastrophe, one election away from their political patrons being thrown out of office. Even the prospect of Senator John McCain winning the GOP presidential nomination is seen as a potential apocalypse by many on the social Right, as McCain's views on religion in politics owe more to Goldwater than to George W.

At the same time, how far the Religious Right's path can lead it into temptation is virtually unlimited. If the proper role of government is no longer simply to leave families and churches alone, in the eyes of social conservatives, but to actively promote morality and fund civic groups and set up savings accounts for every American and to teach kids about abstinence and Intelligent Design—well, then there is simply no logical limit to what government might be asked to do next. And with elaborate political machines running, constantly in need of new controversies and causes to gin up donations and keep themselves running, the "political preachers," in Goldwater's phrase, won't be looking for limits to begin with.

Perhaps, then, it's worth revisiting another letter: Weyrich's 1999 letter to conservatives. In proposing that conservatives should focus on changing America's culture more than on its politics, he put forward the idea of the faithful setting themselves apart. "I believe that we probably have lost the culture war. . . . This is why, even when we win in politics, our victories fail to translate into the kind of policies we believe are important," Weyrich wrote. "Therefore, what seems to me a legitimate strategy for us to follow is to look at ways to separate ourselves from the institutions that have been captured by the ideology of Political Correctness, or by other enemies of our traditional culture. I would point out to you that the word 'holy' means 'set apart,' and that it is not against our tradition to be, in fact, 'set apart.' You can look in the Old Testament, you can look at Christian history. You will see that there were times when those who had our beliefs were definitely in the minority and it was a band of hardy monks who preserved the culture while the surrounding society disintegrated."

What this means, Weyrich said seven years later, is that conservatives should stop fighting battles they'll never win. "We need instead to do what the home schoolers have done," he said, which is spend their time and energy creating their own networks and alternative culture. "Public schools will shape up when enough people have dropped out . . . the strategy is the right one." A similar strategy, he said, can be applied in popular culture. "Instead of fighting the depravity in the movie industry, we need to present an alternative," he said. In that respect, he points to *The Passion of the Christ* and *The Chronicles of Narnia* as having been extremely important in displaying the market power of the moral values crowd. "When enough of these things are highly successful, and enough people go there as opposed to the rest of the junk, all of a sudden it's going to dawn on the folks in Hollywood, maybe we can't make a lot of money with depravity."

Again, Weyrich doesn't support a retreat from politics by social conservatives by any means. Having fought as hard as he has over a lifetime in the realm of politics, that's perhaps to be expected. Nonetheless, the idea that attempting to achieve religious ends through political means is futile—as opposed to simply anathema to American conservatism—is one that might set more on the Religious Right to thinking.

Do they want to continue down the road to Santorumdom, which, with its calls for ever bigger and more intrusive government, can only lead to a rending of the traditional conservative coalition? Or do they want to find a path back—a path, perhaps, to a renewal of the fusionism that has served the conservative movement and the Republican Party so well for the past fifty-odd years?

7

Look to the West

Only a few days after CPAC 2005 and the orgy of GOP jubila-tion that marked those three days in the wake of Bush's second inauguration and the swearing in of a swelled Republican majority in Congress, a far smaller group of young conservatives and libertarians met in a quieter corner of Washington, D.C.

Their purpose: to delve into the issue glossed over at the Reagan Building. As the title of the talk, hosted by the America's Future Foundation, put it, they were gathered there that day to ask: "Can This Marriage Be Saved?"[1]

The event was a typical internecine debate, with a Festivus-like airing of grievances and squabbles over the finer points of right-wing ideology. One conservative and one libertarian each argued for either divorce or reconciliation between the two factions. The "promarriage" conservative, James Antle of the *American Conservative* (Pat Buchanan's magazine), argued that nonlibertarian Republicans could and would go back to supporting small government. ("Things'll change, baby, I promise!") The "prodivorce" libertarian, *Reason* magazine editor Nick Gillespie, argued that the

conservative-libertarian marriage had always been an abusive relationship, and it was time to get some self-respect. ("These boots
were made for walking. . . .") "If that's who we have to sleep
with," Gillespie said, referring particularly to social-right poster
boy, gay-marriage-opponent, and minimum-wage-hike-proponent
Rick Santorum, "I don't think there's enough liquor in the world to
get me through that."

Cutting to the heart of the debate, however, was an audience
member who, in the course of asking a question, threw out the old
Chris Rock line about men and marital fidelity: "A man is only as
faithful as his options." Libertarians, in other words, are the comic-
book nerds of the political world; if they can find an acceptable
partner willing to listen to them prognosticate about who would
win in a fight between F. A. Hayek and Milton Friedman, they
should consider themselves lucky. And with the only other option
around being an ass by turns indifferent or hostile to their core
beliefs, libertarians are destined—whatever their grievances—to
stay put.

That, of course, is the conventional wisdom: that libertarians
are hopelessly trapped in the Republican Party with no reasonable
means of escape—and that even if some libertarians did defect to
the Democratic Party out of sheer pique, their numbers could never
be of enough consequence to cause the GOP any particular electoral discomfort.

In the past, this conventional wisdom was dead-on. Libertarians
fought alongside the Republican Congress in the 1990s as it did
battle with Bill Clinton, and they did not abandon the GOP and
President Bush between 2000 and 2004, despite the turn toward
big-government conservatism.* But as the old fusionism described
by Frank Meyer withers and dies in Bush's second term, as the

---

*This is based on exit polls from 2000 and 2004. While Bush gained ten points between
2000 and 2004 among voters who thought government should "do more," he stayed
essentially even among voters who felt government should *not* do more or should "do
less." (It should be noted, however, that exit poll phrasing was not identical in those two
years.)

nation's population and electoral map shift ever South and West, and as the Republican Party increasingly favors southern values (religion, morality, tradition) over western ones (freedom, independence, privacy), liberty-minded voters are going to play an increasingly pivotal role in the Democratic Party's strategy to turn back the rising Republican tide.

The conventional wisdom that the Republican Party will continue to enjoy a never-ending free ride with libertarians, in other words, is dead wrong. The Democratic Party is not as stupid as it looks, nor is the Republican majority as sound as it looks (or at least as Karl Rove *tells* you it looks). In the short and long term, both parties—whether they like it or not—are going to find themselves forced to follow a simple dictum: look to the West.

The Democrats' Date with Demographic Destiny

America's population is on the move. It's not a new trend, but the pace at which it is progressing is rather stunning—and its implications for the Democratic Party as it is currently constituted are rather bleak. In short, what's happening is this: the Snow Belt (the Northeast and the Midwest, a.k.a. the Democratic Party's power base) is melting, and the Sun Belt (the South and the West, a.k.a. the Republican Party's power base) is heating up. According to the U.S. Census Bureau, America's population center is moving south and west at a rate of three feet an hour, five miles a year.[2] By 2030, two out of every three Americans will live in the Sun Belt, up from roughly 58 percent today.[3]

As shown in the map, based on current population projections, over the next quarter century 29 electoral votes (and congressional seats) are going to shift from the Snow Belt to the Sun Belt. To look at it another way, Brookings Institution demographer William Frey points out that if the Red and Blue states from 2004 were simply carried through to 2030, the Red-Blue Electoral College vote would come to 303 to 235 (as opposed to the actual 286 to 252 count when Bush was reelected, a shift of 17 electoral votes). The biggest gains for the largely Republican Sun Belt will come in

State Electoral College Change, 2000–2030

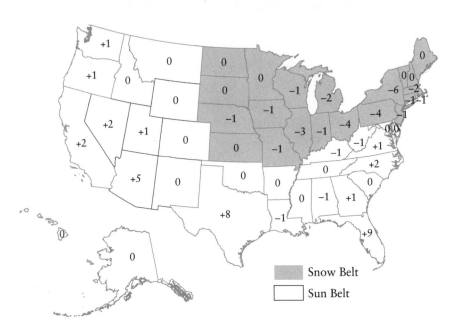

Reproduced courtesy of William H. Frey, Brookings Institution, Washington, D.C. Based on U.S. Census Bureau figures, Census 2000.

Florida (+9) and Texas (+8), but not inconsiderable gains will also be coming to the Southwest, in Arizona (+5), Nevada (+2), and Utah (+1). Meanwhile, Democratic stronghold New York (-6) is in sharp decline, and New England as a whole (-4) is also losing clout. (The sole bright spot for the Democrats is the Pacific Coast, which will gain 4 electoral votes.)

What all this means is that the Democratic Party's problems won't be solved simply by winning back some midwestern swing states that swung Red in 2004—at least not in the long term. Ohio is set to lose 4 electoral votes by 2030 (2 could be gone by 2010), and Iowa and Missouri will lose 1 each. Even if all three states switched to Blue in our fictional 2030 Electoral College map, the GOP would still be ahead, be it by a much narrower margin (271 to 267).

Now, none of this, of course, is to imply that the 2030 Electoral College map actually *will* have the same breakdown of Red and Blue states as the 2004 map (maybe the networks will even choose some new colors by then . . . if network TV still exists). Far from it. What this electoral math does imply, however, is that both parties need a new strategy to keep up with rapid and overwhelming demographic changes coming in the next twenty-five years—but it's the Democrats who have far more incentive to innovate.

To that end, they are destined to look west. After the 2004 election, plenty of people took note of the fact that a shift of 60,000-odd votes in Ohio would have swayed the Electoral College vote to a John Kerry victory. Kerry still would have lost the popular vote by a respectable margin (he put up a good effort in that regard), but perhaps it all would have been fitting payback to Republicans for the Florida recount fiasco—if not exactly healthy for American democracy. Instead, however, people should have been looking at another place where tens of thousands of votes could have turned the election: the Southwest. Some 70,000 votes among Colorado, Nevada, and New Mexico, with their collective 19 electoral votes, would have swung the presidential election just as surely as Ohio's 20 electoral votes. What's more, with margins of 5 percent, 3 percent, and 1 percent, respectively, these were swing states by any definition of the term. Going forward, the reasons for Democratic optimism in these states, as well as in a number of Mountain West states, is solid, as is the case for a serious investment of resources by the Democratic Party—one that is, it seems, already quietly under way.

One reason for Democrats to invest in the Southwest and the Mountain West simply involves a process of elimination: they're already doing what they can in the Midwest, and there's hardly anywhere else they might go to look for votes. Their dominance in the Northeast at the presidential level is all but total; and there are only so many more congressional seats they can pick up in the region. The Pacific Coast paints a somewhat similar picture for the Democrats.

Perhaps most crucial, however—for both parties—is that the

Democrats are now effectively locked out of the South. The story of the Republican Party's coming to dominate national politics at the end of the twentieth century and the beginning of the twenty-first century is the story of the realignment of the South, first at the presidential level in 1968, and then at the congressional level in 1994. But that story looks to be about over, the realignment complete. There is, in short, not much further the Republican Party can go in the region.

In December of 2004, the *Los Angeles Times* conducted an analysis of voting in the South (which it defined as the 11 states of the old Confederacy, plus Oklahoma and Kentucky). It found that in the November election Bush had carried 85 percent of counties in the South; he carried 90 percent of counties where whites were a majority. To put Kerry's performance in the South in another light: Bill Clinton won 510 out of 1,154 white-majority counties down South in 1996; Kerry won 90. After Reagan's 1984 landslide, the GOP held 12 of the 26 U.S. Senate seats in the South; 20 years later, after Bush's 2004 squeaker, the GOP held 22 of the 26 seats. In the House, Republicans have increased their advantage over Democrats in the South from 27 seats before Bush took office to 40 seats after the 2004 election. It was all enough to inspire one Democratic county chairman in Alabama to declare that his party was "out of business" in the South.[4]

Progressive writer Paul Waldman, in his insightful book *Being Right Is Not Enough*, which attempts to draw up a blueprint for how the Democrats can mount a comeback, suggests his fellow travelers must adopt the code of the samurai: "The Samurai considered himself to be already dead. This belief freed him from the fear of death and made him a more effective warrior. Democrats need to free themselves from their fear of losing the South."[5] While perhaps a bit dramatic, Waldman has a point. The South, particularly the Deep South, is so socially conservative that the Democratic Party can do very little to appeal to the region without looking by turns cringe-inducingly ridiculous and stupefyingly dishonest.

Particularly striking is a table Waldman included in his book, reproduced on page 165 based on data from the 2000

National Annenberg Election Survey, showing the percentage of respondents in each state identifying themselves as Evangelical or born-again Christians. The states Bush won in 2004 are shaded. While there are aberrations such as Utah (which doesn't have many Evangelicals because it has Mormons instead, who vote like Evangelicals), the pattern is clear: Republican strongholds have lots of Evangelicals, Democratic strongholds have very few, and swing states are in between. What's most interesting, however, is that while the states

Percentages of Evangelicals in Red and Blue States

State	% Evangelical/ Born Again	State	% Evangelical/ Born Again
Mississippi	73%	Pennsylvania	32%
Alabama	68%	Nebraska	32%
Arkansas	64%	Illinois	32%
Tennessee	63%	Washington	32%
Oklahoma	61%	Maryland	31%
South Carolina	61%	Delaware	31%
Kentucky	59%	Wyoming	31%
North Carolina	57%	Arizona	30%
Georgia	57%	Colorado	30%
West Virginia	56%	Nevada	29%
Louisiana	53%	Idaho	29%
Texas	51%	Wisconsin	29%
Missouri	47%	Minnesota	29%
Indiana	46%	California	28%
South Dakota	44%	D.C.	28%
Kansas	44%	Maine	26%
Virginia	41%	New York	19%
Ohio	39%	New Jersey	18%
Florida	39%	Rhode Island	16%
North Dakota	39%	Utah	15%
Oregon	35%	Connecticut	14%
Michigan	35%	New Hampshire	14%
Iowa	35%	Massachusetts	12%
New Mexico	34%	Vermont	12%
Montana	33%		

Source: Paul Waldman, *Being Right Is Not Enough*. Compiled using data from the 2000 National Annenberg Election Survey. Red states won by Bush in 2004 are shaded.

in the Southwest (Arizona, Colorado, Nevada, New Mexico) would be expected to show up as swingers, the states in the Mountain West (Idaho, Montana, Wyoming) are typically considered solidly Republican—yet there they are, right there in the middle of the pack. These Mountain states might not count for much in Electoral College math, but they've got Senate seats the same as anyone.

While both of these regions went for Bush in 2004, that was in the context of a weak, northeastern Democratic candidate and a strong, Texan Republican candidate. What's more, even within that context, there was some significant tightening of the presidential vote between 2000 and 2004 in the Southwest (Bush actually did worse in Colorado and Nevada his second time around), and Bush's vote in the Mountain West was quite flat compared to his nationwide gains. (Meanwhile, in the South, Bush's margins increased dramatically.)

Another trend is also working heavily in favor of the Democrats in the Southwest and Mountain West: migration within the United States. Specifically, California is overflowing—think of it as a bucket of blue paint spilling all over the West, particularly into Arizona and Nevada. More than 400,000 Arizonans and 360,000 Nevadans were born in California. Demographer William Frey says Arizona and Nevada "are essentially now becoming appendages of California, in terms of the kinds of demography that are shaping them." The numbers in the Mountain states are nothing to sneeze at, either: 122,147 Californians in Idaho (total population: 1.3 million), 47,601 in Montana (total population: 900,000), and 21,096 in Wyoming (total population: 490,000).[6]

Who are these migrants? People who can't afford to live in California anymore, Frey says, typical young people in search of jobs and affordable homes. "A lot of them are from very blue parts of California," he said. "My gut feeling is," he said, that migrant Californians "will hold on to their cultural ideas," even if their economic needs might change. The Republican Party has gotten by on trying to push people's cultural hot buttons, Frey said, but "those kinds of appeals will be less strong in a West that's made up of more Californians." How much less strong? No one knows. The

Inmigration from California to the Interior West

State	Total Population	Born in California	Percentage Born in California
Arizona	5,130,632	407,461	7.9%
Colorado	4,301,261	243,071	5.7%
Idaho	1,293,953	122,147	9.4%
Montana	902,195	47,601	5.3%
Nevada	1,998,257	363,507	18.2%
New Mexico	1,819,046	79,007	4.3%
Utah	2,233,169	153,986	6.9%
Wyoming	493,782	21,096	4.3%

Source: U.S. Census Bureau, "State of Residence in 2000 by State of Birth: 2000," Census 2000.

question is whether the people will change the place, or the place the people.

Then, of course, there's the Hispanic immigration into the Southwest. Here, the picture's a bit more complex, but the Democrats still have plenty of reason to be optimistic. Republicans have been making a lot of noise since the 2004 election about Bush's supposed take of 44 percent of the Hispanic vote. Fred Barnes cites the number in his pro-Bush book, in making the argument that the president has forged a "new majority," and cites the president's showing as "an event of historic proportions."[7] The only problem is that the number is bunk. Almost immediately after the election, researchers questioned the national exit poll numbers. Later reviews of fifty-one state exit polls found that Bush's true 2004 share of the Hispanic vote is likely 40 percent or significantly lower—at best a gain of 5 percentage points, rather than the 9-point gain his supporters were claiming.[8] While this is certainly an improvement on Dole's pathetic 21 percent of the Hispanic vote in 1996, it's comparable to Reagan's 37 percent in 1984. In other words, it's hardly historic.

It's also important to remember, in specifically addressing the Southwest as a swing region, that Bush's Hispanic support has been clustered in Texas and Florida. In Texas, Bush's home state, he's had a chance to cultivate a personal relationship with Hispanic voters over more than a decade. In Florida, his brother Jeb (whose wife was born in Mexico) has done similar bridge-building with a heavily Cuban (and thus heavily Republican-leaning) Hispanic population. In the Southwest, Bush has performed roughly at his nationwide average with Hispanics, or even below it. In Colorado, for instance, he lost the Hispanic vote 30–68.

What's more, for whatever gains Bush has made among Hispanics, they seem to begin and end with him. Hispanic party identification consistently registers roughly two to one in favor of the Democrats and hasn't shown any major swing toward the GOP under Bush; similarly, roughly twice as many Hispanics think the Democrats in Congress represent their views on major issues (the economy, health care, education, immigration) as think Republicans do; and a poll of Latinos in 2005 found that on a generic congressional ballot, Democrats would win the Latino vote 61 percent to 21 percent—a margin of *three to one*.[9]

The Republican Party has done a masterful job at running a disciplined, innovative, and effective political machine in a very closely divided country; if not for their bare-knuckled redistricting in Texas in 2003, they might have lost House seats in 2004 instead of gaining them. But talk of a "new majority" or a "permanent majority" is premature, if not a tad silly. Yes, Bush won reelection; but he was an incumbent president, he'd cut taxes, he had a decent economy at his back, and his opponent was a Massachusetts liberal whose main concern throughout the fall was that he not find himself photographed in any tanks—and even then Bush barely pulled it out. And yes, Bush was the first president to win a popular-vote majority since his father in 1988; but he was also the first not to face a significant third-party challenge (Nader voters by and large learned in 2000 that it really *does* matter whether you vote for Kang or Kodos).

As *National Journal* columnist Jonathan Rauch pointed out in a column shortly after the November election, what the Republicans have achieved is not dominance but parity with the Democrats.[10]

Exit polls found the Republican Party tying the Democratic Party in voter identification for the first time in 2004, 37 percent to 37 percent, with 26 percent of voters calling themselves independents (though, since the election, polls have shown the Democrats still a few points ahead). But this is really just the end of a process that's been under way for decades. In the 1970s, Democrats held a 20-point lead over Republicans in party identification. It shrunk to about 10 points in the 1980s and then to single digits in the 1990s. The driver, however, as with the realignment in Congress, has mostly been the South coming to terms with its new political identity. Party identification in the rest of the country has remained relatively stable.[11]

The question, then, is how either party can get a leg up on the other in a fairly evenly split country. The Republicans have done it so far by organizing and energizing their base—particularly Evangelical Christians in swing states, around contentious issues such as gay marriage. They've also done it by positioning themselves as the tough-on-terror party. Meanwhile, the Democrats have done everything they can to help the GOP by playing into their own portrayal as the soft-on-crime-and-terror, close-pals-with-Michael-Moore, Bush-is-a-bigger-threat-than-al-Qaeda party. This dynamic, however, is not likely to last forever. It might not even last until 2008. As the Democratic Party looks to shift the ground it is fighting on, the West looks abundant with opportunities. And the same might be said of a long-neglected, long-suffering political demographic: libertarians.

How the West Will Be Lost

At the end of 2004, Patton Price, a twenty-seven-year-old Democratic activist living in Portland, Oregon, sat down to analyze what had gone right for his party in the fall elections. "As you can imagine," he said in an interview in early 2006, "it wasn't an analysis that took all that long." But there were some encouraging developments for those willing to look beyond the federal picture, and they would lead him in early 2005 to found Frontier PAC with fellow activist Isaac Goldstein, dedicated to the idea that Democrats can win in the West—and that they can do it, at least in part, by appealing to, as the group's Web site puts it, "libertarian, small-government voters" who once formed the core of the Republican Party.

At about the same time, another group was just getting off the ground: Democrats for the West, the nation's first regional party organization, representing nine states in the interior West (Arizona, Colorado, Idaho, Montana, Nevada, New Mexico, Utah, Wyoming, and Alaska). Backed by a "founders committee" consisting of five Democratic western governors from years past and an assortment of former Democratic senators, congressmen, and mayors from the region, they blasted the Bush administration as "not conservatives by any stretch of the imagination" and promised to develop an overarching western message for the Democratic Party, with a focus on issues such as "balancing the budget" and relieving westerners from "federal mandates" hurting their local communities.

Just what were both of these groups seeing—or, perhaps, smoking?

While the idea of a Democratic resurgence in the West may seem far-fetched—naively optimistic in that way that many young, Democratic, "netroots" activists and even retired, elder-statesmen idealists are sometimes prone to—it's worth looking at the facts on the ground. They're fairly striking, even if most of the action is at the state level.

Most famously out West in 2004, Montana elected its first Democratic governor in twenty years, Brian Schweitzer, a rancher and soil expert who made no secret of his love of guns and supported (along with the state's Republicans) a ballot measure banning gay marriage; Democrats won four out of five statewide offices (including attorney general and superintendent of public instruction) in those elections and also took control of Montana's House and Senate. In 2004, Democrats also took over both houses of the Colorado legislature and sent Democrat Ken Salazar to the Senate to replace retiring Republican senator Ben Nighthorse

Campbell; Salazar's brother John also won the open House seat in
Colorado's third district, which was vacated by a Republican (one
of only two open Republican House seats picked up by Democrats
that year).

These gains came on top of other recent gains for Democrats in
the West. With Schweitzer in Montana, Democrats now hold the
governorships of four of the eight states that make up the interior
West—in 2000, they held none. Bill Richardson, a Democrat, won
the governorship of New Mexico in 2002, succeeding two-term
Republican governor Gary Johnson. Dave Freudenthal was elected
governor of Wyoming in 2002, also succeeding a two-term Republican governor. Janet Napolitano won the governorship of Arizona,
also in 2002, making her the first Democrat elected to that office
since the 1980s.

What's more, going into the 2006 gubernatorial election cycle—
in which thirty-six governorships will be up for grabs nationwide,
including the three western governorships won by Democrats in
2002—Republicans seem to expect to lose more ground in the
region as opposed to gaining any back. "If you look at the polling
data in those states [Arizona, New Mexico, and Wyoming], you
don't really see, at this point in time, any clear challenges on the
Republican side that have got people really focused on those
races," the executive director of the Republican Governors Association, Phil Musser, said in March. Instead, Republicans will have
their work cut out for them just holding on to governorships in two
states out West where their incumbents will be term-limited out of
office: Colorado ("A state where we had a bad year in 2004," in
Musser's words) and Nevada (where, Musser said, Republicans
have a "reasonable shot").

It's possible to read too much into victories at the state level, of
course, but they're not insignificant either. "Governors make a big
difference in states," longtime Democratic pollster and strategist
Celinda Lake said. "They really help, even more than federal races,
build Democratic operations," she said. "They bring in state legislators behind them, they articulate very vividly a Democratic
alternative, which is one of our biggest problems right now, that

voters don't know what the Democratic alternative is." What's more, state-level wins help build a farm team of experienced candidates for federal offices. And while it's still not clear what the Democratic alternative in the West is exactly, it's getting clearer. Specifically, it has a lot to do with appealing to what Lake called a more "secular" and more "libertarian" electorate with an ingrained "culture of live and let live."

If anyone could pin down just what the emerging Democratic alternative in the West might be, it would be Dan Kemmis, former Speaker and minority leader of the Montana House of Representatives and one of the original people who conceived of Democrats for the West. Whereas the West once produced Democratic giants such as Senator Frank Church of Idaho and Senate majority leader Mike Mansfield of Montana, the party lost its way in the region in the 1980s and 1990s. Kemmis recalls how the environmental movement, once a homegrown phenomenon, came to be seen as an alien force and a threat to local jobs and how Republicans successfully used it to brand all Democrats as—how to put this delicately?—owl-fondling gun-grabbers.

But in recent years both the West and the Republican Party have changed—and perhaps begun to drift apart. With the increasing inmigration from California and other congested parts of America, Kemmis said, "People are increasingly concerned about how to manage that growth in a way that both sustains prosperity and sustains the quality of life that's bringing people here in the first place." At the same time, Kemmis said, "Westerners still are pretty much small-government people. . . . They have a tendency to trust the government that's closest to them, rather than a distant government." Given that, and given the performance of the Bush administration over the past five years, "There's been increasing uneasiness about whether the Republican Party hasn't become the party of big brother and big government."

The No Child Left Behind Act, said Kemmis, is "just anathema to the West. . . . What is the federal government doing in the classrooms to that extent?" On the Patriot Act: "People are getting very squeamish about having big brother looking over everybody's shoulder to that extent." On medical privacy: "The Schiavo case did not go down well in the West." On fiscal discipline: "It's become increasingly easy for Democrats to paint the Republican Party as the party of big government." And then some. "I personally think that's fair," Kemmis said. And, he said, after a pause: "It's effective."

Democrats, in other words, are watching the Republican Party tilt on its axis, toward the South and away from the West, and they see an opportunity.

Patton Price, the young activist behind Frontier PAC, who grew up in the South and now lives in the West, said he feels the potential for change in the West "on an emotional level that can't exactly be quantified." For Democrats, it's just an entirely different field of play than the South. "One of the key differences from the South," he said, "is that, yeah, people might be conservative, yeah, people might be religious, but Evangelical religions don't have the same kind of cultural foothold out West. . . . People are a lot more likely to have a fire wall between their religious practices and their secular life."

That leaves rural voters in the West more open to populist economic appeals, in his view. As a worker for MoveOn.org's get-out-the-vote effort in Ohio in 2004, Price saw how, as he put it, "we got absolutely slaughtered" in the rural counties. His hope is that the Democratic Party's pitch on fiscal discipline and corporate responsibility can be more effective with rural voters who are less open to emotional, cultural appeals. "It's more than just yanking away the mantle of being these northeastern, sweater-vest-wearing smart guys who can look at a pile of numbers," he said. "It allows us to communicate with conservatives as conservatives, not as Republicans."

What's more, all the corruption scandals plaguing the Republican Congress going into the 2006 elections aren't hurting the Democrats' chances. "One of the greatest things that's happened in terms of giving Democrats potential for 2006 onward was the K Street Project," Price said, referring to the name of the Republican effort to force corporate lobbyists to deal only with the GOP. "Our biggest problem in terms of connecting with rural voters, and in terms of being real populists, is that we're often seen as the other corporate party . . . the Republicans essentially offered to help us out of that conundrum."

Discomfort with the Bush administration's closeness to corporate America also plays into the environmental issue, which Democrats in the West now believe they can take back. David Sirota, who was a senior strategist to Schweitzer's gubernatorial campaign, has a special feel for how this might work. Not only did the candidate aggressively court Montana's hunters and fishermen by running ads showing himself and his brother trudging through the woods in hunting gear with rifles, but he also put forward a nine-point plan to keep public land in the government's hands and to spend more money to maintain the land for sportsmen. The Republican legislature, meanwhile, had previously tried to sell large chunks of public land. As Sirota explained in an article in *Washington Monthly*, Schweitzer's plan appealed not just to right-leaning hunters but also to left-leaning environmentalists. What's more, it helped Schweitzer tie his opponent in Republican-leaning Gallatin County, one of the fastest-growing counties in America—and one that, like other Rocky Mountain exurbs, has seen an influx of people looking to live somewhere with abundant outdoor recreation.[12]

So Democrats have a theory: libertarian-minded voters are up for grabs in the West, abandoned by the Republican Party. These are not literal, registered, or self-identified libertarians, for the most part—just voters who, whether or not they're particularly conservative in their personal lives, subscribe to a typically western, leave-me-alone philosophy when it comes to government busybodies in Washington, D.C. What's more, the Democratic theory goes, these voters don't trust corporations much, either, so they're open to an environmental message centered around preserving the beauty of the West and an economic populist appeal that says big business is responsible for a whole host of society's woes.

Does it work?

The first part of the theory works pretty well: the West has a socially libertarian and anti-federal-government streak as long as the Rocky Mountains. Nevada, Colorado, and Montana all have medical marijuana laws (along with the Blue states on the Pacific Coast, Alaska, Hawaii, Maine, and Vermont). Resolutions denouncing the Patriot Act have been passed out West by the Republican-controlled state legislature in Idaho and Democrat-controlled state legislatures in Colorado and Montana. And the two states that have openly rebelled against No Child Left Behind's federal testing regime, by passing laws exempting themselves from it (without any sort of federal permission), are Colorado and Utah.

Public-opinion polling also reveals the interior West's libertarian streak on many social issues. Most polling data released to the public, if it includes any regional breakdown at all, tends to divide the country into four regions: Northeast, South, Midwest, and West. The problem with such a breakdown is that it lumps the Blue Pacific Coast with the Red Southwest and Mountain West. At the request of the author, the Pew Research Center for the People and the Press broke down responses to questions from their 2005 political typology survey (discussed in chapter 4), splitting the Pacific Coast (California, Oregon, and Washington) from the interior West (Arizona, Colorado, Idaho, Montana, Nevada, New Mexico, Utah, and Wyoming). The results are fairly revealing, and they particularly show a cultural gulf between the South and the interior West—with the interior West often looking in its attitudes much closer to Blue-state northeasterners and Pacific Coasters than to their fellow Red staters (see the appendix).

For instance, almost twice as many people in the interior West say that religion is "not that important to me" as say the same in the South (30 percent vs. 17 percent); the Pacific Coast and the Northeast both hover at about 30 percent on that question. Relatedly, 61 percent of southerners say it is necessary to believe in God "to be moral and have good values"; only 44 percent in the interior West believe the same. To take the hot-button issue of gay rights, only 39 percent of southerners think homosexuality "should be accepted by society," while 53 percent of folks in the interior West support tolerance of gays (that figure bumps up to 60 percent on the Pacific Coast and in the Northeast). Similarly, 53 percent of southerners think public-school libraries should ban "books that contain dangerous ideas" versus 44 percent in the interior West. Cultural libertarianism, it seems, is pretty deeply ingrained in the West.

It's the Democrats' populist pitch on economic issues that might have a harder time gaining purchase in the region. Only in the Northeast, the party's base, does the Democratic message of doing more to help needy Americans have significant resonance. Meanwhile, westerners seem particularly unlikely to be convinced that Wal-Mart, oil companies, and other "bad corporate citizens" are preventing them from getting ahead—a message that seems more tailored to the dying industrial Midwest. A whopping 74 percent of people in the interior West believe "most people who want to get ahead can make it if they're willing to work hard"; only on the Pacific Coast and in the Midwest does that American faith in hard work waver, and even in those places only down to the low 60s. Likewise, only 10 percent of interior westerners believe that success in life is determined by "forces outside of our control"; almost twice as many believe that in the Midwest.

The environment, likewise, is an area where western Democrats might not want to get too far ahead of themselves. Preservation of the natural environment enjoys majority support in every region of America. But there are still regional differences; the interior West isn't the Northeast. Almost twice as many in the interior West agree with the statement that "This country has gone too far in its efforts to protect the environment" as agree with it in the Northeast (22 percent vs. 13 percent); similarly, almost twice as many in the interior West believe stricter environmental laws will "cost too many jobs" as believe so in the Northeast (40 percent vs. 24 percent). Democrats are probably right about the greening of the West in the long run, as a generation of coastal telecommuters and other job seekers fill up the nation's sparsely populated interior. But for now they're threading a needle, making the case that they'll preserve what's special about the West—by not selling off pristine wilderness to big corporations for oil exploration, logging, mining, etc.— without transforming the region into an industry-and-job-free national park. It's certainly possible to pull it off, as Schweitzer and others have shown, but it's a delicate undertaking.

Last but not least, of course, the Democrats still have a patriotism problem in the West. Whether Democrats think it's fair or not, it's a pretty big problem in America—pretty much anywhere you go—if you're the party that, while it doesn't exactly *hate* America, isn't exactly comfortable *waving the flag* either. People in the interior West are skeptical of domestic terror-fighting measures and worried about giving up liberty and privacy (even more so than people in the Northeast), but they still believe, just as much as southerners, in fighting for your country "whether it is right or wrong." These are not pacifists in the interior West, which shouldn't surprise anyone. And as President Bush continues to enjoy a disproportionate amount of support in the region, particularly from the Mountain West states, it should be clear that these aren't voters likely to be swayed by anti-Bush and antiwar appeals.

The best news for Democrats, then, is that Bush is leaving the scene. Whether they're able to get over a sometimes near-pathological hatred of the president or not, they'll have to start talking about something else come 2008. Conversely, there couldn't be worse news for the Republicans: they're going to have to decide what direction their party is going to move; and if they continue moving in the direction they've been moving, it could have dire consequences out West.

Will they solidify their status as the party of big government? If so, it probably won't hurt them in the South, where most Republican voters have come to identify with the party primarily on cultural issues—and where low-income white women who want more government have been something of a growth industry as of late. But again, it's not as if the Republican Party could do much *better* in the South at this point; it's not really the ideal region to which to pander. While gaining very little in the South, they'll play right into the Democrats' hands in the West.

Will the Republican Party also continue to pander to its Religious Right base? Given the rate at which the GOP makes big promises to Christian conservatives during even-numbered years and then disappoints them during odd-numbered ones, the party's really going to have to amp it up in '08 to get Evangelicals energized. Last election it was gay-marriage initiatives in swing states. Who knows what they'll think of next? Whatever it is, though, it's sure to risk tipping the balance of the GOP too far toward the South and too far away from the West.

It's worth remembering, in that regard, that the Republican Party has already lost California, probably for the foreseeable future, at least in part because of the Republican Party's tilt South. The Sun Belt coalition that Nixon assembled, Reagan renewed, and George H. W. Bush coasted on in 1988 has never been put back together since Pat Buchanan declared a religious war at the 1992 convention in Houston. And ever since Pete Wilson's anti-immigrant gubernatorial campaign in 1994, California's Republican Party has been in shambles and in thrall to a Christian Right wing that will nominate only prolife candidates in an overwhelmingly prochoice state. Arnold Schwarzenegger provides what long-time California political strategist Dan Schnur calls a "pretty good template" for what a candidate—gubernatorial or presidential—needs to do to win in the Golden State. But Schnur admits at the same time that Arnold would have had trouble getting elected governor if he'd had to face off with the fundamentalists in a primary—as opposed to running against Gary Coleman and porn star Mary Carey in the free-for-all 2003 recall. Even with the gubernator on the job, it's not certain the state party is on its way to moderating anytime soon.

Other state Republican parties could share California's fate if they're not careful. In fact, Colorado's has already taken a step in that direction and paid the price. Republicans are largely seen to have lost control of both houses of the legislature in that state in 2004 because they'd spent the previous session on issues such as gay marriage, the Pledge of Allegiance, and the liberal biases of college professors, all while the state faced a monumental fiscal crisis. As the Republican minority leader in the Colorado House said after the 2004 election on NPR, "Our party has basically made the party platform guns, God, and gays, and that wasn't a winning message this election cycle when we should have been talking about jobs, the economy, and health care."

A number of prominent businesspeople, in particular, were motivated to spend big bucks by the lunacy of what was coming out of the legislature. Tim Gill, the founder of Quark, which makes desktop-publishing software, got mad after a bill was introduced to make it illegal to discuss homosexuality in Colorado schools outside the context of STDs. "Before this, I had always been interested in supporting people that were in favor of my views," Gill told NPR. "This year, for the first time, rather than just supporting people that were with me, I decided that we should also try to get rid of the people who had unreasonable views." Gill personally put $1 million into the effort.[13]

Immigration also stands ready to sink the GOP in the West. While control of the U.S. border with Mexico is of concern to many Americans—and has gained new urgency in the minds of some since 9/11—the politics of the issue are extremely tricky for a party with such a checkered racial history. Things are only complicated further for Republicans by the fact that Democrats in the West are moving swiftly to guard their right flank. The Democratic governors of New Mexico and Arizona have made headlines in the past year or so by declaring "border emergencies" in their states and dedicating money and manpower to the problem. "We've developed some immigration positions which I believe, at least in the West, will keep Democrats not just on the right side, but also a bit immune from the attacks from the Right," Governor Richardson said in an interview. Specifically, he points to the border-emergency declarations, calling for crackdowns on businesses employing illegal immigrants, greater cooperation with Mexican authorities, and supporting a guest-worker program. "We all sing this tune," Richardson said, referring to Democrats in the West.

Republicans, however, have very little incentive to push for a tougher crackdown on illegal immigration—at least if they are looking at the electoral map. If the issue gains any traction in the 2008 election, it will be as a pander to the South, not the West.

Voters in the South are far more anti-immigrant than voters in the West. To go back to the Pew numbers, while 44 percent of southerners think immigrants threaten traditional American customs and values, only 32 percent in the interior West think the same. Numbers from Survey USA show a similar pattern. In Alabama, 56 percent think immigrants "take jobs from Americans"; in New Mexico, where there's a "border emergency," only 33 percent think so. One could also look at the makeup of the Congressional Immigration Reform Caucus, chaired by nativist firebrand representative Tom Tancredo (R-Colo.); only eleven of its ninety-one members are from the Interior West, another seven are from the Pacific Coast, and a full fifty-one are from the South.[14] By tilting South on this issue, the GOP could set off a civil war, with small businesses, big business, and upper- and middle-class Republican voters—all of whom depend to some extent on cheap immigrant labor—doing battle with working-class whites, mostly in the South and Midwest. Wouldn't it be something to see local chambers of commerce lining up with Democrats across the West?

It's certainly something Dan Kemmis, of Democrats for the West, would like to see—just another piece of the puzzle out West, as Democrats try to fit together a philosophy that will make their party the natural home of immigrants, small-businessmen, itinerant workers from the coasts, telecommuters, ranchers, hunters, fishermen, and all those coming to the West with dreams of living the good life . . . and being left alone to live it as they see fit.

"This is definitely meant to be a long-term party-building effort," Kemmis said of his group. But the long term is starting today. For the 2006 campaign season there were plans to do regional polling and message development and perhaps even to design and run ads based on the results. Perhaps most importantly for 2008, Democrats for the West also was lobbying to set up a "western caucus," to be held simultaneously in as many of the interior western states as possible—an idea that's also been endorsed by the bipartisan Western Governors' Association—to draw more attention to the region during the presidential primaries. As of this writing, the Democratic National Committee had given the go-ahead to the possibility of a western or southern state holding a caucus between Iowa and New Hampshire. Arizona, Colorado, New Mexico, Alabama, Arkansas, Mississippi, and South Carolina were reported to be under consideration.[15]

Whether or not the DNC approves an early western caucus, however, there's widespread agreement among Democrats that Dean's party apparatus "gets" the opportunity out West. "They've certainly put staff out West to beef up these state parties," Democratic pollster Celinda Lake said. In fact, the Wyoming Democratic Party got a press secretary for the first time in 2005, along with a field director. New Mexico, meanwhile, has gotten four new DNC organizers, one dedicated primarily to the Native American vote. "In the West, you're seeing it in every state," said Luis Miranda, a DNC staffer. "We're not just looking at the West and throwing up our hands, we're actually fighting for it."

And if there's one last factor worth mentioning that makes the West an attractive target for the Democrats: it's a cheap date. Brian Kuehl, a spokesman for Democrats for the West, describes testifying before a DNC committee, urging them to set up a caucus in the region. "I showed them how cheap it is," Kuehl recalled. "You could see people, sort of, their jaws dropping . . . they're ridiculously inexpensive races." The governor's race in Wyoming: $700,000. The governor's race in Montana: $1 million. A House seat in Colorado: $1.5 million. With dispersed media markets, airtime is cheap, and candidate visits have a big impact. "If you go to Salt Lake City as a candidate, your media is covered all over Idaho, it's covered all over Wyoming, and it's up into Montana," Kuehl told the committee.

So as Democrats gear up for competitive Senate races in the West this year, looking to knock off Republicans such as Conrad Burns in Montana (who's been closely tied to disgraced lobbyist Jack Abramoff) and Jon Kyl in Arizona (who faces a serious challenge from real-estate developer and former Arizona Democratic Party chairman Jim Pederson), they'll also have their eyes on the long game—pulling at the fraying threads of the Republicans' strained conservative-libertarian coalition. "Those coalitions might continue to make sense in the South for a long time," Frontier PAC's Patton Price said, "but I think they've stopped making sense in the Mountain West already." The change could happen quickly, but it's more likely to happen in slow motion. "The decline of the party in the West happened over a decade or so, and we expect the rebuilding to take that long," Kemmis said. "But we want to rebuild in a way that will last several decades."

"In Montana, we have a libertarian streak that's a mile wide," Governor Brian Schweitzer said in an interview in mid-March, reached by phone at his office in Helena. "When it comes to government telling you what to do, we're just as likely to tell them to go straight to hell."

"We don't like government lookin' over our shoulder, we don't like'm sneaking around behind our houses, diggin' in our garbage, we don't like'm figurin' out what we read and where we've been . . . that's part of living in Montana," Schweitzer said. "At least in Montana, we represent the values of libertarians better than Republicans do."

Maybe.

The Bush administration has certainly opened the door for the Democrats to come in and make that case. But a Democratic image makeover won't be enough to sway the West. In the course of a twenty-minute interview, Schweitzer feels compelled to give a rundown of what he's wearing: "I'm dressed for the day, I'm wearing a pair of boots, cowboy boots, a pair of jeans, and I wear a bolo tie." The dog, the gun, the folksiness—there are only so many Democrats out West who can pull it off without the image descending into a patronizing shtick.

And beneath the surface are still a lot of the same old policies, dressed up in values-laden language. Schweitzer gives a rundown (unsolicited) of why Jesus would be a Democrat: "What would his platform be? Let's see, I think his platform would be, oh, yeah, it'd be universal health care. . . . It would be investment in quality public education. . . . I think that he'd be concerned about monopolies in the energy business, so that poor families couldn't afford the heat that they need for their homes. . . . You think he'd run as a Republican?"

Republicans make some stupid claims on behalf of the Almighty, but when Jesus has a position on monopolies in the energy business, we're past the point of parody.

Still, the battle is on in the West, and Democrats are making a play for the libertarians. They've appropriated the language of small government, lower taxes, balanced budgets, efficiency, privacy, responsibility, and a whole host of other come-ons designed to lure libertarians into at least a fling. With the situation at home looking like an episode of *Cops*, with the shirtless social conservatives wrestled to the ground and handcuffed outside the trailer, and the libertarians deciding whether to press charges, now is not the time for empty promises. Either Republicans can take the possibility of losing the West seriously, or they can be surprised when their better half walks out the door.

8

Return to CPAC

f these were George W. Bush's friends, it was really no wonder
about his enemies. The broadsides against the president started
almost immediately, as conservative commentator George Will
took the stage as the first speaker of CPAC 2006, at nine-thirty on
a February morning. Left behind was the Reagan Building;
CPACers found themselves back in the relatively cozy Omni Shore-
ham Hotel, the conference's more familiar digs. Just days short of
a year had passed since the Swift Boat Veterans for Truth were subjected to interminable standing ovations, since God was barraged
with unceasing thanks for the return of the Republican president to
the White House and the Republican Congress to Capitol Hill, and
since Karl "The Architect" Rove outlined his plans for the conservatives' new, permanent majority. The mood was less ebullient
now—it could scarcely have been *more* ebullient, of course—and
doubt had begun to set in. After an extremely rough 2005 (the
Katrina debacle, the Miers misstep, Iraq, etc.), a question, or really
a series of questions, was beginning to emerge: What have five

years of Bush-style conservatism gotten us? What *is* Bush-style conservatism, anyway? And does *anyone* want to carry its mantle in 2008?

Will kicked things off by blasting Bush and the Republican Congress for soaring spending, federal intrusion into local schoolhouses, farm subsidies, the Medicare prescription-drug bill, and believing that the U.S. government could "run the Middle East with more skill and dexterity than it can run Amtrak." He blamed the American people, however, as much as (if not more than) the president; they suffered from "cognitive dissonance," as Will put it, "a genteel mental illness" that allows voters to tell pollsters that they hate Washington but simultaneously that they love Social Security, Medicare, Medicaid, and much else that emanates from that fetid swamp.

Will was followed not long after by Representative Tom Tancredo (R-Colo.), whose fondness for walls is well known to rival that of the Ming Dynasty. Though Tancredo's disagreements with the Bush administration on immigration policy garner the most attention in the press, he also laid into the president more generally. "American conservatives have watched dumbfounded as the Congress, their Republican Congress, and the Republican White House, engineered the largest expansion of the federal government in modern history," Tancredo said. "We are not the party of bigger government, and we should prove it by admitting our mistake and repealing the prescription-drug program." For good measure, he also suggested that No Child Left Behind be repealed. Last but not least, he took dead aim at compassionate conservatism: "We should always remember that our party doesn't define compassion by the number of people dependent on government programs."

And this was all before the three-day conference's first hour was out.

Make no mistake. This was, of course, an audience firmly and profoundly sympathetic toward, and admiring of, George W. Bush and his administration. Dick Cheney's annual visit on the first night of the conference just about brought the house down—especially his teasing declaration that "a reception like that almost makes me want to run for office again . . . almost." (Less than forty-eight hours later the vice president would spray a poor old man in the face with birdshot while out quail hunting, perhaps putting a little more emphasis behind that second *almost*.)

But when Virginia's senator George Allen—presumed presidential candidate extraordinaire—took the stage as the dinner speaker that first evening, the dilemma for the GOP's 2008 primary field became clear. As the crowd recovered from a cringe-inducing song about the Pledge of Allegiance, sung live by Pat Boone (sample: "They came to Philadelphia, Our forefathers newly free, To draft a Constitution, But they couldn't quite agree . . ."), Allen attempted a high-wire act. Republicans, particularly of the conservative variety, like to run against Washington; but how can a Republican run against Washington now that Republicans *are* Washington?

Allen tied Bush's quest for democracy in the Middle East to Reagan's winning the Cold War. He called for staying the course in Iraq. He called for a reduction in America's dependence on foreign oil. He called for improvements to the public-education system (out on a real limb there). But when he turned to the issue of spending and the size of government toward the end of his speech, it was almost surreal. "We need to remember that we have a deficit not because we have a revenue problem, but because the federal government has a spending problem," he said. "Government doesn't tax too little, it spends too much."

But just who was spending too much? Perhaps the boss of the man who'd spoken just minutes before Allen, a president who'd refused to veto a single spending bill (or any other bill, for that matter) in five years; or perhaps the Republican majority in Congress, of which Allen had been a member since 2001 (he'd voted *for* NCLB, the Medicare prescription-drug bill, and the 2005 highway bill, all big contributors to the spending problem).

And Allen's solution to the spending problem? Cut the size and scope of government? Nope. He proposed that "we need to spend smarter and learn to do more with less." *More with less* has long been the battle cry of budget-cutting technocrats, such as New York City's barely-a-Republican mayor/monarch Michael

Bloomberg, but it's hardly the stuff conservative dreams are made of. A real Republican should want the government to do *less* with less.

The problem is that there are hardly any real Republicans left.

The Big Picture on Big-Government Conservatism

As Republicans have taken over Washington, they've internalized what Will was saying: that the American people will forever say one thing and do another. They will say they want lower taxes and smaller government, but they will punish the Republican Party if the giveaways it offers are any less generous than those offered by the Democrats; they will say they're against pork and waste, but they'll send their congressman packing if he doesn't bring home that bridge, highway, or stamp-collecting museum to boost the local economy; and they'll say individuals should be self-sufficient, but recoil in horror the second the state allows one human need or desire to go unfulfilled.

It's no wonder Republicans have come to accept without question that there's no constituency for small government. The mistakes of the Gingrich years made them gun-shy, even though the setbacks during those years had more to do with the personalities and political skills at the head of each party than the underlying argument over the role of government. And the political triumphs of the Bush years have led them to believe that there's much to be gained by simply acquiescing to an ever-expanding welfare state, even though the War on Terror has been the key to every Republican political triumph since September 11, 2001. It was not by accident that between 1995 and 2005, Republicans dropped Reagan's axiom that "government is not the solution to our problem, government *is* the problem," and picked up Bush's axiom that "when somebody hurts, government has got to move."[1]

This departure from small government is, however, no small shift for the Republican Party or for the conservative movement. Most conservative voters did not sign up in 2000 for a wholesale abandonment of their long-held principles, even if close listeners to

Bush's rhetoric in that campaign might have detected cause for concern. The Republican base was, as Grover Norquist put it, a "leave-me-alone coalition." That coalition stuck by Bush in 2002 and 2004, but its patience isn't endless.

Four months after musing in the Capitol dining room as to whether the Republican Party could right itself with conservatives, Mike Pence arrived at CPAC as the first speaker on its third and final day in a dour mood. Gone was the note of optimism with which he had addressed the gathering in 2004, and which he had maintained well into the fall of 2005, full of hope that the GOP could return to its roots. Instead, he shocked the hung-over crowd awake at 8:30 A.M. on a Saturday with a fierce declaration of despondence. (Friday night had seen a surprise visit from, and a standing ovation for, Tom DeLay—"I'm not going anywhere!"— along with all other manner of debauchery among the young CPACers, so these folks were groggy.) "Two years ago, when I presented the keynote speech here at CPAC 2004, I likened the state of the Republican movement to a tall ship at sea, a ship that had drifted off-course from essential conservative principles," Pence recalled. "I said we had lost our way, but I believed we could get back on course. . . . I no longer believe that.

"It's one thing to drift off course," he said. "It's quite another thing to continue on that course when half the crew and passengers are pointing out that nothing looks familiar, not to mention the tens of millions of Americans lining the shoreline yelling, 'You're going the wrong way!' . . . In a word, we're no longer adrift. We might've been when we started, but now 'off course' is the accepted course." Pence blasted Bush for calling for more spending, and he blasted his congressional colleagues for heeding Bush's call—and giving him twice what he'd requested, for good measure. He had reason to be angry. His Operation Offset in the aftermath of Katrina had met with stiff resistance from the Republican majority and resulted in only trifling cuts. House leadership elections just days earlier had placed a nominal reformer, Representative John Boehner (R-Ohio), in the majority-leader spot vacated by DeLay, but Pence had endorsed a more radical reformer, Representative

John Shadegg (R-Ariz.), in that contest. All in all, it looked increasingly obvious that the GOP would make the most minimal changes possible going into the 2006 midterm elections.

"Whether it's called 'compassionate conservatism' or 'big-government Republicanism,' after years of record increases in federal spending, more government is now the accepted Republican philosophy in Washington," Pence said. "For the sake of our party and for the sake of the nation we must say, here and now, to all who would lead us in this new century, 'the era of big Republican government is over!'"

To many, of course, Pence is a dinosaur—a throwback to the Gingrich era of the Republican Party, harping on deficits and serving as the nation's fiscal scold. And, in fact, both Gingrich and Dick Armey are quite fond of Pence; Gingrich calls him "the closest thing we've seen to the emergence of the next generation of conservative leader," and Armey offers regular advice to Pence's Republican Study Committee. The current leadership of the Republican Party might want to start asking themselves why, instead of making him an outcast, his invocation of an earlier era has made him the rising star of the conservative movement. The key may well lie in a passage Pence quoted from a 1975 speech, given by Ronald Reagan at CPAC: "A political party cannot be all things to all people. It must represent certain fundamental beliefs which must not be compromised to political expediency, or simply to swell its numbers."

All things to all people is practically the five-word definition of the Bush-Rove governing style. But that governing style has never been developed into anything even approaching a governing philosophy. Pence and those who believe like him are told over and over again that the old conservatism is dead, that arguments about the size of government can never be won, and that the scope of the state can never do anything but expand. At the same time, however, "big-government conservatism"—the de facto philosophy of the White House and the congressional leadership and the explicit philosophy of longtime enemies of limited government, such as the folks at the *Weekly Standard*—has proven an abject failure as a way of going about making policy.

While these conservatives arrogantly believe they have harnessed big government, in reality it has harnessed them. The notion that it's possible to reduce the demand for government without ever reducing the supply (i.e., making people less dependent on government through offering them a wider variety of government benefits) has so far proven a farce and in the long run may well prove a tragedy. The idea, of course, was sheer nonsense on stilts from the start—a clumsy metaphor, utterly incoherent even on its own terms. Seldom does increasing the supply of something reduce the demand for it; rather, it simply makes the good in question more readily available to more "customers."

After five years of Bush, this fundamental problem with big-government conservatism isn't theory, it's fact. Demand for government services certainly hasn't shown any signs of cooling down; in fact, it's heating up. An analysis published in *USA Today* in March 2006 found that federal entitlement spending had grown more between 2000 and 2005 than in any other five-year period since the Great Society. The paper found that enrollment in twenty-five major government programs (such as Medicaid, food stamps, unemployment benefits, Pell grants) increased 17 percent in those years, while the nation's population grew only 5 percent—and while, it should be noted, the economy was fairly strong and unemployment extremely low. "Congress has expanded eligibility for programs in ways that attracted little attention but added greatly to the scope and cost of programs," the paper wrote. Spending on the programs was up 22 percent, adjusted for inflation, and three-quarters of that explosion was fueled by enrollment growth. What's more, the effects of the Medicare prescription-drug program hadn't yet begun to be felt—those were set to wreak havoc in the next five years, about the same time Social Security costs will head for the stratosphere. The only bright spot: welfare rolls had *fallen* 18 percent (a carryover from those awful, awful Gingrich years).[2]

Instead of reshaping government in their own image, today's conservatives are relearning a lesson that wouldn't have been lost on their intellectual forebears. Namely, they're learning that big, interventionist government is inherently corrupt and corrupting. By its very nature it is unconservative. As Peggy Noonan put it in a column at the beginning of 2006, it is a steamroller, rolling over "traditions, shared beliefs, individual rights, old assumptions" and all else that's dear to conservative hearts. "If the problem with government is that it is run by people and not, as James Madison put it, angels," she wrote, "the problem with big government is that it is run by a *lot* of people who are not angels."[3] And the number of those people has just kept growing under Republican rule. According to a column by John Fund, in 2004, a total of 3,521 companies or local governments hired lobbyists to pursue earmarks, up from just 1,865 four years earlier.[4] Matthew Continetti of the *Weekly Standard* pegs the total number of lobbyists to have grown from some 9,000 when the GOP took over Congress in 1994 to more than 34,000 today.[5]

Lobbyists are a class protected by the Constitution as surely as journalists and clergymen (the First Amendment enshrines the right "to petition the Government" along with the freedoms of religion, speech, and the press), but that doesn't mean their integration into the Republican Party machine in Washington, D.C., is something to celebrate. Instead of using lobbyists and the influence to which they have access as a means to an end—perpetuating Republican rule so the party can cut taxes, roll back the size of government, and enhance individual freedom—the GOP has allowed the means to become the end. Using the machinery of government to do favors for lobbyists is now the closest thing Republican politicians have to a reason for getting up in the morning—to keep the wine flowing, the campaign cash rolling in, and the conveyor belt that runs from Capitol Hill to K Street well lubricated. Even for the best-intentioned Republican politicians, life has come to be defined by Dick Armey's famously clumsy but accurate saying: "We come to this town and we do things we ought not to be doing in order to stay in the majority so we can do things we ought to be doing that we never get around to doing."

All the while, the social conservatives who make up an indispensable part of the God-and-government coalition that makes big-government conservatism possible (after all, without them we're just talking about "big government," and Democrats are better at that) are growing increasingly uneasy. At CPAC to promote his new book *America: The Last Best Hope*, Reagan-era education secretary and talk-radio host William Bennett stopped to answer questions about the current state of the conservative movement. Social conservatives have become "entirely too comfortable" with the idea of wielding the government's power toward their own ends, he said. "I'm not a libertarian. I'm with Hamilton, strong government, but limited government, limited to the objects which government should do, people can't do for themselves and so on . . . but things have gotten entirely out of hand." That's not to say that even most social conservatives have turned against the idea of trying to bend government to their own ends. But at the very least, prominent voices such as Bennett and Paul Weyrich are beginning to sound serious doubts.

It remains to be seen whether social conservatives remain susceptible to blatant button-pushing by the national Republican Party. Any time the GOP finds itself in trouble, its strategists cynically trot out a stable of tired old warhorses: gay marriage, the Pledge of Allegiance, flag burning, school prayer, human cloning. It's worked brilliantly in the past, but values voters have grown tired of, as James Dobson put it, the GOP wanting their votes every two years and then saying, "Don't call us, we'll call you." The Republican straddle works by promising to do big things for values voters—writing a ban on gay marriage into the Constitution, writing a right to prayer in school into the Constitution, scrubbing sex and violence from the airwaves, banning abortion—but never actually *doing* those things, for fear of inviting a massive backlash from moderates. This balancing act can take the Republican Party only so far. With the GOP thoroughly in control of every branch of the government, it is running out of excuses to give its friends on the Religious Right.

And so it seems increasingly clear that Bush conservatism is a dead end. Five years of nearly unitary Republican government, agnostic as to the size of the state and powered by the muscle of the

Evangelical Right, have yielded essentially nothing in terms of truly conservative policy. Tax rates are down, but out-of-control spending and a looming entitlement crisis guarantee huge tax increases in the near future. Local schools are now "held accountable" to the federal government (a dubiously conservative achievement in its own right), but that accountability is a sham. Medicare has had planted in it the seeds of reform, but at a tremendous price and at great risk should a Democratic administration come in and tear them up before they grow roots. Social Security remains untouched, and the Bush administration's inept handling of the issue may well have set back free-market reform another decade. The administration's lone achievement in domestic policy may end up being a Supreme Court leaning a few clicks further to the Right—nothing to sneeze at certainly, but hardly a record of accomplishment.

Perhaps most telling, there does not seem to be at this early date a single prospective Republican presidential candidate looking to run on the success of Bush's domestic policies. On foreign policy, most conservatives—regardless of their particular feelings as to how the Iraq war has been handled—believe that Bush has gotten the big picture right, that America has to confront terror-sponsoring regimes aggressively. But on domestic policy, everyone wants to be the heir to Reagan; no one wants to be the heir to Bush.

The reason is rather simple: just as big-government conservatism doesn't work as policy, it falls short as politics as well. Essentially it eschews the old fusionist formulation that has served the conservative movement so well since the start. Instead of allowing the GOP's factions to unite around the concept of limited government, as they have for fifty-odd years, it offers social conservatives little more than the false promise that Washington, D.C., can restore the moral health of the nation, and it offers libertarians . . . precisely nothing. While this may be sustainable in the near term, whether because of the immediacy of the War on Terror or on account of the incompetence of the leadership of the Democratic Party, in the long term continuing down the path of big-government conservatism can only lead to fissure.

A Renewed Fusionism

How, then, can the Republican Party solidify its traditional alliance between social conservatives and libertarians—between, essentially, the South and the West? And how can it pull off this trick without abandoning its strategy of reaching out to socially conservative minorities—a strategy that's particularly crucial in midwestern states such as Ohio? The answer, by and large, is that the conservative marriage *can be saved*, but it will require something like a renewal of vows, a renewal of the fusionism described long ago by Frank Meyer: a recognition that a limited federal government serves the interests of libertarians and social conservatives alike; a recognition that libertarian means still ultimately serve traditionalist ends. But the old formula will need a little tweaking. The pieces don't fit together quite the way they used to. The world has changed. The Cold War is gone. The New Deal is here to stay.

Bush-style, big-government conservatism has attempted to deal with these new realities in two ways, neither of which works very well. First, it has tried to substitute the War on Terror for the Cold War as the centripetal force that will hold together conservatism's competing factions. It's not a one-for-one trade. And second, it has mangled the old fusionist formula, declaring that *big government* can be made to serve *conservative* ends—where conservatism is defined merely as the worship of comfortable notions such as "traditional" family, personal safety, and middle-class financial security, rather than as the principled defense of every American's God-given rights to life, liberty, property, and the pursuit of happiness. This mess needs badly to be untangled.

A turn away from Bush conservatism wouldn't mean a retreat in the War on Terror; nothing could be more counterproductive politically or to America's national-security interests. Nor would it mean on domestic policy a return to the political tone deafness of the Gingrich-Dole years, during which a gloomy and angry conservatism accomplished quite a bit in terms of reforming and reining in government but turned off the American electorate in the process.

Instead, a renewed fusionism would simply mean restoring some balance to the conservative equation: between South and West, between security and freedom, and between political expediency and political principle. An optimistic, fusionist conservatism would revive the best traditions of Ronald Reagan and update them with the most important insights behind the Ownership Society. While renewing the Republican Party's faith in the ability of individuals to make decisions for themselves and its skepticism of bureaucrats' better angels, it would recognize that the New Deal can never be rolled back, but only transcended by a new vision of how individuals should relate to their government. Instead of merely paying lip service to choice in education and health care and retirement while consistently selling out real change in favor of an easier ride in the next election, it would stand firm for real change.

Along those lines, then, outlined below is a minuscule sampling of areas where the Republican Party could shift its policies—or even just its emphases, in some cases—to bridge the gap between social conservatives and libertarians, and to further build bridges to Hispanics and African Americans who have already proven responsive to elements of a fusionist GOP message.

Preserving Freedom *and* Security   "So long as terrorism is a serious threat, it will remain the tie that binds Republicans," writes Fred Barnes.[6] That, to put it mildly, seems doubtful. There's no pro-terrorism party in America (despite what the Republican National Committee might have us believe), but there are deep divisions as to how to fight terrorism, and they cut across party lines. Within the ranks of conservative-movement leaders, William F. Buckley Jr. and Pat Buchanan have said that the Iraq war was a mistake. Dick Armey, in his interview for this book, called it "Bush's adventure in Iraq," and said the war was draining resources from fighting terrorism elsewhere. Conservative columnist George Will has said, in a wonderful turn of phrase, that "nation building" makes as much sense as "orchid building." And on the civil-liberties front, former Georgia congressman Bob Barr, who has even been called an

"ultraconservative" on occasion (with some justification), has carried on a one-man war against the Patriot Act and other attempts
by the Bush administration to increase the president's power to spy
on citizens without any sort of judicial or congressional oversight.

The War on Terror "hasn't had the kind of unifying effect as
much as the late Cold War did," according to conservative movement historian George Nash. For a time after 9/11 it helped to hold
the conservative coalition together, he said, but "it doesn't work
entirely." There's not as much agreement on how to fight the war
as there was during the standoff with the Soviet Union, and there's
far greater concern about war against a stateless enemy becoming
a permanent condition. "The libertarians are uneasy to say the least
. . . it would make anyone with libertarian concerns somewhat
anxious," Nash said, and that includes plenty of people who would
never call themselves libertarians.

The prudence of the war in Iraq and potential future conflicts
with Iran, Syria, North Korea, or other hostile regimes are beyond
the scope of this discussion. But what the Republican Party can do
to make the domestic side of the War on Terror more palatable to
libertarian-minded voters is begin showing at least, say, a passing
concern with upholding the Bill of Rights and protecting American
citizens from warantless wiretapping and other forms of domestic
spying. One way to start might be for Congress to conduct some
actual oversight of the Bush administration—something that
should become increasingly attractive to congressional Republicans
as the outgoing president's power wanes and their concern for their
own political futures waxes.

For instance, in February of 2006, Attorney General Alberto
Gonzales testified before the Senate Judiciary Committee about the
Bush administration's five-year-old secret electronic surveillance
program, but Chairman Arlen Specter (R-Pa.) refused to place him
under oath. In the future, perhaps, key administration officials
could be asked to raise their right hands when giving testimony
about issues of fundamental constitutional importance. Republicans might also sign on to curbs on the Patriot Act, not least of

which should include removing from it all nonterrorism-related provisions, such as those that have been inserted related to meth and cigarette smuggling.

A greater emphasis on civil liberties in the War on Terror would be virtually free of political risk for the Republican Party; the Democrats are thoroughly unlikely to outflank the GOP on the right after five-plus years of complaining about the Patriot Act's excesses. What's more, a concern for limiting the power of the executive branch—which Republicans might do well to remember can be held by members of either party (even by those with the last name Clinton)—is more than in line with the fears of both libertarians and social conservatives of the feds having too much power to snoop and pry into private citizens' personal affairs.

School Choice   Name a controversial issue that pits the Republican Party's deep commitment to family and religious values against the Democratic Party's captivity to single-issue special-interest groups. It's not gay marriage. While the GOP's gains among African Americans in 2004 were widely credited to Bush's support for an anti-gay-marriage amendment to the Constitution and similar initiatives on the ballots in eleven states, there's little reason to buy that story line. Meanwhile, Republicans have been forging meaningful ties to the black community for more than a decade in the fight to give low-income parents—primarily black and Hispanic—a greater say in where their children go to school.

Bush jumped from 9 percent of the black vote to 16 percent in Ohio between 2000 and 2004. Some, such as Ohio secretary of state Kenneth Blackwell, credit the anti-gay-marriage amendment that was on the ballot in that state with boosting Republican turnout and showing African American voters that the GOP was on their side on cultural issues. However, there are a few holes in that story. First of all, turnout in battleground states with gay-marriage initiatives in 2004 actually went up slightly less than turnout in battleground states without such initiatives, according to an analysis by Lake Research Partners. What's more, Bush's share of the black vote was up by roughly the same amount in Florida and California, states without initiatives; meanwhile, his share of the black vote dropped 6 points in Arkansas, a state with a gay-marriage initiative. Essentially, then, there was no meaningful correlation between gay marriage and Bush's share of the black vote, which was up only 2 percent nationally.

Why is all this important? Because if gay marriage is at best a negligible factor in the GOP's outreach to minorities, and if perhaps it didn't bring all that many more Evangelicals out to the polls regardless of race, then the Republican Party's energies would be better spent elsewhere.

Public-opinion polling is tricky on school choice—the public generally has a somewhat shaky idea of how programs such as private-school vouchers and public charter schools work—but African Americans are typically found to have high levels of support for vouchers and charters, especially in states and cities where programs are up and running. And it has often been African American politicians who have taken the lead in establishing these programs, forced to fight the Democratic Party establishment and the teachers' unions every step of the way.

Even Blackwell, who places so much stock in the effect gay marriage had in 2004, is a big believer in the political power of choice. He should be, having seen how it has taken hold in Cleveland, Ohio, home to one of the first voucher programs in the nation. "African American voters in Ohio have become accustomed to voting for Republicans if they address their issues," Blackwell said, issues such as "wanting to get their kids out of dysfunctional schools."

For all the shortcomings in his education policy, Bush at least convinced minority parents that he and the Republican Party cared. "He did something with NCLB that even traditional public school supporters had to at least come away saying, this guy's serious about it," Blackwell said. "At least he was saying, look, these children matter. We take their tax money, and we're gonna say these kids are educable, and we're going to educate them, and we're going to measure it."

Now all Bush, or more likely his successor, needs to do is turn

NCLB into a serious vehicle for promoting school choice. One way to do it would be simply to enforce the law—to threaten districts that don't offer choice to their students in failing schools with losing their federal education dollars. Another way would be to go back to the original proposal that Bush threw out in 2001 at the first objection from Ted Kennedy: turn each kid's share of federal money into a voucher, worth $1,500 or more, that parents could take to any private school (religious or secular) they want.

The politics of the issue are practically designed to wreak havoc on the Democratic coalition. In states such as New York, where charter schools are serving primarily minority populations and turning kids' scores (and lives) around 180 degrees, Democrats representing black and Hispanic parents have had to break ranks with their state and national party. Rarely, however, have they been able to prevail upon the leaders of their party to buck the teachers' unions. The supposed champions of these voters end up selling their poor constituents out time and time again. The loyalty of these voters is up for grabs, in the Midwest, in the West, in the South, even in the Northeast—anywhere schools are failing. It's time to grab it.

Cultural Federalism   All in the same election, Montana reelected Bush by a 20-point margin, elected a Democratic governor by a 4-point margin, defined marriage in the state as between one man and one woman with 66 percent of the vote, and legalized marijuana for medical purposes with 61 percent of the vote. States can be quirky when it comes to cultural issues. That's why both Republicans and Democrats should come around to a much greater appreciation of what might be called cultural federalism.

Both the Clinton and Bush White Houses have gone after doctors and patients and growers in states that have legalized the possession of small amounts of marijuana for medical use. Just why, however, should the Republican Party not be the one to seize the mantle of compassion (it's Bush's word, after all, isn't it?) and give states the freedom to regulate this relatively minor medical matter as they see fit? The beneficiaries would be cancer and glaucoma and AIDS patients who know what the drug does to ease their suffering. Those harmed would be—well, no one. What's more, politically there should be few consequences outside of the states that have voted to change their own laws. What happens in Montana, Nevada, and Colorado *stays* in Montana, Nevada, and Colorado. States in the South and the Midwest that don't want some damned hippie cancer patient smoking a joint don't have to put up with it. In other states, however, the GOP could move one significant step back toward being the party of live and let live.

And speaking of live and let live, the Republican Party could also move toward such an approach on gay marriage and civil unions. The younger the person polled, the more likely he or she is to support legal protection for gay couples; even a significant number of the kids at CPAC take a libertarian view of the issue, supporting civil unions as a reasonable compromise between two extremes. Some form of this or another is coming to the United States. The Republican Party can certainly oppose states being forced to recognize gay marriages from other states (that's what the Defense of Marriage Act that Bill Clinton signed does), but they will only look like overbearing bigots if they try to pass a constitutional amendment that would invalidate marriages from Massachusetts or civil unions from a state such as Connecticut, which in 2005 became the first to ratify such an arrangement sheerly through the popular will expressed in its legislature (no activist judges to blame in the Nutmeg State).

As contentious social issues split the nation, this cultural federalism approach will only become more useful. The Supreme Court has upheld Oregon's right to allow physician-assisted suicide. When the federal government severely restricted its funding of stem-cell research, California passed Proposition 71, a $3 billion bond issue to establish and fund the California Institute for Regenerative Medicine. Red and Blue states can have Red and Blue social policies. As the party that's supposed to value states' rights and the virtues of local government over federal heavy-handedness, the

Republicans should take every opportunity to let this approach flourish. Let the South be the South, the Northeast the Northeast, the Midwest the Midwest, and the West the West.

Breakfast with Newt

The last stop for this correspondent, after a year of meetings and conferences and telephone interviews and correspondence with conservative luminaries of all stripes in search of answers about the past, present, and future of the Republican Party, was the Hyatt Regency Crystal City in Virginia in early March 2006. There, over an hour-long breakfast, the man perhaps more responsible than any other for the Republicans' domination of Washington today sketched out his vision of where the party has been, where it is, and where it is going.

Newt Gingrich—or, as conservative crowds like to call him, "Newt! Newt! Newt!"—had given the closing address at CPAC less than a month before, bounding onto the stage to the strains of a Mighty Mighty Bosstones song and to thunderous applause from the faithful. At the time, he offered up a fairly quick overview of why, as he put it, "conservatism is at a crossroads." In short: government is still too big, government is still too bureaucratic, and the Republican Party still hasn't faced up to globalization, longer life expectancies that will wreak havoc with entitlement programs, and the full implications of the War on Terror.

It was a mouthful, but for Gingrich it was barely even a warm-up. Now he would get to really hold forth.

Two things should be noted up front. First, this is a man who is running for president. "I don't know yet, I'll decide in 2007," is his answer when asked the big question, but he's clearly testing the waters, trying out a platform, and making all the regular rounds. One of his most common targets in speeches and interviews is also suspiciously convenient: the McCain-Feingold campaign-finance-reform legislation signed by Bush in 2002, a signature achievement of another Republican with his eye on a prominent piece of Washington real estate coming on the market in 2008. Second, and crucially, out of all the potential Republican contenders, it is Gingrich who is coming closest not just to running away from Bush but to actually running *against* Bush.

The signs were subtle at CPAC. There was, as is common to many Republicans today, the implicit criticism that if the government is still too big, *somebody* must be to blame. There was also in his speech the derisive reference to "Brownie" and the incompetence of the federal response to Katrina. And last but perhaps not least, there were the Newt-bots out promoting Gingrich's speech for the conference's three days. Along with bright red shirts promoting the title of Newt's book *Winning the Future*, many wore stickers: "Let's begin to win . . . again." If conservatives weren't winning, they must be doing something else. Like losing. And, again, somebody must be to blame.

It was time to find out what exactly Newt! Newt! Newt! was driving at.

"I'm uninterested in who's to blame. I'll let you worry about that," Gingrich said at the outset. But as the interview wore on, and as he was pressed on the issue, the former Speaker's assessment of the man who has occupied the White House and led the Republican Party for the past five years, as well as his assessment of the current congressional leadership, grew increasingly harsh.

"I think the Republican brand is in trouble," Gingrich said. "The party is confused as to its identity . . . and I don't see a very large market for a pro-pork, centrist Republican Party." Republicans in Congress, he said, have come to be "dominated by their incumbency," and no one has had the vision to see that the GOP has "a huge interest in everybody under forty," whether the issue is Social Security privatization, health-savings accounts, home ownership, or making it easier to own a business. Reagan had brought the conservative revolution to Washington. Bush the elder had let it stall. The Gingrich Congress had regained momentum. But now: "You're caught in a muddle that is one part incumbentitis, one part lacking an understanding of venture investment in politics, and one part intellectual shallowness.

"The real breakthroughs we need require a level of intellectual depth that is not one of the strengths of the Republican Party," Gingrich said. And that the GOP hasn't made those breakthroughs is "the collective leadership of the party's fault." And the stakes, Gingrich said, are high even in the short term. "I'm very blunt about the fact that I think this party's in severe danger of losing both the White House and the Congress." If the midterms were held tomorrow morning, he said, "I think we would probably lose seats in the Senate but retain control by a narrow margin, and we could lose the House."

And where has the GOP failed to make breakthroughs? In pretty much every area the president has ever touched.

On health care? "The president's saying the right words," Gingrich said, but he should be working to voucherize Medicaid and open up more choice in Medicare.

On education? "They keep trying to find a way to improve the failure as opposed to finding a way to invent the alternative," Gingrich said. As for NCLB, the president's signature education reform: "The jury's out." But to the extent that school districts aren't facing real consequences, he said, "the program's a failure . . . if the only purpose of testing is to incentivize states to produce new kinds of tests at which they cheat, which is what's happened."

On terrorism? Here Gingrich is quick to say that Bush's decisions have been "profoundly correct" since 9/11. But he's also not shy about criticizing the administration's failure to win the information war. "Nobody's gotten up and said the Danish cartoon offensive is a major military defeat for the United States," Gingrich said, referring to the orchestrated outrage over a series of cartoons in a Danish newspaper that sparked riots across the Muslim world. Our intelligence was so poor that we didn't see it coming, he said, and the administration still doesn't realize how big a defeat it was.

But for all these discrete criticisms, it's Gingrich's assessment of the overall problem with the Bush administration where things get really interesting—and where Gingrich's case for his own presidency begins to emerge. Asked how far Bush has brought Republicans toward being a "governing party" as opposed to an opposition party, his response is harsh and to the point: "Not very." Why? "It's because the most important characteristic of a governing party is that you set the agenda and you win the argument. . . . If you can't win the argument, you can't sustain the agenda. And if you're not setting the agenda, then random chance and your opponents are setting the agenda."

"I have a very mixed emotion about the Bush presidency," Gingrich said. "I think the president, on almost every big decision, has been essentially right. . . . He has really had the moral courage to rise to some huge decisions." But there's a but. A big one. "He has not had the drive and the understanding to force the level of change those decisions imply," Gingrich said. "I think his big decisions are right, but I think his ability to understand how difficult and how complicated follow-through is is a major limitation."

The Republican Party lacks "intellectual depth"? The president can't "win the argument"? The president lacks "drive" and "understanding," which limits his effectiveness? It all comes dangerously close to an assertion that Bush & Company aren't up to the job intelligencewise, or at least that they're too intellectually lazy to govern. And it leads to a surprising rationale for a Gingrich candidacy.

"We're looking for a next cycle of intellectual politics," Gingrich said, in the tradition of Lincoln, Teddy Roosevelt, and Ronald Reagan. "I don't mean this in an abstract, French-university sense," he said. "I mean this in the sense of what are the key ideas that underpin where we are going, and how do we make them understandable to the average person, and how do we make them popular? . . . That's the heart of where we have to go to in the next phase." Gingrich doesn't mention himself as the standard-bearer for this conservative intellectual revival, but if there's one thing the former Speaker has always fancied himself, not without some justification, it's as an ideas man and a visionary.

As for predictions about the future, beyond the 2006 midterms, Gingrich thinks Senator John McCain looks strong, though he takes what might be interpreted as a dig, comparing him to Bob Dole. "He is sort of where Dole was in '95," Gingrich said. "The Republican Party often gets a sense of exhausted acceptance and decides, oh, yeah, you've earned it." He also sees a chance for a conservative revival in Congress, though he admits it will take a post-Gingrich generation, not shell-shocked by perceived losses in the 1990s (he's still perplexed why winning on welfare reform, tax cuts, and balancing the budget counts as losing), to mount it. He also sees Democrats in the West as competitive, though he questions "How does the party of Vermont and San Francisco reach out over time?"

Above all, however, he sees the coming years as a major time of transition for the Republican Party, one that will require a period of intellectual openness and debate that has been missing for a long time. "Republicans ought to be having loud, noisy arguments right now," Gingrich said.

It seems unlikely he'll be disappointed.

Gingrich is certainly right about one thing: the Republican Party hasn't been doing enough thinking lately. There's an elephant in the room, and conservatives are only now beginning to muster up the will and the courage to talk about it and to start dealing with it. The current leadership of the Republican Party has betrayed the spirit of the conservative revolution of 1964, 1980, and 1994. Up to now, the problem has been papered over, one election after another. No one has wanted to rock the boat. No one has wanted to risk drawing too much attention to a problem that could rend the conservative coalition in two.

But problems like this don't go away on their own—not in a movement that has long been committed more to principle than to winning at any cost, and not in a family whose method of dealing with conflict has always been to throw dishes, not to throw in the towel. Libertarians and social conservatives belong in the same party, but only if it's a party with reverence for the ideal of limited government. Big-government conservatism, the conservatism Bush has brought us, might be something—but it's not conservative in any way, shape, or form. Conservatism, from its earliest days, has always meant a fusion between liberty and tradition, freedom and responsibility. To dismantle the edifice built by Buckley and

Meyer and Goldwater and Reagan and to replace it with one built by Bush and Rove and DeLay and Santorum is to replace the authentic with the inauthentic, the noble with the misguided and opportunistic.

At the very end of CPAC 2006, after Newt! Newt! Newt! had left the building and most of the crowd was heading for the doors, the results of the annual CPAC straw poll (it's mostly the younger CPACers who participate) were presented to those still paying attention. George Allen was in the lead of the presidential poll, with 22 percent, followed by McCain at 20 percent and Giuliani at 12 percent. Bush's approval numbers were good on the War on Terror, judges, taxes, and Social Security; they were poor on cutting spending, cutting the size of government, and stopping illegal immigration.

Most interesting, however, was a question where respondents were asked what was more important to them: promoting individual freedom or traditional values. Fifty-one percent took the freedom position, 45 percent chose values. It was pretty much the mirror image of the results CPAC pollster Tony Fabrizio gets when he polls Republicans nationally; values have been winning in recent polls by a healthy margin. The gap tells us something important. While a fusionist Republican Party will see some conservatives emphasize freedom and some emphasize values, there has to be a balance. If the Republican Party tilts too far toward values, it risks losing not just moderates, but also its own youth. And when they become disaffected, the party risks, as Newt might say, losing the future.

The Republican Party has been heading in the wrong direction for a long time. Toward big government and away from small government. Toward politics and away from principle. Toward the South and away from the West. Toward moralism and away from morality.

It's not too late to turn back. But time is growing short.

Acknowledgments

I would like to thank the Academy . . .

Any book, though attributed to one author, is inevitably the product of a collaborative process. With that in mind, I'd like to briefly mention those who had a hand in this one.

My agent, Eric Lupfer at the William Morris Agency, saw the potential of this project when it was just a crabby column I wrote on the train back from three days at CPAC 2005 (speaking of which, thanks to Nick Schulz, my editor at *TCS Daily*, who put me up in a fancy hotel for said three days). Eric's suggestions from the beginning were instrumental in shaping the book and its underlying arguments.

The other Eric responsible for this book, my editor Eric Nelson at Wiley, also was incredibly supportive from day one. His macheteing of overly long discourses on Robert A. Taft and the finer points of F. A. Hayek have saved you, the reader, some serious pain. If it's not too much trouble, you might consider dropping him a line to say thanks.

I'd also like to thank the countless interview subjects, whose sitting for lengthy sessions enhanced my own, and hopefully the reader's, understanding of the state of the modern conservative movement immeasurably. In particular, I'd like to thank two historians of the conservative movement, Lee Edwards and George H. Nash, whose excellent books (much recommended) and in-depth answering of queries were indispensable. I'd also especially like to thank Michael Dimock of the Pew Research Center for the People and the Press, who provided the breakdowns of public opinion in the West that serve as a key piece of the analysis in chapter 7. Also in chapter 7, Brian Kuehl of Democrats for the West provided irreplaceable assistance in putting me in touch with, well, Democrats *in* the West.

Also especially generous with their time were (alphabetically, not by the number of minutes): former majority leader Dick Armey, Kenneth Blackwell, my old boss David Boaz of the Cato Institute, Michael Cannon, Mike Franc, William Frey, Newt Gingrich, Krista Kafer, Dan Kemmis, Annette Kirk, David Kuo, Frank Luntz, Representative Mike Pence, Patton Price, William Rusher, David Sirota, Paul Weyrich, David Winston, Marshall Wittmann, and the late Lyn Nofziger.

On a more personal level, I'd like to thank Seth Lipsky and Ira Stoll, my old bosses at the *New York Sun*, who, when there were perilously few jobs for young journalists, started a new paper and gave a lot of us our starts. As with any founding generation, we stand on their shoulders.

I'd also like to thank my colleagues on the *New York Post* editorial page, especially our fearless leader, Bob McManus, who was exceedingly generous with time off to work on this project, and also Adam Brodsky, Mark Cunningham, Eric Fettmann, Tom Elliott, and Abby Wisse Schachter. Also, my former cubicle neighbor, Robert George, who objected to Bush before objecting to Bush was cool, and who took an early look at this manuscript.

On an even more personal level I'd like to thank my wonderful mother, Geri, who, more than anyone else, taught me how to write. And I'd like to thank the lovely and talented Emily Gitter, my first, last, and most important editor—she is, by the way, the one who came up with the title for the book (which is, in fact, a little like writing the whole book) in a little under five minutes, after I'd banged my head into a wall for about as many months.

Also: Owen, Jacob, Eileen, Dave, Darcy, and my father, David. All provided various forms of moral support during a grueling year.

Last, and also least, I'd like to thank the Starbucks corporation. Their cozy cafés have provided a welcome escape from the home office—even if much of one's time there inevitably consists of staring at a spot on the wall while lulled into a trancelike state by generically hip music.

In the spirit of fusionism: God bless capitalism.

Political and Social Attitudes in the South and the Interior West

Regional breakdowns courtesy of the Pew Research Center for the People and the Press, based on data from its 2005 Political Typology. Interior West is defined as Arizona, Colorado, Idaho, Montana, Nevada, New Mexico, Utah, and Wyoming. Pacific Coast is defined as California, Oregon, and Washington.

	Northeast	Midwest	South	Interior West	Pacific Coast
The government should do more to help needy Americans, even if it means going deeper into debt.	65%	57%	55%	55%	54%
The government today can't afford to do much more to help the needy.	27%	34%	36%	35%	34%
We should all be willing to fight for our country, whether it is right or wrong.	41%	48%	51%	52%	38%
It's acceptable to refuse to fight in a war you believe is morally wrong.	51%	45%	40%	41%	54%

	Northeast	Midwest	South	Interior West	Pacific Coast
Most people who want to get ahead can make it if they're willing to work hard.	71%	63%	71%	73%	64%
Hard work and determination are no guarantee of success for most people.	25%	33%	25%	22%	34%
Success in life is pretty much determined by forces outside of our control.	18%	18%	16%	10%	13%
Everyone has it in their own power to succeed.	77%	76%	78%	84%	83%
This country should do whatever it takes to protect the environment.	81%	76%	76%	72%	78%
This country has gone too far in its efforts to protect the environment.	13%	19%	18%	22%	18%
Stricter environmental laws and regulations cost too many jobs and hurt the economy.	24%	31%	34%	39%	30%
Stricter environmental laws and regulations are worth the cost.	66%	60%	58%	56%	62%

	Northeast	Midwest	South	Interior West	Pacific Coast
Homosexuality is a way of life that should be accepted by society.	60%	46%	39%	53%	60%
Homosexuality is a way of life that should be discouraged by society.	30%	47%	54%	40%	34%
Books that contain dangerous ideas should be banned from public school libraries.	43%	39%	53%	44%	35%
Public school libraries should be allowed to carry any books they want.	51%	58%	42%	52%	61%
Religion is a very important part of my life.	68%	78%	81%	69%	64%
Religion is not that important to me.	29%	21%	17%	30%	34%
It *is not* necessary to believe in God in order to be moral and have good values.	53%	46%	37%	52%	59%
It *is* necessary to believe in God in order to be moral and have good values.	44%	49%	61%	44%	39%

	Northeast	Midwest	South	Interior West	Pacific Coast
The government should do more to protect morality in society.	41%	43%	45%	32%	32%
I worry the government **is getting too involved** in the issue of morality.	52%	50%	46%	59%	63%
The growing number of newcomers from other countries threaten traditional American customs and values.	37%	42%	44%	32%	34%
The growing number of newcomers from other countries strengthens American society.	51%	49%	45%	59%	59%
Americans need to be willing to give up more privacy and freedom in order to be safe from terrorism.	39%	34%	37%	33%	29%
Americans shouldn't have to give up more privacy and freedom in order to be safe from terrorism.	56%	62%	58%	64%	67%

NOTES

1. Live from the Reagan Building

1. Karl Rove, interviewed by Tim Russert, *Meet the Press*, NBC, November 7, 2004.
2. Dan Balz and Mike Allen, "Four More Years Attributed to Rove's Strategy; Despite Moments of Doubt, Adviser's Planning Paid Off," *Washington Post*, November 7, 2004.
3. Editorial, "The Urban Archipelago: It's the Cities, Stupid," *Stranger*, November 11–17, 2004. http://www.thestranger.com/seattle/Content?oid=19813.
4. David Frum, "The Libertarian Temptation," *Weekly Standard*, April 21, 1997, p. 19.
5. David Brooks, "How to Reinvent the G.O.P.," *New York Times Magazine*, August 29, 2004, p. 32.
6. Catalina Camia, "Armey Says Callers to His Offices Support GOP in Budget Impasse," *Dallas Morning News*, November 16, 1995.
7. Brooks, "How to Reinvent the G.O.P."
8. Ibid.
9. Craig Gilbert, "Battles Likely as GOP Plots Its Post-Bush Course; President's Efforts to Redefine Modern Conservatism Prompt Dissent," *Milwaukee Journal Sentinel*, February 20, 2005.
10. Ibid.
11. Wes Allison, "With Conservative Jubilation, a Bit of Concern," *St. Petersburg Times*, February 19, 2005.
12. Deroy Murdock, "Rudy '06: A Giuliani Win over Senator Hillary Will Go Far Toward a 2008 Victory," *National Review Online*, March 1, 2005.
13. Russell Kirk, *The Conservative Mind: From Burke to Eliot* (Washington, D.C.: Regnery, 2001), p. 8.

2. United against Communism

1. John Micklethwait and Adrian Wooldridge, *The Right Nation: Conservative Power in America* (New York: Penguin, 2004), p. 8.
2. Ibid.
3. Lionel Trilling, *The Liberal Imagination* (New York: Viking Press, 1950), p. ix.
4. Lee Edwards, *The Conservative Revolution: The Movement That Remade America* (New York: Free Press, 1999), p. 15.
5. Richard A. Viguerie and David Franke, *America's Right Turn: How Conservatives Used New and Alternative Media to Take Power* (Chicago: Bonus Books, 2004), pp. 49–50.
6. Whittaker Chambers, *Witness* (New York: Random House, 1952), p. 793.
7. George H. Nash, *The Conservative Intellectual Movement in America since 1945* (Wilmington, Del.: Intercollegiate Studies Institute, 1998), p. 89.
8. Ibid., p. 97.
9. Kevin J. Smant, *Principles and Heresies: Frank S. Meyer and the Shaping of the American Conservative Movement* (Wilmington, Del.: Intercollegiate Studies Institute, 2002), p. 21.
10. Nash, *The Conservative Intellectual Movement*, pp. 20–21.
11. Ibid., pp. 32–33.
12. Ibid., pp. 64–65.
13. Edwards, *The Conservative Revolution*, pp. 53–54.
14. Ibid., pp. 62–65.
15. Roy Cohn, *McCarthy* (New York: New American Library, 1968), p. 208.
16. Edwards, *The Conservative Revolution*, p. 85.
17. Rick Perlstein, *Before the Storm* (New York: Hill & Wang, 2001), pp. 110–119.
18. William F. Buckley Jr., "Publisher's Statement," *National Review*, November 19, 1955, p. 5.
19. William A. Rusher, *The Rise of the Right* (New York: William Morrow, 1984), p. 73.
20. Edwards, *The Conservative Revolution*, p. 81.
21. Micklethwait and Wooldridge, *The Right Nation*, p. 51.
22. Edwards, *The Conservative Revolution*, p. 82.
23. Ibid., p. 86.
24. Nash, *The Conservative Intellectual Movement*, p. 272.
25. Perlstein, *Before the Storm*, pp. 247–248.
26. Edwards, *The Conservative Revolution*, pp. 114–115.
27. Perlstein, *Before the Storm*, pp. 248–249.
28. Edwards, *The Conservative Revolution*, p. 103.

29. Perlstein, *Before the Storm*, pp. 253–254.
30. Micklethwait and Wooldridge, *The Right Nation*, p. 59.
31. Edwards, *The Conservative Revolution*, p. 102.
32. Frank S. Meyer, *In Defense of Freedom and Related Essays* (Indianapolis: Liberty Fund, 1996), p. 155.
33. Nash, *The Conservative Intellectual Movement*, pp. 146–147.
34. Ibid., pp. 143–144.
35. Alvin Toffler, "The Playboy Interview with Ayn Rand," reprinted in *The Libertarian Reader*, ed. David Boaz (New York: Free Press, 1997), pp. 161–168.
36. Ronald Hamowy and William F. Buckley Jr., "'National Review': Criticism and Reply," *New Individualist Review* 1, no. 3 (November 1961): 83–91.
37. Smant, *Principles and Heresies*, p. 20.
38. Meyer, *In Defense of Freedom*, p. 183.
39. Ibid., p. 158.
40. Ibid., p. 78.
41. Ibid., p. 40.
42. Ibid., p. 162.
43. Ibid., p. 17.
44. Rusher, *The Rise of the Right*, p. 84.
45. Edwards, *The Conservative Revolution*, p. 94.
46. Ibid., pp. 97–99.
47. Ibid., pp. 103–104.
48. Ibid., pp. 111–116.
49. Ibid., pp. 121–122.
50. Barry Goldwater, 1964 Republican National Convention address, delivered July 16, 1964, San Francisco. Audio recording, mp3, http://www.americanrhetoric.com/speeches/barrygoldwater1964rnc.htm.
51. Edwards, *The Conservative Revolution*, p. 127.
52. Micklethwait and Wooldridge, *The Right Nation*, p. 57.
53. Edwards, *The Conservative Revolution*, p. 131.
54. Perlstein, *Before the Storm*, pp. 472–473.
55. Edwards, *The Conservative Revolution*, p. 138.
56. Viguerie and Franke, *America's Right Turn*, pp. 98–99.
57. Smant, *Principles and Heresies*, p. 154.
58. Micklethwait and Wooldridge, *The Right Nation*, pp. 52–54.
59. Perlstein, *Before the Storm*, p. 21.
60. Nash, *The Conservative Intellectual Movement*, p. 260.
61. Edwards, *The Conservative Revolution*, p. 123.
62. Micklethwait and Wooldridge, *The Right Nation*, p. 54.
63. Rusher, *The Rise of the Right*, p. 195.
64. Edwards, *The Conservative Revolution*, p. 163.

65. Ibid., pp. 163–165.
66. Rusher, *The Rise of the Right*, pp. 239–240.
67. Nash, *The Conservative Intellectual Movement*, pp. 295–297.
68. Jerome Tuccille, *Radical Libertarianism* (Indianapolis: Bobbs-Merrill, 1970), pp. 106–108.
69. Nash, *The Conservative Intellectual Movement*, p. 296.
70. Rusher, *The Rise of the Right*, pp. 296–297.
71. Micklethwait and Wooldridge, *The Right Nation*, pp. 84–85.
72. Edwards, *The Conservative Revolution*, pp. 183–190.
73. Ibid., p. 285.

3. United against Clintonism

1. Kim Painter, "Joycelyn Elders Looks Back with No Regrets," *USA Today*, October 7, 1996.
2. Elizabeth McCaughey, "No Exit," *New Republic*, February 7, 1994, p. 21.
3. Elizabeth Kolbert, "New Arena for Campaign Ads: Health Care," *New York Times*, October 21, 1993.
4. American Health Line, "HIAA: Ad #2 Creates Controversy as Well," October 14, 1993.
5. Kolbert, "New Arena for Campaign Ads."
6. John Micklethwait and Adrian Wooldridge, *The Right Nation: Conservative Power in America* (New York: Penguin, 2004), pp. 109–110.
7. Testimony of Stephen Moore, director of Fiscal Policy Studies at the Cato Institute, before the Committee on the Judiciary, U.S. Senate, February 14, 1995. Via the Cato Institute Web site: http://www.cato.org/testimony/ct-mr-3.html.
8. Micklethwait and Wooldridge, *The Right Nation*, p. 110.
9. Richard A. Viguerie and David Franke, *America's Right Turn: How Conservatives Used New and Alternate Media to Take Power* (Chicago: Bonus Books, 2004), pp. 176–182.
10. Ibid., pp. 183–184.
11. Ibid., pp. 185–187.
12. Dan Balz and Ronald Brownstein, *Storming the Gates: Protest Politics and the Republican Revival* (New York: Little, Brown, 1996), p. 190.
13. Lee Edwards, *The Conservative Revolution: The Movement that Remade America* (New York: Free Press, 1999), p. 239.
14. Balz and Brownstein, *Storming the Gates*, pp. 318–319.
15. David Plotz, "Ralph Reed's Creed," *Slate*, May 4, 1997.
16. Ralph Reed, "Casting a Wider Net," *Policy Review* (Summer 1993): 31–35.
17. Ibid.
18. Balz and Brownstein, *Storming the Gates*, pp. 35–36.

19. David Maraniss and Michael Weisskopf, *Tell Newt to Shut Up!* (New York: Simon & Schuster, 1996), p. 5.
20. Balz and Brownstein, *Storming the Gates*, pp. 118–119.
21. Ibid., pp. 19–25.
22. Ibid., p. 26.
23. Ibid., p. 32.
24. Ibid., p. 23.
25. Micklethwait and Wooldridge, *The Right Nation*, pp. 110–112.
26. Balz and Brownstein, *Storming the Gates*, p. 47.
27. Ibid., pp. 37–38.
28. Maraniss and Weisskopf, *Tell Newt to Shut Up!*, p. 83.
29. Tim Curran, "Perot's Call for GOP Control More Bad News for Weak Democrats. Here's Who Specifically," *Roll Call*, October 10, 1994.
30. Balz and Brownstein, *Storming the Gates*, p. 55.
31. Edwards, *The Conservative Revolution*, p. 301.
32. Balz and Brownstein, *Storming the Gates*, p. 56.
33. Robert A. Rankin and Ranny Green, "Clinton Not Necessarily News, Say Networks," *Seattle Times*, April 19, 1995.
34. Gallup, "The New Republican Mandate," November 1994, Question 12.
35. Text of Clinton's speech to American Association of Community Colleges, CNN transcript, April 23, 1995.
36. Micklethwait and Wooldridge, *The Right Nation*, p. 117.
37. Maraniss and Weisskopf, *Tell Newt to Shut Up!*, p. 8.
38. Ibid., pp. 129–30.
39. Dick Morris, *Behind the Oval Office: Getting Reelected against All Odds* (Los Angeles: Renaissance Books, 1999), p. 139.
40. Ibid., p. 151.
41. Ibid., p. 150.
42. Maraniss and Weisskopf, *Tell Newt to Shut Up!*, pp. 142–143.
43. Morris, *Behind the Oval Office*, p. 184.
44. Kevin Merida, "Gingrich Pledges to Find 'Common Ground' with Clinton," *Washington Post*, November 7, 1996.
45. Major Garrett, *The Enduring Revolution: How the Contract with America Continues to Shape the Nation* (New York: Crown Forum, 2005), p. 107.
46. Ibid., p. 159.

4. The Breaking Apart

1. Patrick J. Buchanan, "Coming Home," *American Conservative*, November 8, 2004. http://www.amconmag.com/2004_11_08/cover.html.

2. Robert A. George, "Conscientious Objector," *New Republic*, October 25, 2004, p. 20.

3. Amy Fagan and Stephen Dinan, "DeLay Declares 'Victory' in War on Budget Fat," *Washington Times*, September 14, 2005.

4. Peggy Noonan, "Whatever It Takes," *OpinionJournal*, September 22, 2005; http://www.opinionjournal.com/columnists/pnoonan/?id=110007291.

5. David Brooks, "A Bushian Laboratory," *New York Times*, September 18, 2005.

6. "2005 Political Typology," Pew Center for the People and the Press, May 10, 2005; http://people-press.org/reports/display.php3?ReportID=242.

7. Fred Barnes, *Rebel-in-Chief: Inside the Bold and Controversial Presidency of George W. Bush* (New York: Crown Forum, 2006), pp. 175–176.

8. Daniel J. Mitchell, Ph.D., "The Impact of Government Spending on Economic Growth," Heritage Foundation Backgrounder 1831, March 15, 2005; http://www.heritage.org/Research/Budget/bg1831.cfm.

9. Office of Management and Budget, *Budget of the United States Government, Fiscal Year 2005: Historical Tables* (Washington, D.C.: U.S. Government Printing Office, 2004), p. 128, table 8.4, at http://www.gpoaccess.gov/usbudget/fy05/pdf/hist.pdf.

10. Ramesh Ponnuru, "Why Conservatives Are Divided," *New York Times*, October 17, 2005.

11. "U.S. Representative Dennis Hastert (R-IL) Delivers Remarks on the Budget," Federal Document Clearing House Political transcript, October 1, 1999.

12. Walter R. Mears, "Bush Makes Early Move to Center an AP News Analysis," Associated Press, October 7, 1999.

13. Deborah McGregor, "Bush Keeps His Distance from Republicans on the Hill," *Financial Times*, October 8, 1999.

14. Editorial, "Why W.?," *National Review*, July 12, 1999.

15. Editorial, "Philadelphia: The Big Speech," *National Review*, August 28, 2000.

16. David S. Broder, "Stakes High in 2000; Voters Can Redirect 3 Federal Branches," *Washington Post*, June 21, 1999.

17. Brian M. Riedl, "Federal Spending—By the Numbers," Heritage Foundation WebMemo #989, February 6, 2006; http://www.heritage.org/Research/Budget/wm989.cfm.

18. Bruce Bartlett, *Impostor: How George W. Bush Bankrupted America and Betrayed the Reagan Legacy* (New York: Doubleday, 2006), pp. 85–101.

19. Bill Beach, Rea Hederman, and Tim Kane, "The 2003 Tax Cuts and the Economy: A One-Year Assessment," Heritage Foundation WebMemo #543; http://www.heritage.org/Research/Taxes/wm543.cfm.

20. George F. Will, "On K Street Conservatism," *Newsweek*, October 17, 2005, p. 78.

21. Jonathan Rauch, "Why Republicans Can't Cut Spending," *National Journal*, January 21, 2006.

22. Editorial, "GOP, MIA: Taking the Road Most Traveled," *Manchester Union Leader*, August 31, 2003.

5. The Ownership Society and Its Discontents

1. Milton Friedman, "The Role of Government in Education," originally published in 1955. Published online by the Milton and Rose Friedman Foundation, http://www.friedmanfoundation.org/50/1955.pdf.

2. David Boaz, "Defining an Ownership Society." Cato Institute Web site, http://www.cato.org/special/ownership_society/boaz.html.

3. Fred Barnes, *Rebel-in-Chief: Inside the Bold and Controversial Presidency of George W. Bush* (New York: Crown Forum, 2006), pp. 138–139.

4. Kathleen Lucadamo, "Harlem Parents File School Choice Suit," *New York Sun*, January 28, 2003.

5. Barnes, *Rebel-in-Chief*, pp. 164–165.

6. Kate O'Beirne, "Weak Non-Reformer: W. Caves on Education," *National Review*, May 28, 2001.

7. Siobhan Gorman, "The Education of House Republicans," *National Journal*, March 31, 2001.

8. Krista Kafer, "A Small but Costly Step toward Reform: The Conference Education Bill," Heritage Foundation WebMemo #66, December 13, 2001; http://www.heritage.org/Research/Education/WM66.cfm.

9. David Espo, "House Panel Strips Vouchers from Education Bill," Associated Press, May 2, 2001.

10. Pamela Benigno, "No Child Left Behind Mandates School Choice: Colorado's First Year," Independence Institute, Issue Paper 9-2003, June 2003, p. 8; http://i2i.org/articles/9-2003.pdf.

11. "From the Capital to the Classroom: Year 3 of the No Child Left Behind Act," Center on Education Policy, March 2005, p. 107; http://www.cep-dc.org/pubs/nclby3/press/cep-nclby3_21Mar2005.pdf.

12. Ibid., p. 109.

13. Krista Kafer, "No Child Left Behind: Where Do We Go From Here?" Heritage Foundation Backgrounder #1775, July 6, 2004; http://www.heritage.org/Research/Education/bg1775.cfm.

14. David S. Broder, "Time Was GOP's Ally on the Vote," *Washington Post*, November 23, 2003.
15. Michael Tanner, "Medicare Drug Debacle," Cato Institute Daily Commentary, June 27, 2003; http://www.cato.org/dailys/06-27-03.html.
16. Grace-Marie Turner, "A Sense of Entitlement," *National Review*, December 22, 2003.
17. Joseph Antos and Jagadeesh Gokhale, "Medicare Prescription Drugs: Medical Necessity Meets Fiscal Insanity," Cato Institute Briefing Papers, Number 91, February 9, 2005.
18. Michael F. Cannon and Michael D. Tanner, *Healthy Competition: What's Holding Back Health Care and How to Free It* (Washington, D.C.: Cato Institute, 2005), pp. 66–67.
19. Ibid., p. 68.
20. Robert Novak, "Shall Bush Reform?," *Chicago Sun-Times*, June 14, 2004.
21. Amy Goldstein, "AARP to Seek a Better Drug Benefit," *Washington Post*, January 28, 2006.
22. Barnes, *Rebel-in-Chief*, pp. 135–136.
23. Michael Tanner, "The Long, Winding Road to Social Security Reform," in *The Republican Revolution 10 Years Later: Smaller Government or Business as Usual?*, ed. Chris Edwards and John Samples (Washington, D.C.: Cato Institute, 2005), p. 94.

6. Dancing with an Elephant

1. Devlin Barrett, "Senators Exchange Child-Rearing Views in Capitol Hallway," Associated Press, July 13, 2005.
2. Russell Kirk, "The Essence of Conservatism," adapted from *The Intelligent Woman's Guide to Conservatism* (New York: Devin-Adair, 1957). Reprinted online by the Russell Kirk Center for Cultural Renewal, http://www.kirkcenter.org/kirk/essence-1957.html.
3. Jerry Kammer, "1953: Matt Dillon Goes to Washington," *Arizona Republic*, January 18, 1987.
4. Rick Perlstein, *Before the Storm* (New York: Hill & Wang, 2001), p. 33.
5. Ibid., p. 484.
6. Ibid., pp. 485–486.
7. Dan Balz and Ronald Brownstein, *Storming the Gates: Protest Politics and the Republican Upheaval* (New York: Little, Brown, 1996), p. 55.
8. John Micklethwait and Adrian Wooldridge, *The Right Nation: Conservative Power in America* (New York: Penguin, 2004), p. 12.
9. Ibid., p. 185.
10. Peter Baker and Amy Goldstein, "Nomination Was Plagued by Missteps from the Start," *Washington Post*, October 28, 2005.
11. Micklethwait and Wooldridge, *The Right Nation*, pp. 186–187.

12. Grover Norquist, "Dobson and the GOP," *American Spectator*, July 1998.

13. David D. Kirkpatrick and Sheryl Gay Stolberg, "Backers of Gay Marriage Ban Use Social Security as Cudgel," *New York Times*, January 25, 2005.

14. "Religion and Politics: The Ambivalent Majority," Pew Research Center for the People and the Press, September 20, 2000. http://people-press.org/reports/display.php3?ReportID=32.

15. "National Security More Linked with Partisan Affiliation: Politics and Values in a 51%–48% Nation," Pew Research Center for the People and the Press, January 24, 2005; http://people-press.org/reports/display.php3?ReportID=236.

16. "Excerpts from Goldwater Remarks," *New York Times*, September 16, 1981.

17. Michael Jonas, "Senator Clinton Urges Use of Faith-Based Initiatives," *Boston Globe*, January 20, 2005.

18. Perry Bacon Jr., "Trying Out a More Soulful Tone," *Time*, February 7, 2005, p. 32.

19. John DiIulio, "Faith, Hope, and Government," *Boston Globe*, June 22, 2003.

20. Peter Wallsten, Tom Hamburger, and Nicholas Riccardi, "Bush Rewarded by Black Pastors' Faith," *Los Angeles Times*, January 18, 2005.

21. Thomas B. Edsall and Alan Cooperman, "GOP Using Faith Initiative to Woo Voters," *Washington Post*, September 15, 2002.

22. Tom Hamburger and Peter Wallsten, *One Party Country: The Republican Plan for Dominance in the 21st Century* (Hoboken, N.J.: John Wiley & Sons, 2006), p. 117.

23. "President Speaks with Faith-Based and Community Leaders," January 15, 2004. White House transcript: http://www.whitehouse.gov/news/releases/2004/01/20040115-7.html.

24. Hamburger and Wallsten, *One Party Country*, p. 123.

25. Wallsten, Hamburger, and Riccardi, "Bush Rewarded by Black Pastors' Faith."

26. David Kuo, "Please, Keep Faith," *Beliefnet*, 2005; http://www.beliefnet.com/story/160/story_16092_1.html.

27. "Grants to Faith-Based Organizations FY 2004," White House Office of Faith-Based and Community Initiatives; http://www.whitehouse.gov/government/fbci/data-collection-2004.html.

28. Peter Wehner, "A Screwtape Letter for the Twenty-first Century," in *What's God Got to Do with the American Experiment?*, ed. E. J. Dionne Jr. and John J. DiIulio Jr. (Washington, D.C.: Brookings Institution Press, 2000), pp. 41–45.

7. Look to the West

1. America's Future Foundation debate, "Can This Marriage Be Saved?," February 23, 2005, Washington, D.C., audio recording, mp3, http://www.americasfuture.org/events-archive/archives/019534.php.
2. John Micklethwait and Adrian Wooldridge, *The Right Nation: Conservative Power in America* (New York: Penguin, 2004), p. 20.
3. William H. Frey, "The Electoral College Moves to the Sun Belt," Brookings Institution, May 2005; http://www.brookings.edu/metro/pubs/20050504_electoralcollege.htm.
4. Ronald Brownstein, "GOP Has Lock on South, and Democrats Can't Find Key," *Los Angeles Times*, December 15, 2004.
5. Paul Waldman, *Being Right Is Not Enough: What Progressives Must Learn from Conservative Success* (Hoboken, N.J.: John Wiley & Sons, 2006), p. 35.
6. "State of Residence in 2000 by State of Birth: 2000," U.S. Census Bureau, http://www.census.gov/prod/cen2000/doc/sf3.pdf.
7. Fred Barnes, *Rebel-in-Chief: Inside the Bold and Controversial Presidency of George W. Bush* (New York: Crown Forum, 2006), p. 188.
8. Roberto Suro, Richard Fry, and Jeffrey Passel, "Hispanics and the 2004 Election: Population, Electorate and Voters," Pew Hispanic Center, June 27, 2005; http://pewhispanic.org/reports/report.php?ReportID=48.
9. 2005 National Latino Survey, The Latino Coalition, released January 5, 2006; http://www.thelatinocoalition.com/news/pdf/2005NationalLatino Survey.pdf.
10. Jonathan Rauch, "In 2004, the Country Didn't Turn Right—but the GOP Did," *National Journal*, November 13, 2004.
11. Waldman, *Being Right*, p. 54.
12. David Sirota, "Top Billings: How a Montana Democrat Bagged the Hunting and Fishing Vote, and Won the Governor's Mansion," *Washington Monthly*, December 2004.
13. Robert Siegel and Linda Wertheimer, "How Voters in Colorado Split Their Tickets in the Last Election," *All Things Considered*, NPR, December 21, 2004.
14. http://tancredo.house.gov/irc/members.html, accessed March 11, 2006.
15. Chris Cillizza, "Democrats to Alter Caucus Schedule to Boost Diversity," *Washington Post*, March 12, 2006.

8. Return to CPAC

1. "President's Remarks on Labor Day," September 1, 2003. White House transcript: http://www.whitehouse.gov/news/releases/2003/09/20030901.html.

2. Dennis Cauchon, "Federal Aid Programs Expand at Record Rate," *USA Today*, March 13, 2006.

3. Peggy Noonan, "The Steam Roller: The Road to Big Government Reaches a Dead End at Jack Abramoff," *OpinionJournal*, January 5, 2006.

4. John Fund, "Marks for Sharks," *OpinionJournal*, January 9, 2006.

5. Matthew Continetti, "Contract Killers," *New York Times*, October 1, 2005.

6. Fred Barnes, *Rebel-in-Chief: Inside the Bold and Controversial Presidency of George W. Bush* (New York: Crown Forum, 2006), p. 191.

INDEX